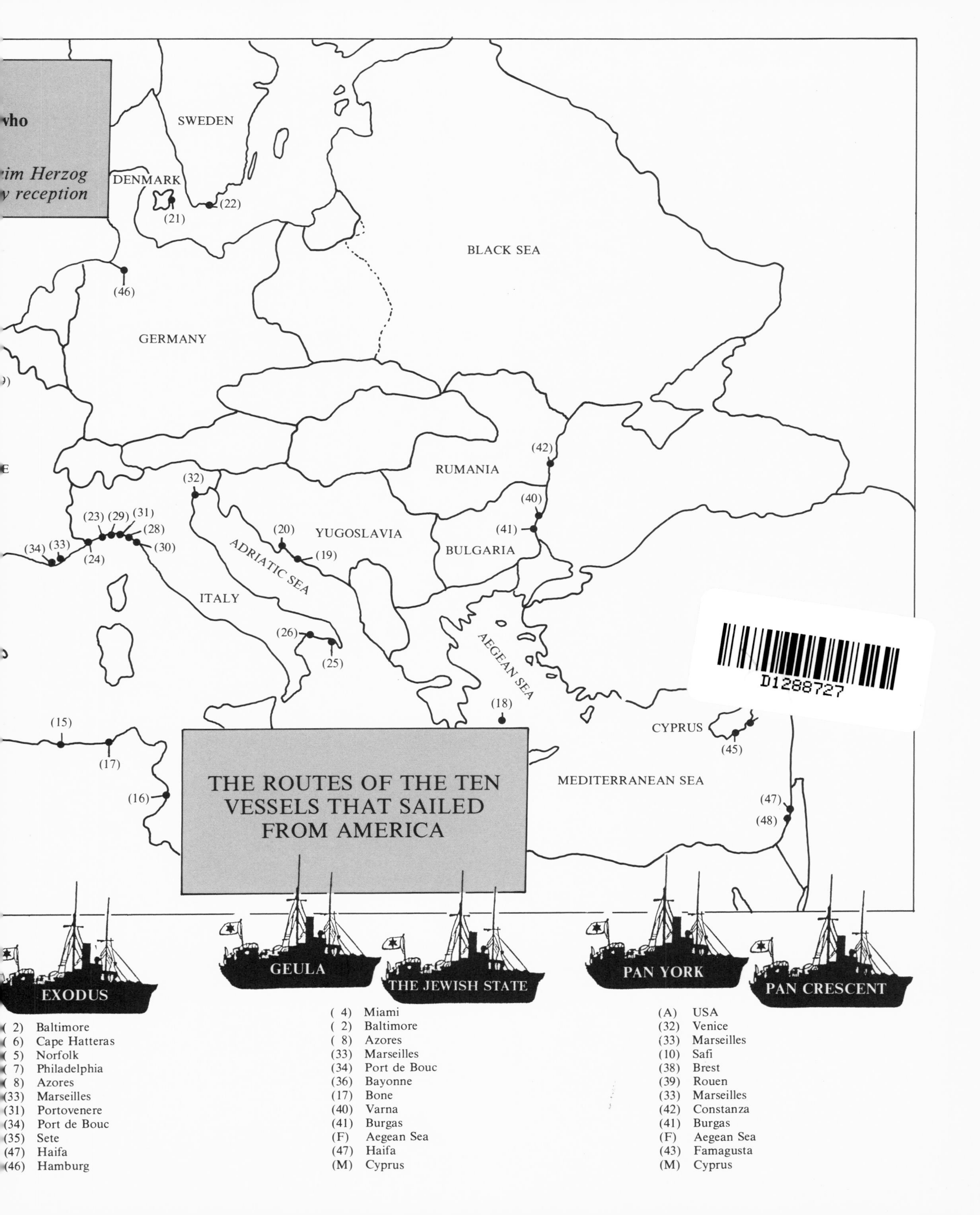

who
im Herzog
y reception
SWEDEN
DENMARK
(21)
(22)
BLACK SEA
(46)
GERMANY
RUMANIA
(42)
(40)
(41)
(32)
(23) (29) (31)
(28)
(30)
(24)
(34) (33)
(20)
(19)
YUGOSLAVIA
BULGARIA
ADRIATIC SEA
ITALY
(26)
(25)
AEGEAN SEA
(18)
CYPRUS
(45)
(15)
(17)
(16)
MEDITERRANEAN SEA
(47)
(48)
THE ROUTES OF THE TEN VESSELS THAT SAILED FROM AMERICA
EXODUS
GEULA
THE JEWISH STATE
PAN YORK
PAN CRESCENT
(2) Baltimore
(6) Cape Hatteras
(5) Norfolk
(7) Philadelphia
(8) Azores
(33) Marseilles
(31) Portovenere
(34) Port de Bouc
(35) Sete
(47) Haifa
(46) Hamburg
(4) Miami
(2) Baltimore
(8) Azores
(33) Marseilles
(34) Port de Bouc
(36) Bayonne
(17) Bone
(40) Varna
(41) Burgas
(F) Aegean Sea
(47) Haifa
(M) Cyprus
(A) USA
(32) Venice
(33) Marseilles
(10) Safi
(38) Brest
(39) Rouen
(33) Marseilles
(42) Constanza
(41) Burgas
(F) Aegean Sea
(43) Famagusta
(M) Cyprus

Praise for *The Jews' Secret Fleet*
and the Heroic Sailors who Navigated 32,000 Jews to Safety

The Jews' Secret Fleet is full of stories as dramatic as that of the *Exodus*. It reminds us that American Jews played a small, yet significant role in the creation of the Jewish state. Four of the American vessels became the first warships in the fledgling Israeli navy. The bravery displayed by these American volunteers for Zion should not be forgotten, and this book helps make certain they will receive their historical due.

Henry Srebrnik
Washington Jewish Week, December 10, 1987

The Ministry of Defense is well aware and appreciates the personal contribution made by each one of you; there is no doubt that this contribution as well as the personal sacrifices were all part of the great endeavor made at the time to build the new State of Israel and the Israel Defense Forces, and you should all be proud of the role you played towards achieving this goal.

Prime Minister Yitzhak Rabin
Minister of Defense, Israel, May 11, 1988

Murray Greenfield, one of 240 volunteers, took it upon himself to document in writing this unknown story, which has been omitted from the history of the Zionist struggle. Greenfield describes in short the history of the organized maritime immigration to Eretz Israel, and then goes to the core of his book: The role of North Americans, mostly Jews but some non-Jews, in this exodus operation. It is difficult to imagine this immigration without the ships which became world famous such as the Exodus, the Pan York and the Pan Crescent. These are only three out of the 11 ships, purchased in the United States, which transported 32,000 Jewish refugee survivors of the Holocaust into Palestine at the conclusion of World War II and played a crucial part in the founding of the State of Israel.

Dr. Mordechai Naor
Ha'aretz (Hebrew Daily Paper), May 13, 1994

The saga of all 11 North American ships, including the immortal *Exodus*, and of the volunteers was generally unknown until it was beautifully summarized in the 1987 book, *The Jews' Secret Fleet* by Joseph Hochstein and Murray S. Greenfield, the latter having served aboard one of them, the *Hatikva*. Issued by Gefen of Jerusalem and New York and in Hebrew translation (*Hatzi Hasodi Shel Hayehudim*) by the Defense Ministry, it has an introduction by Prof. Sir Martin Gilbert, Winston Churchill's official biographer, and a foreword by one of those volunteers, Paul Shulman, a graduate of the US Naval Academy at Annapolis and World War II combat veteran, who was the Israel Navy's founder and first commander.

Moshe Kohn
Jerusalem Post, February 7, 1997

The Jews' Secret Fleet

MURRAY S. GREENFIELD
JOSEPH M. HOCHSTEIN

Photo Typeset by Gefen Ltd.

ISBN 965 229 023 8

Edition 9 8 7 6

Gefen Publishing House
POB 36004
Jerusalem 91360, Israel
972-2-538-0247
isragefen@netmedia.net.il

Gefen Books
12 New Street
Hewlett, NY 11557, USA
516-295-2805
gefenbooks@compuserve.com

Printed in Israel

Contents

Addendum

There are two important incidents that concern Cyprus. The decision to bring the two ships, Pan York and Pan Crescent, direct to Cyprus was one that did not go down easily with the Captains of both ships. The British came on board to make the final arrangements in Famagusta and together with the British came an official representing the Joint Distribution Committee which had a special position on Cyprus. It was the Joint that helped get better rations for the detainees, improved health facilities where some two thousand children were born, and also educational facilities were created.

The British wanted to take over the vessels and demanded that the captains and the crews leave the ship until they decided to return them. Sea lawyers know that if you leave a ship with no crew it is considered an abandoned ship and one must go to court to regain possession. The captains refused to accept the British Commanders position and the Joint, not knowing the rules, sided with the British. The captains said there will be no disembarkation of the 15,000 passengers thereby creating a very big health and public relations problem for the British. An agreement was finally reached that a skeleton crew should remain on board and keep the engines running. Because the agreement called for the running of the engines, fuel had to be brought regularly to the ships. When May 15, 1948, came about, the ships were full of fuel and both ships could immediately take the survivors, who were prisoners on Cyprus, to Israel without any questions asked and without any help from the British authorities. It was in this manner that many men and women came to Israel and were able to help the fledgling state in its fight for life.

In the final act of nastiness the British would not allow men and women of military age to leave Cyprus. For the British this was a way of living up to the ban that was imposed on the area against bringing weapons in. Of course, the Arab forces came in by land and were even assisted by the British in Jordan. Some 10,000 men and women were held on Cyprus behind barbed wire until February 1949, nearly nine months after the State was declared.

David Livingston was a crew member of the ship Haim Arlosoroff. From research we have learned since the publication of the last updated book *'The Jews' Secret Fleet'* that David sailed another voyage and this time on the Pan Crescent. He went with the passengers to Cyprus and after several weeks was released and came to Israel where he joined a Kibbutz and subsequently joined the Palmach's Yiftach Brigade. He was killed in the defense of Mishmar Ha'emek.

It was the meeting of the Jews of Palestine who served in the British Army in WWII with the survivors that gave them real hope. Then the persons involved in the *Bricha* (escape) that strengthened the survivors but in turn made those involved more fully realize how important their work was. The enlistment of North American Jewish volunteers manning the ships from the USA to Europe and then Palestine gave an unbelievable impetus to both the *Bricha* and *Polyam* volunteers. But in the final analysis it was the determination of the survivors that gave it all more meaning. *If there are any heroes, it is the survivors.*

Introduction

Sir Martin Gilbert

Biographer of Winston Churchill

With the end of the war in Europe on 8 May 1945, Jews all over the world hoped, and expected, that the doors of Palestine would be opened for the survivors of the holocaust. The number of people involved was not much more than 150,000; their suffering had been terrible, and their survival little short of miraculous. Neither their political views, their professions, their place of birth, their class or their diverse ways of life had played any part in their fate: only their Jewishness. The attraction of building a new life in Palestine derived almost entirely from this fact: as Jews, they had been singled out for the most evil torments devised by man; as Jews, therefore, they wished to live in dignity, protected by their own people, and not dependent upon the approval or sufferance of any non-Jewish majority.

On 22 May 1945, two weeks after the German surrender, Dr Weizmann wrote direct to Churchill, to ask that Jewish immigration be resumed. But in his reply on June 8, Churchill informed Weizmann that there could be 'no possibility of the question being effectively considered' until the proposed Peace Conference. Weizmann was appalled by this decision to delay what was, for the survivors of the holocaust, a matter of urgency. On June 13 he replied to Churchill that the contents of Churchill's letter had come 'as a great shock' to him, and he went on:

"I had always understood from our various conversations that our problem would be considered as soon as the German war was over; but the phrase 'until the victorious Allies are definitely seated at the Peace table' substitutes some indefinite date in the future. I am sure that it cannot have been your intention to postpone the matter indefinitely, because I believe you realise that this would involve very grave hardship to thousands of people at present still lingering in the camps of Buchenwald, Belsen-Bergen etc., who cannot find any place to go if the White Paper is to continue for an unspecified period."

The Jewish Agency, and the Zionist leaders, continued to press for an end to the immigration restrictions of the White Paper. In London, a special Palestine Committee of the Cabinet reported, on October 19, that Britain would support the appointment of an Anglo-American Commission, to examine 'the situation of the Jews in Europe', and to make recommendations 'for its alleviation'. The Chairman of the Palestine Committee, Herbert Morrison — the Lord President of the Council — warned, however, in his report, of Muslim opposition to any relaxation of the immigration restrictions. President Truman's wish that the survivors of the concentration camps should be allowed into Palestine had, Morrison pointed out, already led to protests not only from the Arab States, but also from 'the Congress in India.'

On October 10 Weizmann went to see Bevin, in the hope of changing the British Government's mind, but his effort was in vain, and a month later, on November 13, Bevin announced that the White Paper policy would continue.

The Labour Government carried out the policy it has announced. Although nearly 100,000 Jews moved through Europe during 1945, in search of the routes, ports and ships for Palestine, by the end of the year only 13,100 had been allowed by the British to enter; this was 1,500 *less* than had been allowed in during 1944.

With Palestine so effectively barred to Jewish refugees, and the American quota system still rigidly enforced, it might be thought that, as compensation, the British immigration laws would be relaxed. But in a Cabinet memorandum of October 30, the Home Secretary, J. Chuter Ede, set out the principal basis of Labour's immigration policy, that it would not be 'right', as he thought, for Britain to contemplate 'any large-scale addition to our foreign population at the present time.'

* * * * *

During the winter of 1945 the British Government became concerned by the exodus of the 80,000 surviving Polish Jews, many of whom sought to escape not only the evil memories all around them, but also the growing Polish anti-semitism. On 8 December 1945 the Commander-in-Chief of the British Forces in Berlin informed the Foreign Office that six thousand Polish Jews had reached Berlin from Poland in the previous month. 'As these persons are Polish citizens,' the Commander-in-Chief declared, 'they cannot be described as persons displaced from their homes by reason of the war, nor as refugees from persecution instigated by Germany or her allies. We are therefore refusing them food and accommodation in our sector of Berlin and onward transit into our Zone.'

The head of the Refugee Department at the Foreign Office, Douglas Mackillop, understood more clearly the reasons for the exodus of Polish Jewry, noting on January 12, 1946 that it arose 'partly for racial & economic reasons, readily understandable since the new Poland does not offer them the same opportunities as the old, and there is a spontaneous general wish on the part of European Jewry to go to Palestine.' Mackillop added: 'Though it is magnified & artificially fostered by Zionist propaganda, it is a real aspiration.'

Despite Mackillop's understanding of the 'real aspiration' of Polish Jewry, the Foreign Office continued to examine every possible pressure to keep the Polish Jews inside Poland. Even the British Treasury was involved in these efforts. On January 18 a Treasury memorandum suggested applying pressure by means of the funds being made available by the Interim

Treasury Committee on Polish Questions. According to the Treasury, some Polish Jews had already been refused funds, and the memorandum explained: 'The non-payment of allowances from ITC sources to Polish holders of Immigration Certificates was based on the assumption that they were embryonic Palestine citizens...' The Treasury memorandum continued: 'Certificate holders who wish to receive maintenance from the ITC must relinquish their claim to Palestine citizenship and revert to refugee status.'

On 25 January 1946 the Cabinet's Overseas Reconstruction Committee met in London, with Bevin as chairman. The purpose of the meeting was to discuss what Bevin described as 'the serious problem' caused by the exodus of Jews from eastern Europe into the British and American Zones of Germany and Austria, and into Italy. The Chancellor of the Duchy of Lancaster, John Burns Hynd, told his colleagues that during his own recent visit to Germany 'he had spoken with Jews at Belsen Camp, and these were all in favour of going to Palestine.' Hynd gave as his personal advice:

"It would be undesirable to let it be thought that there would be an early opportunity for large numbers of Jews to go to Palestine, as this would not only encourage the present movement, but would also encourage Polish Jews forming part of the large mass of Poles who were now being repatriated from our Zone in Germany to Poland, to refuse to go home."

Bevin told the Cabinet Committee that the Foreign Office had considered sending 'an appeal' from the British to the Soviet Government 'to suspend the movement of Polish Jews from Poland,' but felt that such an approach would be 'unprofitable.' They had also considered asking the Polish Government to create 'more tolerable conditions' for Jews already in Poland, but feared that if they did this, the Poles 'would resent the imputation' of anti-semitism. Bevin, however, did not believe that Polish anti-semitism was the principal cause of the Jewish desire to leave, telling his colleagues that, according to his information, 'most of the Jewish migrants from Poland were influenced by political rather than racial motives in their efforts to reach Palestine.'

According to the Chancellor of the Duchy of Lancaster, the British authorities in Germany and Austria 'were already tightening the control arrangement;' nevertheless, some Jews were still managing to cross from Eastern Europe into the British Zones. The Chancellor of the Duchy wondered 'whether such persons should be treated as displaced persons;' he himself 'felt that they should not be so treated but should be dealt with on the same basis as German refugees and provided with rations on the reduced scale for Germans.'

A Jewish member of the Government, Lord Nathan, told the Cabinet Committee that:

"...for generations Poland had been a centre of anti-semitism. Many Jews who had returned to Poland or had emerged from concealment had found their businesses and homes in the hands of others and on this account were not received with any great favour.

He did not believe that there had been any organised evacuation. In the past, Jewish propaganda had sought to create a Jewish majority in Palestine by introducing one million Jews into that country out of a European pool of five million Jews. That pool had disappeared and to achieve such a majority in Palestine it would now be necessary to get almost all surviving European Jews to go to Palestine."

Lord Nathan suggested, however, that in order to halt 'the illegal departure of Jews from Italy,' the British Government should concert measures with the Italian Government 'to ensure that the arrangements made to prevent illegal emigration of Jews were effective'.

The Cabinet accepted Lord Nathan's suggestion to enlist Italian support in stopping Jews leaving Italy for Palestine. They also accepted the Chancellor of the Duchy of Lancaster's proposal that Jewish refugees 'filtering through our control zones' should be 'dealt with' by a reduction in rations, so that henceforth they would be treated, not as displaced persons, but as Germans.

A struggle now began, in Palestine and in Europe, between the British Government and the Jews: a struggle marked by increasing bitterness and extremism on both sides. The British, determined to halt the now swelling tide of 'illegal' immigration from liberated Europe to Mandatory Palestine, went so far as to return captured immigrants from the waters of the eastern Mediterranean to which they had sailed, to the displaced camps in Germany from which they had fled. In Europe itself, at the frontier crossings between Austria and Italy, British troops halted concentration camp survivors who were on their way to the Adriatic, and to Palestine, and held them in former prisoner-of-war camps.

In April 1946, while the Anglo-American Committee had been preparing its report, which included the recommendation of an immediate grant of 100,000 immigration certificates to the Jews of the D.P. camps, British pressure on the Italian Government grew. As had been suggested by the British Ambassador, a diplomatic protest had led to the Italians refusing to allow two 'illegal' immigrant ships, called by the Jews the *Dov Hos* and the *Eliahu Golomb*, to leave the port of La Spezia, on the Italian Riviera. For their part the 1,014 refugees, most of whom were from Poland and central Europe, refused to leave the ships, and declared a hunger strike. If force were used against them, they declared, they would commit mass suicide, and sink the ships. In Palestine, Golda Meyerson proposed a hunger strike by fifteen Zionist leaders, as a gesture of support with the refugees, and as a means of forcing the British to allow the ships to sail. Before starting the strike, the leaders went to see the chief Secretary of the Palestine Government, Henry Gurney. In her memoirs Mrs Meyerson recalled how:

"He listened, then he turned to me and said: 'Mrs Meyerson, do you think for a moment that His Majesty's Government will change its policy because *you* are not going to eat?' I said, 'No, I have no such illusions. If the death of six million didn't change government policy, I don't expect that my not eating will do so. But it will at least be a mark of solidarity'."

The hunger strike was, in fact, successful, and on May 8 the *Dov Hos* and the *Eliahu Golomb* sailed for Palestine, their 1,014 passengers having been granted immigration certificates from the next month's quota.

The Anglo-American Committee published its Report on 1 May 1946. Among its recommendations were the end to the land purchase restrictions of the 1939 White Paper, and the immediate grant of 100,000 immigration certificates to the Jewish survivors. The Jews of Palestine were bitterly disappointed that their hope of statehood was not endorsed by the Committee, which recommended a continuation of the Mandate. The Arabs of Palestine, opposed to the entry of a further 100,000 Jews, rejected the Report and declared a general strike.

On June 12, at the Labour Party Conference at Bournemouth, Ernest Bevin rejected even the 100,000 extra certificates, and declared that the reason why the Americans had wanted Palestine to take 100,000 Jewish refugees was that they did not want 'to have too many of them in New York.' Bevin also claimed that it would cost £200 million to finance the transfer and settlement of the 100,000, and involve the despatch to Palestine of another Division of British troops: both burdens that the British taxpayer ought not to have to bear.

During the Cabinet's discussion of 'illegal' immigration, on July 30, it was agreed, despite Attlee's own doubts as to the wisdom of the measure, to deport to Cyprus all 'illegal' refugees who were caught trying to enter Palestine. At the same time, it was suggested that Dr Weizmann be asked to use his influence 'to persuade illegal immigrants not to resist transfer to staging camps in Cyprus,' on the understanding that they would soon be transferred to Palestine as part of the 100,000. But Jewish fears were now too roused to trust such a proposal, which both Weizmann himself, and the Jewish Agency, were unwilling to accept. For them, immediate and unimpeded immigration to Palestine itself was the dominant need, on which no compromise was possible.

A serious blow to Zionist hopes of Labour Government support had come on July 24, with the publication of a plan drawn up by yet another Cabinet Committee on Palestine, and announced in the House of Commons on July 30 by Herbert Morrison, the Lord President of the Council and Deputy Prime Minister. Under this new plan, Palestine was to be divided into three areas. The first area, constituting 43 per cent of the Mandate area, and including Jerusalem, was to remain under British control. The second area, making up 40 per cent of the country, was to become an area of Arab provincial autonomy. The third area, the remaining 17 per cent of Palestine, was to become the area of Jewish provincial autonomy: all three areas to be under British rule.

Only if the Jews accepted this plan, Morrison announced, would the 100,000 refugees of the Anglo-American Committee recommendation be allowed into Palestine. Even so, those allowed in would have to be refugees primarily from Germany, Austria and Italy. Adult refugees from Poland, Rumania and eastern Europe would not be included in the total, only orphan children from these areas. Nor would Britain agree to receive these refugees, even under these restrictions, unless the United States Government agreed in advance to undertake 'sole responsibility for the sea transport of these refugees', as well as providing them 'with food for the first two months after their arrival in Palestine.'

* * * * *

During 1946 the position even of the surviving Jews in Germany became subject to the dictates of a harsh policy, illustrated by a Foreign Office confidential note sent to the Control Office for Germany and Austria on 5 July 1946. The note stated, tersely, 'We must have... a clear definition of the term German JEW and must prevent German JEWS from emigrating to PALESTINE.'

As before the war, the British Government's pressure against the 'illegal' Jewish immigrants was intense. But with each month the organizers of the 'Bricha', or 'Flight', as it was called, were able to mobilize their resources, driven forward by the determination of the survivors to reach Palestine, whatever the hardships of the journey. For most of them, there could never be a peril so foul as that from which they, the mere remnant of European Jewry had escaped. Between August 1945 and May 1948, sixty-four ships set off, from ports in France, Italy, Yugoslavia, Greece, Bulgaria and Rumania, bearing almost 70,000 men, women and children to Palestine.

Some Jews found refuge elsewhere than Palestine. More than 15,000 went to Latin America; nearly 13,000 reached the United States; 7,000 went to Canada; and 6,000 went to Australia. But the majority wanted to go to Palestine, where, despite British opposition, the groundwork of Jewish statehood was being laid with deliberation and careful planning.

Foreword

Paul N. Shulman
First Commander of the Israeli Navy

When this century finally finds itself in the pages of history it will probably, and sadly, not be recalled for the achievements in science and technology, or medicine, nor for the broadening of cultural interest in all its forms. No doubt our century will be remembered for two dominant features: continuous warfare; and the individual's struggles for material advancement.

There was hardly a period during which two or more wars were not fought. These wars brought a new dimension in destruction and a new measure of human suffering and cruelty. The epitome was the slaughter of 6,000,000 Jews in the Nazi Holocaust. Even President Roosevelt, the leader of the free world, callously chose to close his nation's eyes to this brutal slaughter during the war and refused shelter to survivors following the actual fighting. The British Government by its White Paper denied entry of these victims to their spiritual promised homeland. To right these wrongs and to rescue the European remnant of this noble Jewish nation, a new and strong force was formed manned by volunteers from Palestine and abroad. The force was the Mossad for Aliyah Bet. This book recounts the saga of those American and Canadian members of that force.

I have stated that the struggle for material security was the second phenomenon of this century. Our fathers, many of whom came to America from the Old World, struggled to secure for themselves and their families a firm footing in the new land; to conquer a new language, and to blend into a new composite of cultures. People of our generation and probably that of our children, built upon the achievements of our fathers, in seeking higher education and pursuing remunerative professions. In their success they contributed financially to many worthy causes. In their free time they took up these causes as part of their life's motivation. Surely one of these causes was the Zionist aspiration and the support of Jewish refugees, whether from Hitler's Nazis or from Russian oppression. The work was noble and the contribution meaningful. The men whose stories are found in this book were not satisfied with the mere giving of money. Perhaps they had little to give. In these circumstances, they saw the futility of the printed word and of well turned speeches. They believed direct action and personal involvement were morally imperative, and they did what was necessary for the success of the Aliyah Bet cause. They gave their time and their will; their strength and their determination. They worked without pay, without fanfare, without reward or praise, and were undeterred by the risks to their lives.

In all, this daring band was comprised of more than 200 officers and men together with shore based supporters of many skills and equal dedication. They were mainly Jews but there were also Christians among them; men whose sense of justice transcended parochial identification.

With the passing of time, the number of these volunteers has been depleted and so, before the parade passes on, this book tells their story; not for their self-aggrandisement, but to inform their grandchildren and to record in history these great, noble, and historic years which helped change the future of the Jewish people. A period when the will of a few moved the might of governments. At the time it was not foreseen that world sympathy and understanding of the plight of the Illegal Immigrants would be so great as to cause the British Government to be willing to give up its Palestinian Mandate.

Much has been written in the annals of the Mossad for Aliyah Bet. A list of books for further reading is to be found in this book. By additional suggested reading, it is hoped that the reader will continue to find interest in this subject. Here, in addition to the sagas of each vessel and some of the crew, this book sets out the data of facts and figures as well as a chronological chain of events. Many writers have divided the history into several phases depending on the political climate prevailing, the bases of operation or even the changes in the Mossad leadership. To comprehend better this book an alternative division should be considered: Before and after the decision to purchase ships in the United States.

In the earlier period the ships were small, seldom exceeding a few hundred tons, and never carrying more than a few hundred refugees. Of course there were good reasons for the selection of small vessels. They were relatively easy to acquire; the investment put less money in 'each basket;' the logistic operation, including the handling of the 'human cargo,' was more manageable; the vessels were less conspicuous and could move about with less chance of detection. Hopefully, they could complete more than one voyage. However, the end of the Second World War brought about major changes. Refugees could be moved more freely and the 'shipping' requirements exploded. There simply were not enough ships available in Europe and those that were available became more expensive, often going outside the so called budget of 125 dollars per refugee. But equally important the end of the War allowed the British Naval forces to make men and warships available to oppose actively the Mossad operations. The British government was more able to exert more political pressure on European governments to obstruct Aliyah Bet work ashore.

With diminishing chances of successfully running the blockade the Mossad for Aliyah Bet decided to massively flood refugee camps both in Palestine and Cyprus, and thus hopefully forcing the Mandatory authorities to release the refugees and allow them to settle in Palestine.

Meanwhile in America at the end of the war, there was a tremendous surplus of vessels, many of which were heading for the scrap yards. Vessels could be bought by weight for a few dollars on the ton. The Pan Ships, for example, were bought for $ 125,000 each. They later each carried 7,500 refugees; thus the cost 'per passenger' was now only $16.66.

In addition Jewish political pressure could be applied to counteract its British war time ally. Local authorities were not intimidated by CID agents, and the ship owners made their decision to sell, based upon commercial considerations, often influenced by their sympathy for the plight of the refugees. These vessels were manned, in the main, by volunteers and this is their modest story. It is an essential part of history.

I can only end with a personal note. It was an honor to have served with these fine men, both in the Mossad for Aliyah Bet, and in the Israel Navy, and to have been asked to write this Foreword.

Preface

The truth about the role North American volunteers played in Aliyah Bet has been lost in a historical shuffle for four decades.

More than 32,000 immigrants, almost 50 per cent of the refugees who sailed from post-Nazi Europe for Palestine before Israel came into existence, traveled on vessels purchased in the United States and manned by American volunteer sailors. Yet this fact cannot be found in any history book.

To set the record straight, 40 years after the fact, is a task that carries with it some built-in difficulties. Not only are history books short on dependable information. Key participants have died. Those who remain alive cannot always be sure of their memories. Archival material is incomplete. The operations in which the Americans took part were secret at the time. Extensive record-keeping was not practiced. Of the records that were kept, many have been lost or destroyed.

Elusive as the facts may be, they are there. They emerge from archives, from conversations with volunteers, from recollections of others who had contact with the volunteers, from passing mentions in books, from newspaper clippings. Each of these sources has limitations, but in combination they yield a richly detailed picture of what happened 40 years earlier.

Documents listing the crews of some of the ships have been found. Interviews and correspondence have yielded the names of more than 200 volunteers. With the aid of a microcomputer, crew lists have been compiled and circulated three times to known crew members, resulting in the addition of new names and in the deletions of errors. Press articles and letters to the editors of publications elicited additional names. Similarly, a process of interviewing and document research has reconstructed much of the story of the purchasing of the ships and of their voyages. Wherever possible, we cross-checked participants' accounts with at least two other sources. In rare instances, we used information that was contradicted by other sources, and we have indicated this in the text.

This book does not recount every detail of every voyage. We have tried to avoid repetitious narration of events that were essentially the same from one vessel to another. But the chapters, taken together, provide a composite picture of the entire operation.

Interviews with the volunteers themselves, tape-recorded over the past decade, provided a detailed and representative picture of the Aliyah Bet voyages. But not all participants responded to requests for information. This created a possibility that the narrative would appear to overstate the roles of some volunteers while ignoring others. To avoid such an imbalance, we have not identified individual volunteers by name in most narrative sections of the text.

The unnamed sailors who appear in these chapters were part of a combined effort. A list of all known crew members and their vessels appears in an appendix. These men took part in the incidents described in the text. All of them share in the recognition resulting from publication of this book.

With one exception, the events in this book are described as they actually occurred. The exception is the opening shipboard narrative in Chapter One. This description is based on a real event, but the musings attributed to an American sailor are a composite gleaned from interviews with volunteers and other research.

Our objective has been to tell what the Americans did, without distortion, and without omitting major elements of the story. We hope the appearance of this book will encourage other researchers to fill whatever gaps remain in the story.

A few definitions

For brevity and ease of reading, some terms are used in this book with special definitions:

"Aliyah Bet" was a clandestine movement that brought Jews from Europe to Palestine by sea from 1934 to 1948. The British called this "illegal immigration." Unless otherwise specified, references to Aliyah Bet in this book denote the three-year period between the defeat of the Nazis in 1945 and the establishment of the State of Israel in May 1948.

"American" in this book means North American. The volunteers referred to as American in these pages were from the United States and Canada, plus a small number from Mexico.

"Displaced Persons" refers to Jews made homeless in Europe during the Nazi era and its aftermath. Many were confined in camps operated by the United Nations Relief and Rehabilitation Administration.

"Mossad" is short for the Mossad for Aliyah Bet, the agency that directed the operations of Aliyah Bet. The term is sometimes used interchangeably in this book with Haganah, the Jewish underground military organization. While the Mossad for Aliyah Bet was technically separate from the Haganah, its officers were all Haganah members, and it functioned as part of the Haganah during the period covered in this book.

"Palestine" in this book means the part of British Mandatory Palestine that became the State of Israel on May 15, 1948.

"Shu-shu boy" was the American sailors' term for a representative of the Haganah or the Mossad for Aliyah Bet. The origin of the term is obscure. It is said that the term expresses the

Americans' impression that the secrecy-minded Palestinians were continually saying, "sshh-sshh."

A word about "ships" and "boats" is also in order. In nautical terminology, a ship is a deep-water craft; a boat is a smaller vessel that can be carried aboard a ship. Many of the vessels used in Aliyah Bet, and sometimes referred to in this book as ships, were not ships in the strict sense of the term.

A few names

Descriptions of the persons named in this book appear where they are first mentioned. Some names appear in more than one chapter without repeated description:

Ash, Captain William C.—An American professional mariner, of Eastern European Jewish extraction, who served as a key Aliyah Bet volunteer. He was instrumental in buying and equipping Aliyah Bet vessels in the United States, and in recruiting and training their crews.

Ben-Gurion, David—The head of the Jewish shadow government in Palestine, as Chairman of the Jewish Agency Executive. In 1948, he became Israel's first Prime Minister and Minister of Defense.

Bevin, Ernest—British Foreign Secretary, a vocal opponent of Aliyah Bet and Jewish immigration to Palestine.

Schind, Ze'ev (Danny)—Palestinian director of Aliyah Bet activities in the United States. A member of Kibbutz Ayelet Hashahar, he went to New York in 1946 to organize the buying and equipping of vessels and recruiting of crews.

Weizmann, Chaim—Zionist leader and head of the scientific research institute that bears his name. In 1948, he became Israel's first President.

The Blockade Runners

Blood ran down the sailor's face and soaked into his shirt. Pain shot through his head, radiating from the spot where the attacker's club had landed. The sailor's skin smarted from tear gas.

Anger followed the pain, coursing through him like hot liquid. There was no time to think, only to react. A violent rage took over his entire body as the fire in his head turned to a throbbing pulse of pain. The rage went to his fists. He wanted to hit someone.

The urge to hit back forced his thoughts to work again. He had no weapon. Below, in the ship's galley, there were butcher knives. He threw himself into the passage-way, pushing past the men battling one another on the deck.

He ran to the galley and looked for a knife.

Some way to fight, he thought.

* * *

Like most of his shipmates, the sailor had been in the last war. He had been injured in that war, too.

But this conflict was different. In the last war, you had weapons and uniforms. And the enemy spoke a different language.

This time, your weapons were kitchen implements, potatoes and cans of food for throwing, and wooden sticks for clubs. This time, you had no uniform. This time, your enemy spoke English, with a British accent, and wore the uniform of the Royal Navy. This time, the ones who spoke a different language were your commanders, the "shu-shu" boys from Palestine.

In the last war, your life may have been in danger, but at least you could hope to look out for yourself. Before you went to war, you learned a military specialty from instructors who drilled it into your head that what you were learning could save your life some day. And the men around you knew what to do.

This time, it seemed as if you faced impossible odds. You were unarmed, and you weren't trained for the job you had to do. As for your shipmates, some were the greatest buddies you could ever hope to find, but others left much to be desired as seamen. Some distinguished themselves by being seasick most of the time. Like you, they were volunteers; most of them hadn't even been to sea before. They meant well, but, as a group, they did not seem to add up to enough to overcome the Royal Navy, the elements, and your own ignorance of how to operate a ship.

Except for one thing, it could have been every man for himself.

* * *

What kept the crew together was the job to be done: bringing Jewish refugees to Palestine from post-war Europe. This meant crossing the Atlantic on a dilapidated rust-bucket, loading the ship in Europe with many times the number of people she could safely carry, and sailing straight into a Royal Navy blockade of Palestine. When you signed up as a volunteer, you were warned the job could be dangerous, and you agreed to submit to Haganah discipline. Giving up your identity as well as your family, you turned over your passport to the Haganah and agreed not to tell anyone where you had gone. Your family could write to you through a mailing address in New York City. Your young Jewish commanders from Palestine reinforced this air of conspiracy, repeatedly admonishing you to follow rules of secrecy. You and the other American volunteers kiddingly referred to them as the "shu-shu boys;" they seemed to be forever telling you "sshh, sshh." But the Palestinians' intensity rubbed off on everyone. You and your shipmates took the job seriously.

* * *

Wiping the blood from his face, the sailor found a large kitchen knife. He took a last look around the little galley where he had drunk so many cups of coffee over the past few months. He knew it was a last look, because this voyage to Palestine was a one-way, one-time affair.

Not that your ship wasn't in shape for another trip. Despite her age and other shortcomings, she had made it across the Atlantic, and a return trip to Europe across the Mediterranean would be no problem. The only obstacle was the British Empire.

Only the night before, your commanders had called the crew together and explained that seizure of your ship by the British was virtually inevitable. The Royal Navy's blockade of the Palestine coast, supported by a widespread British intelligence network, made escape almost impossible. If the British boarded your ship at sea and captured her, as usually happened, she would be interned at Haifa. Even if you managed to outrace the pursuing British warships in a final dash for the beach, as the refugee vessel Haim Arlosoroff did in early 1947, your ship would fall into British hands. An ever-growing collection of captured refugee vessels along the jetty protruding into the sea at Haifa bore silent evidence to the determination of both sides to press the confrontation further; the Jews vowed to keep on challenging the blockade, and the British were not yet ready to accept the end of their rule in Palestine.

As for the passengers and crew, a British prison camp was most likely your destination. The goal was Palestine, of course, but few refugee voyages could accomplish it these days. Before the larger, American-manned ships joined the immigration fleet early in 1946, a series of smaller craft had made it to shore with lesser numbers of refugees. As the refugee traffic increased, so did the efforts of the British to seal the coast of Palestine. Not since December 25, 1945, when 252 immigrants made it ashore, had a refugee craft gotten through. Today, the chance of a successful landing on a beach in Palestine was small in the face of the overwhelming superiority of the blockading British forces.

* * *

Although this would be good-bye to the ship, the crew would stay together, at least for a while.

You had to avoid being identified as a crew member. When the British captured a ship, they tried to find and arrest the American crew members and Haganah leaders. For most volunteers, the way to escape was to pass yourself off as a refugee; you could accomplish this by melting into the crowd and not speaking English. The British would take the refugees to prison camp, and you would be among them.

A few volunteers might escape directly at the harbor in Haifa. It was customary for a small number of men, generally Haganah commanders and key crew members, to elude the British by concealing themselves aboard ship in a water tank or other specially prepared hiding place. There they would wait for a day or more until the cleaning crew came aboard. The ships were in a filthy state when they arrived in port, and the British left the nasty job of cleaning them to local Jewish workers. The Haganah controlled the port work force and was able to send its agents aboard in the cleaning crews. When the cleaning staff walked off the ship, the ship's hidden crew members were among them. They would walk through the port gates, past British guards who did not count them or ask questions.

For the other crew members, your next step was a British internment camp in Cyprus. Most of the passengers and volunteers on the first two American-manned ships had been sent to prison camps in Palestine. Not long after that, as the number of arriving refugees increased sharply, the British in the summer of 1946 adopted a new policy of transporting the refugees to the nearby island colony of Cyprus. As soon as a refugee ship arrived at Haifa, its passengers would be herded aboard prison ships and dispatched to Cyprus, where they would be confined in internment camps. Barbed wire and lookout towers surrounded the camps, and British soldiers maintained an armed guard to prevent escapes.

Although the British controlled the supply of food and water to the camps, they allowed the Jews to administer their own affairs inside the barbed-wire enclosures. This put the actual control of conditions inside the Cyprus camps in the hands of the Haganah. When you reached Cyprus, Haganah agents would note your arrival at camp and equip you with false identification. Later, when the time came, the Haganah would put you on a list of refugees to be admitted to Palestine under the meager monthly quota allowed by the British. Some of the American volunteers stayed in Cyprus for months; others, especially those needed by the Haganah for duty on another refugee ship, might find themselves in Palestine in a matter of weeks. One American whose tall, mustachioed figure gave him a distinctive appearance was questioned and beaten in Cyprus by British guards who recognized him from an earlier shipment of refugees; he had escaped from Cyprus, returned to Palestine, and joined another refugee vessel that was captured. In all, he made three voyages.

When you arrived at the port in Palestine, the British would put you on a bus to Atlit transit camp. Eventually, you would be released from this camp and would be free to make your way back to Haifa. Some of the American volunteers chose not to wait and managed to slip away from the bus taking them to the transit camp.

In Haifa, you would go to the Carmelia Court Hotel, where the Haganah maintained a secret center for volunteers from refugee ships. If you were planning to remain in Palestine, you would receive new identity papers and about $100 in pocket money. If you were returning to the United States, you would receive false identification sufficient to take you to Europe, where you would report to the American consul with a made-up story to explain why you had no passport. The consular officer would issue you a travel document valid only for your return to the United States. Later, you might be questioned by agents of the Federal Bureau of Investigation; the FBI men would want to know whom you had met during your voyage, and particularly whether you had contact with Russian agents.

* * *

Not more than minutes ago, the British destroyer had attacked, sending Marines in battle dress across specially constructed boarding bridges onto the refugee ship. The assault brought an abrupt end to the sailor's feeling of refuge and sanctuary on this old ship.

After living aboard the ship and helping take care of her for so many months, you had long since come to think of the old hulk as home, first in port in the United States, then crossing the Atlantic, later refitting her in Europe to carry her horde of refugees, and finally steaming toward Palestine with survivors of the Nazi Holocaust crammed into every available space. Even the top of the deck was filled with refugees. The last few days had been particularly congenial, sitting on deck at night with your shipmates, learning the stories of the refugees, joining in songs, and talking about the ever-closer goal of Palestine. Your language of communication with the passengers was Yiddish; most of them spoke it fluently. With Yiddish-speaking crew members serving as interpreters, the refugees gave you and your shipmates first-hand accounts of the horrors the Nazis had visited upon the Jews of Europe. You learned how the refugees survived the Holocaust, and you heard for the first time about Jewish heroism and resistance during the darkest days of the Nazis' rule. Some Jews who had joined bands of partisans told you of their experiences in the forests fighting a guerrilla war against the Nazis. Others explained to you how Jewish survivors were consigned after the war to the miserable status of "displaced persons" living in camps established by the victorious Allies. Determined to go to Palestine, tens of thousands of Jews streamed across post-war Europe toward seaports where Haganah ships operated.

These revelations of the European Jews' struggle gave a further dimension of meaning to your decision to volunteer. Many of the passengers were your own age, young people whose lives had taken an entirely different course from yours only because of geography; they grew up in Europe, while fate had placed your home beyond the reach of the Nazi death machine. Members of youth groups and political movements, they had linked up with the Jewish underground network that developed in Europe after the war, and they had made their way to the coast. And now their lives were joined with yours, aboard this creaking old vessel. Until the British attacked a few minutes ago, the ship seemed to have become an inseparable part of your existence.

The battle on deck could not last much longer. Already, the sailor could hear gunfire. His shipmates were unarmed, as were the passengers. The British had all manner of weapons, and only restraint on both sides could keep the confrontation from turning into a bloodbath. At the moment, the din of battle from the deck above did not bear the sounds of restraint.

In a short while, the aging ship would be immobilized, and you would be separated from her forever.

* * *

Clutching his knife, the sailor bolted into a passageway to the upper deck. His rage to lash out had subsided, and his head was calmer now. He had a single thought: to rejoin the defense of the ship. As he reached the scene of the fighting, he saw one of his shipmates struggling with a British Marine. A tingle of pride surged through the sailor as his buddy knocked the Marine to the deck.

You had to admire those shipmates of yours. They were fighters.

Like the American volunteers on other refugee ships, most had served in World War II. They represented virtually every branch of the armed forces. A few were real sailors. Some had been naval officers or enlisted men. Others had served in the Coast Guard. Still others were veterans of the Merchant Marine, including men who had become ship's officers after graduating from the Kings Point Merchant Marine Academy. But, on ship after ship sailing from America, most of the volunteers had no experience at sea. They included former infantrymen, paratroopers, marines, aviators, medics, and technicians. Among them were men who had seen action in major engagements including the Battle of the Bulge, the Anzio beachhead, and the island war in the Pacific. The volunteers on one ship included an ex-paratrooper planning to study marine biology, a Marine wounded on Guadalcanal, a sailor who won the boxing championship aboard a Navy cruiser, two former Merchant Marine officers in their early 20s, a European-born soldier who had risen to the rank of major in the U.S. Army, and a Navy pharmacist's mate whose wartime background helped him organize medical services for his refugee passengers.

In addition to being war veterans, most of the sailors had another common characteristic: almost all of the volunteers were young Jews. Some were members of Zionist youth groups and planned to make their lives in Palestine; a few came from religiously observant backgrounds; many had no formal affiliation with Jewish life. There were also non-Jews who signed up along with Jewish friends or took up the cause on their own. What united them was a deep impulse to take positive action to help the survivors of the Nazi holocaust. Six million Jews had been murdered while the rest of the world looked the other way or failed to take actions that could have saved countless victims. After the war, the homeless survivors were confined in wretched camps while the failure to act continued. The list of those who seemed unable to do more than debate or appoint study committees was long; it included their own American government and the leadership of the organized Jewish community. The volunteers confronted the general impotence with a simple, if rare, response: They took action, doing what they personally could.

* * *

Suddenly, the battle was over. The British had won control of the ship, and the resistance halted as the order to stop fighting passed among the well-organized fighting groups of passengers.

The sailor tossed his knife over the rail and walked into the midst of a cluster of refugees. If he had ever doubted whether he and these Jews from Europe had very much in common, the time of doubting was over. Like the others crowded together on the deck of the old ship, he was one more Jew about to be imprisoned. In time, they would all be in Palestine.

'Illegal Immigration': An Overview

And if those ships are illegal, so was the Boston Tea Party.
—*I.F. Stone, Underground to Palestine.*

Like so much else in the history of modern Israel, this story of Aliyah Bet is filled with people who made the seemingly impossible happen.

By ordinary standards, the whole venture should have been impossible. By ordinary standards, the Aliyah Bet fleet could not have been assembled. By ordinary standards, the predominantly untrained volunteer crews could not have operated a ship. By ordinary standards, the inadequate vessels of Aliyah Bet could not have carried the number of passengers who crammed aboard them. By ordinary standards, the Aliyah Bet voyages could not have proceeded after British agents persuaded European port officials to detain the antiquated vessels on grounds of insufficient sanitation or other infractions. By ordinary standards, the effort would have been stifled by the Royal Navy's blockade.

But this was no ordinary operation. When Aliyah Bet resumed after the German surrender in 1945, two unequal antagonists faced each other in Europe and the Mediterranean. On one side stood the British Empire, battered but triumphant after more than five years of war against the Axis powers. On the opposing side were the Jews — homeless refugees in Europe, the Zionist settlement in Palestine, and a scattering of activists in other parts of the world. Much to the surprise of many, including more than a few Jewish leaders, the Jews set out to challenge the Empire with a makeshift fleet of daring blockade-runners. In less than three years, the seemingly hopeless Jews prevailed over the power and prestige of the British.

* * *

At the end of the war in 1945, large numbers of Jews who had managed to survive the Nazi Holocaust found themselves outcasts in Europe. Unable to return to their former homes, they became Displaced Persons in Allied-occupied areas, living in camps operated by the

United Nations Relief and Rehabilitation Administration.

Of more than 7 million persons who had been uprooted in Germany by the war, most were quickly repatriated. By the end of 1945, some 6 million had returned home. Of those who remained without homes, only 10 to 20 per cent were Jews, but their problem was not on the way to solution. The number of homeless Jews actually was increasing, as anti-Jewish outbreaks in post-war Europe added to the survivors' difficulties of resuming their former existences. For many of these Jews, their only real homeland was the Zionist settlement in British-controlled Palestine. And Palestine

Passengers of the Wedgwood, the first of the American Aliyah Bet vessels

was closed to large-scale Jewish immigration.

In July 1945, an American investigating commission toured more than 30 Displaced Persons camps and urged admission to Palestine for those who wanted to go there. The commission reported that in the camps "we appear to be treating the Jews as the Nazis treated them except that we do not exterminate them." The Jews lived under guard, behind barbed wire fences, unable to send or receive mail, unable to receive help from social service agencies. In some cases, Displaced Persons lived in former concentration camps, housed together with their former guards. Housing and medical care were inadequate, and no improvements were being made.

The first step in the Jews' rescue was one of self-help. European Jews organized an underground network known as the Brichah ("flight," in Hebrew), which moved thousands of these Displaced Persons across Europe to coastal areas. Their objective was to reach Palestine by sea. Clandestine voyages from Europe had brought refugees to Palestine as early as 1934, when the Nazis were only beginning their persecution of Jews. In 1945, with the Nazis defeated and Jews streaming toward the ports of Europe, the stage was set for a resumption of the immigrant voyages.

The British strongly opposed this movement. In 1945 they reaffirmed a pre-war policy restricting Jewish immigration to Palestine. The British would permit only 1,500 Jews a month to enter Palestine. As the clandestine immigration voyages resumed, the British prepared a massive naval and military force to turn the refugees back. They declared it "illegal immigration." The Jews, rejecting the concept of "illegal immigration," called the movement "Aliyah Bet," a Hebrew term indicating that this was a legitimate return of Jews to their own homeland.

Through its agency known as the Mossad for Aliyah Bet, the Haganah underground in Palestine chartered boats for transport across the Mediterranean. But charters in Europe proved expensive, and crews were not always available or dependable. Nor were the boats big enough to meet the need of large-scale transport.

In an attempt to find a solution, the Mossad sent emissaries to the United States. There they found Jewish ship-owners, officers, seamen, and people of good will. Many were ready to help, without pay. Others were prepared to contribute money. The buying of ships and the recruitment of American volunteer sailors began. Starting in 1946, a fleet of aging vessels purchased by Americans and manned by American volunteer sailors joined the Aliyah Bet effort.

* * *

North Americans first put their mark on Aliyah Bet with the voyages of the former Canadian corvettes Wedgwood and Haganah. In barely more than one month in mid-1946, the two sister ships transported almost 5,000 refugees, nearly as many as had been carried by the entire post-Nazi Aliyah Bet effort until then.

Immigrants take a turn above deck

With the advent of the American vessels, Aliyah Bet entered its transformation into an operation involving larger and larger numbers of refugees, eventually overflowing the British camps in Palestine and then the camps in Cyprus. The number of passengers carried was only one indication of the American impact on Aliyah Bet. Not only the greater speed and capacity of the ships, but the high motivation of their volunteer crews, presented a new challenge to British efforts to maintain the blockade of Palestine.

The third American ship, the Haim Arlosoroff, dramatized the rising violence of the conflict between the British and the Zionists. After a fierce fight in which the British opened fire with machine-guns, the Arlosoroff outran her larger pursuers and beached herself at Bat Galim in view of thousands of Jewish residents of Haifa. American crew members of the Hatikvah, captured less than three months after the Arlosoroff, took part in making a bomb that sank their British prison ship in Haifa harbor.

Three other escalations of Aliyah Bet followed the Arlosoroff battle. Each involved American vessels. More than 4,500 refugees arrived aboard the Exodus in July of 1947. After a battle in which one of the American crew members was killed, the British sent the Exodus passengers to Germany. Aliyah Bet answered the deportation of the Exodus passengers by bringing more than 4,000 additional refugees from Eastern Europe to Palestine aboard the American vessels Geula and The Jewish State. Then, after the United Nations General Assembly on November 29 approved the partition of Palestine into independent Jewish and Arab states, Aliyah Bet reached flood tide with the dispatch of the Kibbutz Galuyot and the Atzmaut carrying more than 15,000 refugees, who swamped the British camps on Cyprus.

Although the volunteers' activity was clandestine, it was not illegal under United States law. In full legality, the American vessels obtained Panamanian or Honduran registry and sailed from the United States for Europe under their foreign flags. The sailors were duly signed on as crew members. In this regard, the voyages were no different from the large volume of American maritime activity conducted under foreign flags of convenience. The British term "illegal immigration" did not imply that the American volunteers were violating the laws of their own country. When the British labelled Aliyah Bet as "illegal immigration," they referred to their refusal to permit Jewish immigrants from Europe to enter Palestine legally. Canadian volunteers among the American crews had a special status; as British subjects, they could enter Palestine legally. In the later stages of Aliyah Bet, the British persuaded the United States government to use its law-enforcement apparatus in investigating the American volunteer effort. But this was an empty threat; no volunteer was ever prosecuted under United States law for his Aliyah Bet activities.

One American volunteer was killed and others injured in battles with the British. Many were captured and interned behind barbed wire in detention camps in Cyprus. Six later lost their lives in Israel's War of Independence.

* * *

The clandestine sealift achieved its purpose of refugee relief. Although most of the passengers were captured by the British and detained in Cyprus, they reached their destination—no longer as refugees, but as citizens of Israel—after the Jewish State declared its independence on May 15, 1948. The immigrants went immediately into service in the new army of Israel; some 800 of these newcomers lost their lives as soldiers in Israel's 1948-49 War of Independence.

In simple arithmetic, the American role was significant. More than 32,000 refugees —more than 46 per cent of 69,563 so-called "illegal" immigrants in 1945-48—escaped from Europe on 10 ships bought in America and manned by American volunteers. Other Americans, not recruited for these 10 ships, served as individual volunteers on other refugee vessels.

In impact, the American role was greater than its numerical proportions. The Americans' contribution provided a critical factor that enabled the 1945-48 immigration effort not only to continue but to go forward in the face of close British surveillance of immigration activities in Europe, and in spite of the non-availability of suitable ships in a depleted European maritime market.

Although some Aliyah Bet vessels succeeded in 1945 in running the Royal Navy blockade of the Palestinian shores, it was clear at the time of the American-manned voyages that this was not possible. Britain had substantially increased her naval power to oppose Jewish immigration: more radar stations, more warhips, improved intelligence, and earlier contact with the refugee ships, near or at the ports of embarkation. The Royal Navy's objectives were to prevent sailings, or, at worst, to prevent arrivals in Palestine.

The refugee voyages were far more than an annoyance to Britain; they directly challenged the Empire's ability to control entry to British-held territory. While Britain possessed an incomparably superior force, this did not deter the desperate and determined refugees from trying to reach Palestine. Britain used her military might as a threat, and she employed it to capture ships and imprison their passengers, but the British were not prepared to sink ships or unleash their firepower against unarmed refugees. As the refugee ships continued to arrive on the shores of Palestine, the human cargo filled the internment camps in Palestine and Cyprus and, as a result, weakened the British resolve.

American-manned ships were involved in episodes that helped discredit British policy and eventually broke the British hold on Palestine. The story of the Exodus 1947, and particularly the deportation of its refugee passengers back to Germany, rallied world public opinion in favor of a Jewish state. The concentration of immigrants, including more than 15,000 who arrived in one day on two American ships, broke down the British administrative and military ability to combat Jewish immigration. Maintaining the blockade became an economic burden. Britain not only failed to stop the transports but was subjected to increasing pressure and embarrassment which contributed to the end of the British presence in Palestine.

* * *

Every Aliyah Bet vessel had Palestinians aboard, serving alongside the Americans. Normal seagoing activities were the responsibility of the captain, who was a professional sailor, usually recruited in the United States. In addition to the captain, a Haganah representative from Palestine was aboard each vessel as its commander. It was the Haganah commander's job to deal with political decisions. He gave the order to resist or not resist when the British attacked. Under him served other Palestinians, usually two or three in number, who escorted and commanded the refugee passengers. The Americans called the Palestinians the "shu-shu boys." This good-humored appellation reflected the Americans' perception that the Palestinians were obsessed with secrecy. Their favorite expression seemed to be "sshh-sshh."

Although they were working for the same goal and shared a common heritage, these two groups of Jews had their differences. The two factions, the Americans and the Palestinians, eyed each other with skepticism, and sometimes with mistrust.

To the Palestinians, indoctrinated to austerity in Socialist youth movements and hardened by underground conflict with the British and Arabs, the freewheeling Americans were an unfamiliar element. They sometimes seemed naive, undisciplined, uncontrollable.

The Americans, on the other hand, were from a different background. They had grown up breathing the air of the richest and most powerful nation on the globe. They were open, warm, imbued with a self-assurance that sometimes came across as over-confidence. To them, the determined Palestinians seemed arrogant, narrow-minded, overly secretive and conspiratorial.

To one group of Americans, their Palestinian commander seemed stubborn, pig-headed, never willing to admit that he did not know everything. Americans who were professional seafarers looked down on the

Crowded conditions below deck

sailing ability and professionalism of the Palestinians. Inexperienced Palestinian commanders, by the same token, were unfamiliar with the ways of sailors and unprepared for the profanity of some Americans and their use of alcohol. Each group regarded the other as a bit reckless in the face of the life-or-death challenges that continually confronted the Aliyah Bet crews.

This clash of traits could have been expected. Even now, four decades later, some of the the differences between the two groups stand out as national characteristics of Americans and Israelis. At least once, when tempers flared and American volunteers in one crew were ordered before the Haganah equivalent of a court martial, the conflict threatened to disrupt a voyage. But, in the end, American-Palestinian misunderstandings amounted to no more than a footnote to the story of Aliyah Bet. The vessels sailed, and the Aliyah Bet crews fulfilled their missions.

In the reports they filed after each voyage, Palestinian commanders sometimes commented unfavorably on the American crew members. In more than one report, the Americans' lack of experience at sea was a mark against the volunteers. Individual Americans who got drunk or whose behavior otherwise offended the Palestinians' sensibilities were singled out in these reports, with recommendations that they not be invited to sail on future voyages. But, in the main, the Palestinian commanders' reports merely noted the composition of the crews and remarked on the presence of Americans. These reports did not quarrel with the principle of using American volunteers. Later, looking back on what had been accomplished, Palestinian commanders praised the Americans. A Mossad official commented that the Americans appeared better qualified than the Palestinians who commanded them. Another Palestinian noted the willingness of the Americans to undertake seemingly impossible assignments, without complaint. He doubted that hired crews would have done the same.

* * *

Although journalists discovered the American sailors and wrote about them at the time, the role of the volunteers quickly faded from public memory. After Israel's War of Independence, in which many of the volunteers fought, the Aliyah Bet crews no longer existed. The volunteers were never to sail together again. A majority of the volunteers dispersed and returned home to America. A substantial minority stayed in Israel and embarked on new futures as citizens of the young nation. Some who were members of Zionist youth groups clustered together in pioneering settlements. Others went their individual ways. In America and in Israel, almost all of the volunteer sailors resumed the landlubber's life. Only a few men continued to go to sea. When the history of Aliyah Bet came to be written, the American sailors were essentially a forgotten group.

The story of how Americans bought and equipped the vessels was never well enough known to be forgotten. Journalists at the time uncovered only small parts of this secret operation. Later, follow-up research into Aliyah Bet purchasing was not of major interest to reporters or historians. The story remained untold, and few people were aware of the full measure of the clandestine purchasing activity.

The first warships of the Israeli navy consisted of four of the 10 Aliyah Bet vessels from America: the Wedgwood, the Haganah, the Ben Hecht, and The Jewish State. Three of these craft took part in the Israeli Navy's most noted action of the 1948-49 War of Independence, the pursuit and sinking of the Egyptian flagship Al Faruk.

Just as American vessels became the new Navy, so did Israeli passenger and cargo shipping become a reality with the American-purchased Atzmaut and Kibbutz Galuyot. Until these American vessels joined the Zim lines, the Israeli merchant fleet consisted of one boat that could carry 300 people.

The Exodus and the Haim Arlosoroff were too severely damaged to sail again, and the Geula and Hatikvah were deemed too dilapidated for further use. Like the receding memories of the American contribution to Aliyah Bet, they were consigned to scrap.

CREATING THE FLEET IN AMERICA

> We had the feeling that in America we could do something that would have been impossible in another place.
>
> —*Ze'ev (Danny) Schind, head of Aliyah Bet operations in the United States.*

One of the bright spots of cafe society in New York City at the end of World War II was the Copacabana night club, home of the Copa Girls chorus line and performers such as Lena Horne and the comedy team of Dean Martin and Jerry Lewis. A few floors above the famous night club, Haganah agents from Palestine came and went in 1945 and early 1946. The Palestinians were arriving in New York with a secret mission: organizing American assistance for the coming struggle for a Jewish state.

The Palestinians' choice of one of Manhattan's most celebrated addresses as their secret base came about through personal connections. The Copacabana occupied the basement level of 14 East 60th Street. The night club leased its quarters from the Hotel Fourteen, built in 1902 as a residential hotel catering to rich widows and other members of upper-class society. The landlords of the Copacabana and of the Haganah agents were Fanny Barnett and her husband, Ruby, who had bought the hotel in 1944. In the past, Fanny Barnett had sometimes worked at the offices of the Jewish Agency, serving there in World War II as secretary to Chaim Weizmann. In 1945 the Jewish Agency asked her to come back to work to help a Palestinian who had arrived in New York to begin organizing American Jewish support for the Haganah. Fanny took the assignment; in the spring of 1945, she arranged a room at the hotel for the Palestinian, Reuven Shiloah. Then known as Reuven Zaslansky, Shiloah was later to become the first head of the Shin Bet, Israel's General Security Service. Shiloah's boss, David Ben-Gurion, arrived in the summer to stay at the Hotel Fourteen while conferring with American friends. One of Ben-Gurion's meetings was with 19 American Jews at the Manhattan apartment of Rudolph Sonneborn; Ben-Gurion told them the Jews of Palestine would soon have to fight for survival, and he asked the Americans to be ready to help. More Palestinians arrived at the Hotel Fourteen; it became the meeting place of many future leaders of the State of Israel.

The Palestinian Jews who came and went at "Kibbutz 14," as the 300-room Hotel Fourteen came to be called, undertook a variety of secret projects to mobilize American Jews. The man in charge of this activity was Yaakov Dori, who moved into the Hotel Fourteen in January 1946. Dori, who was to become Israel's first military chief of staff, was known as Jacob Dostrovsky when he arrived in New York. He headed a clandestine organization concentrating on four major functions: acquiring military equipment, recruiting military manpower, collecting and disseminating information, and helping Aliyah Bet.

Acquiring ships for Aliyah Bet was among the first urgent tasks of Dori's secret mission in New York. In September 1945 the British Cabinet had rejected American President Harry S Truman's proposal that 100,000 Jewish refugees be admitted to Palestine. The British imposed a limit of 1,500 Jews per month. This set the stage for the expansion of Aliyah Bet. In Europe, the Brichah network was functioning, and Jews from Palestine had already arrived to organize Displaced Persons for transport. Ben-Gurion, at first opposed to attempting large-scale immigration, later agreed to a goal of 10,000 immigrants a month. The Haganah, which had been using small craft such as fishing boats and chartering commercial ships with foreign crews, needed larger vessels and its own crews.

The work of the clandestine Aliyah Bet section in the United States entailed not only buying ships but refitting them, equipping them, registering them under foreign flags, and arranging the numerous details ordinarily involved in international maritime commerce. The job came to include the unconventional task of recruiting crews, clandestinely, from a highly varied collection of Zionist youth group members, professional sailors, Jewish volunteers, and others interested in signing on.

* * *

One of the new faces at Hotel Fourteen in 1946 was Ze'ev Schind, a congenial redhead from Kibbutz Ayelet Hashahar, who came to New York to take charge of the Aliyah Bet section. Known as "Danny," the 36-year-old Schind had an Aliyah Bet background that went back to 1937 in Europe. Schind, who was born in Vilna and emigrated to Palestine at age 20, did not speak English well when he arrived in New York, but he managed to get his points across; the first time he showed up to purchase a ship, Schind was asked whom he represented. His reply: "The Jewish people." Schind put his personal stamp on the American operation. To one colleague, Schind was a charismatic wonder worker with "natural executive ability, a ready smile, and an affable personality that made people want to help him." Years later, coworkers would recall him with affection and admiration bordering on awe; they remembered his sense of humor, and his determination to let nothing stand in the way of Aliyah Bet.

Schind acquired a key aide, Joe Buxenbaum, who was recruited for Aliyah Bet shortly after his discharge from the World War II U.S. army. Together, Schind and Buxenbaum found ships, inspected them, arranged their refitting, and visited them at dockside as they prepared to weigh anchor for Europe.

One of Schind's contacts in New York was Morris Ginsberg of the American Foreign Steamship Corporation, who assumed an important role early in the operation. A committed Jew, Ginsberg was a member of a respected family in the shipping industry. He knew the business, and he had connections which could be invaluable. For one thing, he could buy ships. With Ginsberg as the intermediary, Aliyah Bet acquired the former Royal Canadian Navy corvettes Norsyd and Beauharnois, which were refitted early in 1946 as cargo vessels and provided with Panamanian registry. They became the Wedgwood and the Haganah, the first two Aliyah Bet ships manned by American crews.

Ginsberg's service to Aliyah Bet extended far beyond acquiring ships. He was a frequent source of expertise and advice, and his company gave the clandestine operatives of Aliyah Bet an aboveground channel for making business contacts. His name carried weight in the industry, and his prestige enabled him to function both as a financial guarantor and as a channel for disbursing funds. Schind said his grandfather came from the same Eastern European community as Ginsberg's family; Buxenbaum was never sure whether Ginsberg believed this. About another personal connection, no doubt existed: Ginsberg, who entered Aliyah Bet as a bachelor, later married Schind's secretary, Pepe.

Another American Jew who played an important role almost from the beginning of the United States operation was a professional sailor, William C. Ash. Born in Poland, Ash had become a sea captain, a wartime officer in the U.S. Maritime Service, and an officer of the Masters, Mates and Pilots Union. He served briefly after World War II as port captain for Morris Ginsberg's American Foreign Steamship Corporation. Then he set up his own business as a marine surveyor at 24 Stone Street in the Wall Street district of New York.

Captain Ash received a telephone call one day from the Jewish Agency for Palestine, inviting him to an important meeting. The next day, at the Agency office at 342 Madison Avenue, Danny Schind filled Captain Ash in on the activities of the Aliyah Bet mission and sought his assistance. To the gruff-spoken American sea captain, Schind's approach leaned too heavily in the direction of conspiracy, furtiveness, and illegality. Captain Ash refused to become involved in anything illegal; he advised Schind that there was no need to break the law. Aliyah Bet could operate in America in full legality, as American shipowners did when they obtained foreign flags of convenience by organizing dummy foreign companies. Ash explained that a foreign company could be created on paper for the modest cost of

$500. Morris Ginsberg recalled a similar conversation with Schind, who suggested Aliyah Bet could earn money by dealing in tobacco, at the time a valuable black-market item in Europe. Ginsberg said no; he told Schind that everything should be done in full legality.

The Palestinian took the advice of the Americans. A new Panamanian company, hardly more than a mailing address, came into existence under the name of Arias and Arias. Schind and Ash also set up an American corporation, the Weston Trading Company, and put its name on the door of Captain Ash's office at 24 Stone Street. Captain Ash was company president. American Jews who had come into the Aliyah Bet orbit were listed as the directors of the company. Nowhere did Schind's name appear on company papers.

The sole stockholder listed on the Weston Trading Company's incorporation papers was Dewey Stone, of Brockton, Mass. A friend of Chaim Weizmann and a future national chairman of the United Jewish Appeal, Stone provided the clandestine Aliyah Bet mission with another respectable means of access to the above-board world. As a prominent businessman, philanthropist, and community leader, Stone was in a position to write checks for large sums without causing inconvenient questions to be asked. When agents of the Federal Bureau of Investigation came to see Stone about one of the American ships being fitted out for Haganah service, Stone's involvement in a bona fide textile company gave plausibility to his response that the ship was being readied to transport clothing to refugees in Europe.

* * *

Aliyah Bet had two basic needs in America: ships capable of carrying large numbers of refugees, and sailors to man the ships. Danny Schind's newly acquired high-level American business contacts might find the ships, but these were not the people who could form the crews. To find the sailors, it was necessary to turn elsewhere, to the working level of the industry. Aliyah Bet needed men to navigate, handle a sextant, steer, swab decks, chip paint, operate an engineroom, and carry out the many other functions of the sailor's trade.

As with the buying of ships, the recruiting of crews was complicated by the need for subterfuge. Balancing the requirements of secrecy with the need to spread the word among potential crewmembers was a delicate task. Unlike the purchasing operation, which could be quietly carried on under the cover provided by a few key people such as Morris Ginsberg and Dewey Stone, the job of recruiting carried with it a built-in need to tell more and more people about Aliyah Bet. Had Aliyah Bet been a conventional shipping business, it would have been simple to go to the seamen's hiring halls and straightforwardly circulate the word that crews were needed. But the underground was in no position to publicize the needs of Aliyah Bet. Moreover, recruiters had to be highly selective in whom they approached: Aliyah Bet needed crewmen who could be depended upon not only to do their shipboard jobs under difficult conditions but to keep secrets. Aliyah Bet had to take care to avoid hiring anyone who might be an informant for the British. The volunteers chosen for Aliyah Bet would work without pay and face a strong possibility of going to jail in Europe or Palestine.

Although the obstacles were formidable, Aliyah Bet came to the hiring task with certain compensating advantages. American Zionist organizations, particularly youth groups, could be approached discreetly; their members were highly motivated, and they had their own channels of communication. And there were Jewish sailors; although seafaring was not widely regarded as a Jewish occupation, one Palestinian sea captain who had served in the Merchant Marine estimated that Jews constituted ten per cent of the American merchant fleet at the time. There was also Captain Ash; as an official of the Masters, Mates, and Pilots Union, he was in an especially good position to identify men who might serve as captains, mates, and other key members of the Aliyah Bet crews. And there were many other American Jews, members of the world's largest Jewish population, more than 500,000 of whom had just returned from World War II. Most of these returning war veterans were young men. From all of these sources, it should be possible to assemble a few crews. Captain Ash and Zionist youth movement activists began lining up the crews.

Captain Ash used his knowledge and contacts in the shipping industry to find experienced seafarers. He found captains, mates, engineers. He did not restrict his recruitment efforts to Jews: Captain Ash hired non-Jewish captains, agreeing that their role would be to take the ships to Europe, where volunteer captains would take over.

Palestine Vocational Services, another front organization, came into existence to recruit crews for Aliyah Bet. Its director was Ralph Goldman, who later became Executive Director of the American Jewish Joint Distribution Committee, the overseas relief organization.

Akiva Skidell, who recruited sailors through Palestine Vocational Services, used his contacts in Zionist groups to put out the word that volunteers were needed. One feature of Zionist youth movements at the time was the preparation of groups for aliyah to Palestine. To this end, the Hehalutz pioneering movement had bought farms where prospective immigrants to Palestine could learn agriculture and organize themselves into nuclei of future settlements. Youth movement members from two New Jersey training farms, at Creamridge and Hightstown, became a source of manpower for Aliyah Bet in 1945 and 1946. Volunteering for Aliyah Bet offered these young men a means of transportation to Palestine and a chance to be of service on the way.

Volunteers agreed to serve without pay except for pocket money for cigarettes and sundries, and to subject themselves to Haganah discipline. Recruiters explained that there was no way of knowing how much time a voyage might take. They warned the volunteers not to tell anyone including their families where they were going. Skidell admonished volunteers to stay out of bars when in port; Jewish boys could not hold their liquor, he told them. Before signing on, volunteers had to be interviewed personally by Danny Schind. The Palestinian also did some recruiting on his own; on a trip to Canada, he found time to line up three volunteers for the first American-manned voyage.

Not surprisingly, the first American crews were made up from the most readily available sources. Many were Zionist youth group members with no seafaring experience. Others were war veterans whose eagerness to serve the Jewish cause far exceeded their experience at sea. Supervising the landlubbers were non-Zionist professional sailors recruited by Captain Ash.

Before the volunteers sailed, they were sworn into the Haganah. A modest shipboard ceremony would take place, attended by members of the top management such as Yaakov Dori, Danny Schind, or perhaps Joe Buxenbaum.

I.F. Stone, an American journalist, sailed on the first two American-manned volunteer ships and wrote a book about his experiences (*Underground to Palestine,* New York, 1946.) Stone described the Wedgwood as "manned by about as odd a collection of seamen as ever sailed the seas."

Of the captain and first mate, both of whom were professional sailors and former members of the militant International Workers of the World, Stone wrote: "Like many of the sailors I was to meet on these illegal ships, neither of these officers was Jewish by anything but an accident of birth. They had little Jewish upbringing and no Jewish education, and were, of course, not at all religious. But they had left families in America and taken the risk of long sentences in British prisons if caught. They said they were 'sore as a —— boil' about the treatment the Jews had received in Europe. They spoke a thick Brooklynese, heavily seasoned with favorite GI expletives."

As to the crewmen, Stone described the sailors of the Wedgwood's sister ship Haganah as follows:

> Many of the crew members were New Yorkers. Others came from Chicago, Los Angeles, Baltimore, Washington, Boston, Jersey City, and New Haven. There was a Canadian boy from Toronto. Only our chief engineer was non-Jewish.
>
> Most of the crew had served in the Army, Navy, or Merchant Marine during the war. Some joined the crew because they were Zionists. A lot of them were American *Chalutzim* (Hebrew for "pioneers") who intended to remain in the collective settlements in Palestine.
>
> The rest were simply American sailors who happened to be Jews, boys with little if any past contact with Jewish life. They spoke neither Yiddish nor Hebrew. They were not very articulate, but for them the trip was more than a heroic adventure. They all felt deeply about the treatment of the Jews in Europe, and this was their way of doing something about it.

Later, as the word went out through ever-widening Jewish circles and then became public knowledge, the makeup of the crews became more diversified. Jewish ex-servicemen signed up from a variety of backgrounds. Some of the Jews were moved to action by two books by non-Jews who criticized Britain's policies in Palestine: *Behind the Silken Curtain,* by Bartley C. Crum, and *The Forgotten Ally* by Pierre Van Paassen. At Harvard Law School, a rabbi's son who had been a U.S. Navy officer in Pacific combat learned about Aliyah Bet by reading I.F. Stone's book in 1946; he and an Irish-American non-Jewish classmate sought out the Aliyah Bet recruiters and signed up. On Okinawa, a Palestinian serving in the U.S. Merchant Marine received a telegram from the Hehalutz office in New York to come home; he headed for New York and learned about Aliyah Bet on Guam from a newsletter for Jewish servicemen. In New York, he discovered that an elderly aunt was babysitting for the family of Danny Schind, the Haganah agent to whom he had been instructed to report.

Volunteers also came to Aliyah Bet through another front, Land and Labor for Palestine, Inc., which was set up to recruit Americans with military experience for the Jewish army in Palestine. Land and Labor opened its head office at the Hotel Breslin in New York and quickly set up branches in Chicago, Boston, Philadelphia, Baltimore, Pittsburgh, Cleveland, Detroit, and Miami.

Eventually, volunteers who had entered Aliyah Bet with no seafaring background became old hands who returned for second voyages. Some sailed three times or more. One volunteer, who first learned of Aliyah Bet at a Zionist youth movement's convention during the 1945-46 Christmas holidays, made his first voyage in 1947 and kept on going back for a total of five sailings.

Other American volunteers came to Aliyah Bet by roundabout routes. One left his U.S. army unit in Europe after meeting a group of Palestine-bound refugees and learning of the Holocaust; stranded in Europe for half a year, he worked at a refugee camp until he finally went to Palestine as a crew member of an Aliyah Bet ship. Many years later, returning to the U.S. for a visit, he was arrested as an army deserter but went free after telling his story. Another volunteer went to Europe to visit the grave of a soldier brother killed in World War II; instead of returning to the United States, he helped manage refugee camps in Europe and later joined an Aliyah Bet ship bound for Palestine. A youth-group member seeking passage to Palestine got there 13 months later by way of Europe and Cyprus. First, he went to France to help manage secret refugee camps. There, he was selected for a radio operators' course, and later he and his American volunteer instructor took charge of the radio room on an Aliyah Bet ship purchased in Florida by the Weston Trading Company. Another youth-group volunteer who went to France and managed a refugee camp later was assigned to the same job on

Cyprus after his Aliyah Bet ship was captured by the British.

Difficult as the recruiting task may have seemed at the start, Aliyah Bet found its men. Most were Jews who had served in World War II with experience ranging from combat in the Pacific to sea duty on the Murmansk run. Not all of those who offered to volunteer were accepted. In fact, most wound up being turned down for one reason or another. The recruiting records have vanished, and the list of men who sailed the ships in this book is the most extensive compilation available of the names of Aliyah Bet volunteers. Veterans of the recruiting effort say that for each volunteer who was accepted, as many as nine or ten were turned down.

* * *

After Aliyah Bet acquired two Canadian corvettes with the help of Morris Ginsberg, The Weston Trading Company's first purchase was the Unalga, an out-of-service Coast Guard cutter berthed in Baltimore. Captain Ash moved into the Mount Royal Hotel in Baltimore and set up an account for the Weston Trading Company with the Chemical Bank and Trust Company. The ship underwent refitting and received a Honduran flag and a new name. She was now the Ulua, named for a river in Honduras. Later, making the longest voyage of Aliyah Bet, she would become the Haim Arlosoroff.

The fourth American volunteer craft that sailed to Palestine was a former yacht purchased by Revisionist Zionists, militant ideological adversaries of the Haganah and Ben-Gurion. Far from operating clandestinely, the Revisionists advocated a more provocative posture; they publicly raised funds for refugee transportation by producing a pageant, *A Flag is Born,* written by the novelist and playwright Ben Hecht. Along with the publicity achieved by staging the pageant, the American League for a Free Palestine claimed a breakthrough on the American scene: the first racially integrated theater audience in the history of the State of Maryland. According to the producers of the pageant, the National Theatre in Washington, D.C., insisted on segregated seating, so a performance scheduled for the national capital was moved to Baltimore, where the color line was broken. Despite their differences on tactics as well as Zionist ideology, the Haganah cooperated with the Revisionists in the refugee traffic. When the Revisionist group asked Morris Ginsberg's assistance in refitting a vessel, Ginsberg checked with Danny Schind, who told him to help. And in Europe, Aliyah Bet workers cooperated in embarking refugees for the voyage to Palestine on the former yacht, which was renamed in honor of Ben Hecht.

Purchases for the Haganah continued, including the soon-to-be-famous Exodus and culminating, on March 17, 1947, in the acquisition of the largest Aliyah Bet ships, the Pan York and the Pan Crescent. While the Weston Trading Company figured in one purchase after another, an aide to Schind recalled that a separate dummy company was set up for each ship in an effort to insulate each vessel from the others in the event of capture or legal difficulty. Names of companies remembered as figuring in the American volunteer effort include Caribbean Atlantic Shipping Company, FB Shipping Company, Montrose Shipping Company, Nautical Supply and Shipping Company, Pine Tree Industries, Ships and Vessels Ltd., Tyre Shipping Company, and Weston Trading Company. The list is almost certainly incomplete.

Two ships were acquired in Florida and outfitted in Miami at Moody's shipyard on NW North River Drive. Shepherd Broad, a Florida lawyer who was one of the 19 American Jews who met with Ben-Gurion at Rudolph Sonneborn's apartment, took responsibility for these two vessels, buying supplies with money he raised from contacts in the area. Sometimes he raised $2,000; sometimes, $10,000.

In the case of the Pan York and Pan Crescent, the purchasing entity was the fictitious FB Shipping Company. Different participants in Aliyah Bet had different understandings of what FB signified. One explanation was that the initials stood for Fanny Barnett, chatelaine of the Hotel Fourteen. A generally accepted version was that FB meant either "F—k Britain" or "F—k Bevin." According to Joe Buxenbaum, this meaning of the name originated at a Paris bar where he and a Palestinian leader of Aliyah Bet one afternoon vented their frustrations by drinking cognac and muttering imprecations at British Foreign Secretary Ernest Bevin and the Empire he served. Buxenbaum later talked with attorney Maurice Boukstein about the need to set up a new company; Buxenbaum suggested calling it FB Shipping. The lawyer wanted to know what the initials stood for. Embarrassed to explain their obscene meaning, Buxenbaum observed that FB coincided with with the initials of Fanny Barnett's name.

Another Aliyah Bet worker who had to deal with the question was Paul Shulman; when he presented the checks to buy the Pan York and Pan Crescent for the FB Shipping Company, Shulman was asked what the company initials represented. "Far Better," he replied. Shulman said the purchase price was $125,000 for each ship. The cost of refitting the two freighters was more than $500,000. Shulman, a graduate of the U.S. Naval Academy at Annapolis, helped in a variety of tasks connected with acquiring ships and preparing them. He later became the first Commanding Officer of the Israel Navy. In 1948 shortly before Israel became independent, Schind gave a talk reviewing some of the accomplishments of Aliyah Bet. Of the Americans who helped, Schind singled out three men for special mention. They were Morris Ginsberg, Joe Buxenbaum and Paul Shulman.

Obtaining foreign registry for each ship was another job of the American section. After the necessary arrangements had been negotiated, an assistant to Schind would go to a Latin American consulate in New York. There, he would hand an envelope to an official and receive in return an envelope containing the papers entitling the Aliyah

Bet ship to sail under its foreign flag. More than one nation figured in this part of the process. Panama supplied the first two flags; Honduras, the next three. The sixth ship, the Exodus, left the United States with a Honduran flag after her Panamanian registry was withdrawn; the Honduran government, also responding to British pressure, tried to revoke the registration at the last moment, but the Exodus sailed before the paperwork could be completed. The next two ships sailed with Panamanian flags. According to Joe Buxenbaum, the two final ships were to acquire Colombian flags. But Aliyah Bet agents learned from a Colombian diplomat in Bulgaria that Britain had persuaded his government to rescind the registrations. Buxenbaum took a trip to Panama to arrange Panamanian flags. Money changed hands in the acquisition of foreign papers; the amounts are not known. Buxenbaum recalled that a foreign flag could be obtained for a comparatively small sum.

Another American Jew who became involved with Aliyah Bet was Samuel Zemurray, the owner of the United Fruit Company with extensive operations in Honduras. An immigrant from Eastern Europe, Zemurray began in business at age 20 as a banana peddler in Alabama and rose quickly to a position of wealth. Early in 1948, Schind gave co-workers the following account of a visit to Zemurray:

When Aliyah Bet representatives were negotiating to buy the Pan York and Pan Crescent, Schind went to Louisiana to see Zemurray. Since the ships belonged to his United Fruit Company organization and Zemurray himself was a great admirer of Chaim Weizmann, Schind concluded it would be politic to let Zemurray know that the vessels would be used for Aliyah Bet.

Schind flew to New Orleans and then drove to Zemurray's summer estate. When Schind explained the purposes of Aliyah Bet, Zemurray summoned a servant to bring a bottle of his best whisky from the cellar. Then, half in Yiddish and half in English, Zemurray related the story of his youth in Bessarabia and how he came to the United States and worked his way up to ownership of the United Fruit Company. After this, Schind brought up a problem of the Exodus' foreign flag. Zemurray said he personally could do nothing, since his top managers were Englishmen who put the interests of the Empire first, and Zemurray himself was paying $125 million a year to the British government for a commercial concession. Zemurray gave Schind the name of a non-Jew who could arrange the matter in return for money. (This non-Jew, whom Schind did not identify, later solved other problems for Aliyah Bet.) Zemurray wished Schind success with the ships he was buying and said that both Schind and he could have a laugh at the expense of the British, since the manager of Zemurray's shipping interests in Boston was an Englishman who had collected a salary from Zemurray while serving as chief of British naval intelligence in America during World War II. If this Englishman were the seller of the ships, no one would imagine that the vessels were entering the service of Aliyah

Bet. Zemurray and Schind shook hands on their secret, and Schind left.

David Macarov, who worked for Schind from the fall of 1946 until going to Palestine in May 1947, heard a different version of this story, more in keeping with the legend of Zemurray as an international wheeler and dealer whose banana monopoly gave him the power to overturn governments. The story Macarov heard at the time was as follows: Zemurray telephoned a military head of state in Central America and notified him that the price of bananas was falling. The reason for the drop in prices, Zemurray told the ruler of the banana republic, was a delay in the sailing of a ship in which Zemurray was interested. Zemurray said he would have to recoup his losses by paying less for bananas. The general replied that he could arrange the flag and papers. Whereupon, Zemurray told the general that the price of bananas had just gone back up.

Meyer W. Weisgal, at the time executive director of the Jewish Agency and Chaim Weizmann's personal representative in the United States, later said he once accompanied Schind to Louisiana to discuss a problem with Zemurray: three ships purchased in South and Central America were being prevented from leaving Philadelphia. According to Weisgal, Zemurray told them the problems would disappear if they paid $10,000 to one man, $7,500 to another, and $5,000 to a third. This may have been the same visit recounted by Schind. If so, Weisgal's memory missed the mark on at least one point; he wrote in his memoirs that one of the ships was the Exodus, but the Exodus was purchased in the United States, not Latin America.

Weisgal had other connections to Aliyah Bet. Schind once sent an assistant to find Weisgal in an emergency. Schind, whose command of languages other than his own left much to be desired, told his aide Weisgal would be at a restaurant called the Mezzanine. But no such placed existed, and some confusion ensued before Schind's assistant finally located Weisgal at La Maisonette, one of New York's more celebrated restaurants.

Another prominent American Jew whose path crossed with Aliyah Bet was Herbert H. Lehman, former five-term Governor of New York State. Schind was arrested once in the United States. The incident is obscure; Schind's wife, Hava, did not know why he was arrested. But she recalled that Lehman obtained her husband's release. At the time Lehman, although not a Zionist, was an outspoken advocate of unrestricted Jewish immigration to Palestine.

* * *

Dewey Stone, the New Englander whose public activities in business and philanthropy gave an innocuous cover to his work for Aliyah Bet, had a financial function that was secret at the time. He was a conduit for American contributions spent for Aliyah Bet.

Stone opened an account for this purpose in the New England Trust Company, of Boston. Into this account went funds

הסוכנות היהודית לארץ ישראל

The Jewish Agency for Palestine

New York Office: SUITE 1205, 342 MADISON AVENUE, NEW YORK 17, N. Y., MUrray Hill 2-8803

Washington Office
1720 SIXTEENTH ST., N.W.
MIchigan 4480

January 31, 1946

Mr. Dewey Stone
53 Arlington Street
Brockton, Mass.

Dear Mr. Stone:

This will confirm our several conversations at which it was agreed as follows:

1. The Jewish Agency for Palestine hereby appoints you to act on its behalf in the administration of a fund which shall not exceed the sum of Four Hundred Thousand ($400,000.00) Dollars, and which shall be known in the books of the Jewish Agency for Palestine as "Investment Account, Dewey D. Stone, in charge".

2. From time to time sums of money will be transmitted to you by the Jewish Agency for Palestine to be credited to the above account.

3. You are hereby authorized to invest funds transmitted to you, as aforesaid, in whole or in part, in any real estate, securities (stocks, bonds, notes, receivables and other evidences of indebtedness), or other investments, with a view to obtaining a reasonable return on the funds invested. The choice of investment, or reinvestment, is left entirely to you and you may buy, sell, exchange, or otherwise dispose of assets acquired with said funds in such manner and at such time and on such terms and conditions as you see fit, and will not be responsible for capital losses, if any.

4. You are expected to report and render an account directly to the Treasurer of the Jewish Agency for Palestine on your administration of said account every three months.

5. You were kind enough to undertake the management of said account without compensation.

The Jewish Agency for Palestine has agreed to entrust you with the administration of said funds because of its unqualified trust and confidence in you and because of its knowledge that you will exercise your best judgment in the administration thereof.

Will you please sign a copy of this letter at the place indicated therefor, as evidence of your agreement to the contents of this letter.

Very truly yours,
E Kaplan
Eliezer Kaplan

I hereby agree to the administration of the Investment Account in accordance with the terms and conditions hereinabove set forth.

January 31, 1946: Dewey Stone is authorized to "invest" Jewish Agency funds

הסוכנות היהודית לארץ ישראל

The Jewish Agency for Palestine

New York Office: Suite 1205, 342 Madison Avenue, New York 17, N. Y., MUrray Hill 2-8803

Washington Office
1720 Sixteenth St., N.W.
Michigan 4480

February 4, 1946

Mr. Dewey Stone,
53 Arlington,
Brockton, Mass.

Dear Mr. Stone:

Enclosed you will please find check for $16,000 making a total of $128,000 turned over to you to date.

Will you please draw a check on your account for $125,000 to the order of the Caribbean Atlantic Shipping Co. leaving you with a balance of $3,000.00.

Sincerely yours,

Gottlieb Hammer

Gottlieb Hammer

February 4, 1946: The Jewish Agency asks Stone to transfer $125,000 to an Aliyah Bet front

New England ~~Bristol County~~ Trust Company 53-200/113

Boston ~~Taunton~~, Massachusetts Jan. 28, 1947 No.

Pay to the order of Weston Trading Co. $50,000.00

The sum of $50000 and 00 cts Dollars

Dewey David Stone
Special Account

Boston, Mass. 2/5 1946 No. 1

The New England Trust Company

Pay to the order of Carribean Atlantic Shipping Corp $110000 xx/100

One Hundred & Ten Thousand & no/100 Dollars

Dewey David Stone
Special Account

Specimens of Dewey Stone's disbursements for Aliyah Bet

transferred from the Jewish Agency, which in turn received its money from the United Jewish Appeal. Eliezer Kaplan, Jewish Agency treasurer, authorized Stone, in a letter dated January 31, 1946, to "invest" this money as he saw fit. Kaplan wrote that Stone would have at his disposal up to $400,000, which would be carried on the Jewish Agency's books as "Investment Account, Dewey D. Stone, in charge." Stone would not be responsible for losses resulting from his investment decisions. He would serve without pay and furnish a financial report every three months.

Two days later, in a letter dated February 2, 1946, the Jewish Agency asked Stone to send $125,000 to the Caribbean Atlantic Shipping Company. Over a period of more than a year, Stone wrote at least 15 checks totaling $740,000 to Aliyah Bet shipping companies from "Dewey Daniel Stone - Special Account."

In two separate periods for which records have been found, Stone disbursed money to the Aliyah Bet companies at a rate of about $100,000 a month. In three and one-half months between February 5 and May 18, 1946, Stone wrote eight checks totaling $350,000 to the Caribbean Atlantic Shipping Company, an Aliyah Bet commercial front. The checks ranged in amount from $15,000 to $110,000. In a four-month period from November 7, 1946, through March 7, 1947, Stone wrote seven checks totaling $390,000 to Aliyah Bet's Weston Trading Company; these checks ranged between $40,000 and $100,000. These transactions remained secret for four decades and came to light only in the course of research for this book.

Other transfers presumably took place on behalf of Aliyah Bet. The 15 checks with Stone's signature spanned a period of barely 13 months, whereas the purchasing activities of Aliyah Bet took place over a longer time. A gap of almost half a year intervened between the first group of checks for $350,00 and the second batch for $390,00. The purchase of the sister ships Pan York and Pan Crescent did not take place until after Stone wrote the last of these 15 checks; Morris Ginsberg put up a personal check as a guarantee of payment for the Pan York and Pan Crescent.

Whether records of other transactions exist is not known. Those who handled the clandestine affairs of Aliyah Bet in the United States took care to leave as few visible traces of their activity as possible. Each section of Dori's operation was tightly compartmentalized from the others. Maurice Boukstein, an American-born lawyer who had lived in Palestine as a boy, served as legal advisor to Dori's mission; Gottlieb Hammer, comptroller of the Jewish Agency's American Section, was designated by Jewish Agency Treasurer Eliezer Kaplan to handle all monies for Dori's mission including the Aliyah Bet section. Aside from Dori, only Boukstein and Hammer were aware of the full scope of the mission's work, and the two Americans were not informed of the details of each section's activity. When Federal Bureau of Investigation agents questioned Hammer in the fall of 1947 and showed him photographs of suspected members of the underground, Hammer could truthfully reply that he did not recognize the faces.

Detailed financial records were kept, but in secret. These records were in a safe deposit box rented by Hammer and Sidney Green, an accountant who worked closely with the United Jewish Appeal. In July 1948 an auditor arrived from Israel to review these records and found adding-machine tapes, invoices, requisitions, memoranda, and other details of American expenditures for the Haganah. The records later were transferred to Israel and could not be found when the research for this book was undertaken. Many records were destroyed in a fire at the the Tel Aviv offices of Zim, the state-controlled shipping company which took over the business files of Aliyah Bet.

According to Hammer, the primary source of funds for Dori's mission was the United Jewish Appeal.

Money and business connections were provided by "the Sonneborn Institute," a volunteer network known for its founder, industrialist Rudolph G. Sonneborn. This *sub rosa* organization was born at a meeting of 19 American Jews with Ben-Gurion and two Palestinian aides (Eliezer Kaplan and Reuven Shiloah) at Sonneborn's Manhattan apartment in the summer of 1945. Ben-Gurion asked the Americans to be prepared to help the Jews of Palestine. Sonneborn and his circle developed a network throughout North America, recruiting key contacts in more than three dozen industries. The "Institute," as it came to be known, concentrated on acquiring military equipment and weapons, in addition to supporting the activities of Aliyah Bet. Starting in July 1946, members of the Institute met at lunch every Thursday at the Hotel McAlpin to discuss what needed to be done next.

Among those who knew of the Sonneborn group's existence, the general belief was that the Institute helped buy the two Canadian corvettes that became the Wedgwood and the Haganah. Sonneborn was among the dignitaries who met with the volunteer crew of the Wedgwood before she sailed for Europe in April 1946. The purchase of the Exodus was also understood to be the work of the Sonneborn Institute; Sonneborn was a guest at a presailing ceremony aboard the Exodus on February 16, 1947. The Institute bought other ships; it even purchased an aircraft carrier for $125,000. Louis Rocker, a New York stockbroker who received and disbursed money for the Institute, was also a money-handler for Danny Schind's shipping office. How many ships for Aliyah Bet were among the Institute's purchases remains a matter of conjecture; a full and final accounting of the Institute's purchases never became public knowledge.

According to one researcher, the Institute's contribution to Aliyah Bet was mainly in the form of assistance to the overall fund-raising process:

> Initiated by members of the Sonneborn Institute or their trusted friends, there were gatherings in the living rooms of private homes in many cities—in New York, Philadelphia, Boston, Baltimore, Washington, among others—to raise the funds necessary for the purchase of perhaps a dozen ships in the United States and their outfitting.... Everywhere there were groups of prominent people—Zionists and sometimes Gentiles—who many years later were to say that they bought a Haganah ship and sent it to Palestine. The truth of the statement rests in the fact that the money came from a huge pot, the results of contributions from all over the United States. (David Holly, *Exodus,* Boston and Toronto, 1969, pp. 122-3.)

According to Gottlieb Hammer, who had

day-to-day responsibility for juggling the available money to make sure the bills of all sections of Dori's mission were paid, the Sonneborn Institute's major contribution was not in money but in making the personal and business connections necessary to find specific items. Hammer said the sums required became so large that ultimately the source became the United Jewish Appeal, whose collections rose to $35 million in 1945, $100 million in 1946, $135 million in 1947, and $154 million in 1948.

A complete list of Americans who helped Aliyah Bet will probably never be compiled. Along with those who gave money, many others responded to requests for special help. In Baltimore, where several of the ships were berthed, members of the Jewish community took responsibility for such activities as providing kosher food for the Exodus. Dr. Herman Seidel, a Baltimore physician, collected medical supplies for the ships, inoculated and examined crew members, and coached a former Navy pharmacist's mate in obstetrics to prepare him to care for pregnant women aboard ship. Moses I. Speert, a Baltimore clothing manufacturer, collected bedding, rations, and other equipment, which he stored secretly in a special warehouse. The son of a Baltimore lumberyard owner recalled his father's receiving a telephone call one midnight with a request for wood and workmen; at 2 a.m. the materials and a work crew were at the dock.

Others offered to help without being asked. In New York, Siegfried Kramarsky hired Paul Shulman to work for his export-import company after Shulman returned from service in World War II as a naval officer. A few days later, Teddy Kollek of the Haganah mission approached Shulman to help inspect vessels being considered for Aliyah Bet purchase. This began as a part-time activity, but soon it was taking more than weekends, and Shulman decided he had to quit his job. Kramarsky wanted to know if his new employee's reason for leaving had to do with Zionism. On learning that this was the case, Kramarsky continued to pay Shulman's salary while Shulman devoted his time to Aliyah Bet.

* * *

Years after Aliyah Bet ended, a legend persisted that Danny Schind had been sent to America by accident. According to the story, which has been printed in at least two books, Schind was a kibbutz shepherd who had no knowledge of ships or the sea. The story went as follows: The mission in New York telephoned Palestine to request the services of an expert on ships. But the request was spoken with an accent, and the word ships came out as "sheeps." Schind was recruited for the job because he had a reputation for dealing in sheep at his kibbutz. In one version of the story, it was Ben-Gurion who mispronounced ships as "sheeps."

But there was no truth to any version of that story, according to Danny Schind's widow, Hava. Aside from the impossibility of such a verbal confusion in Hebrew, the fact is that Danny Schind was no newcomer to Aliyah Bet. When he arrived in the

United States in 1946, Schind had been involved with Aliyah Bet for almost a decade.

Schind was succeeded in New York in 1947 by David "Davidka" Nameiry of Kibbutz Ashdot Yaakov. Nameiry recalled that the actual change of command took place in Europe, where Schind was recuperating from surgery. Nameiry went to Europe and met with Schind. They talked about the job, and Schind jotted names of key contacts and other highlights on pieces of scratch paper. He gave the notes to Nameiry, along with some word-of-mouth explanations, and Nameiry was off to New York. Schind returned to Palestine.

These two men, who probably knew more than any other Palestinians about the American contribution to Aliyah Bet, both died long before anyone made a serious effort to tell the story. After Israel won her independence, Schind served briefly as Director-General of the Ministry of Defense. He later became executive vice president of Zim and president of the American-Israel Shipping Co. He died December 20, 1953, at 44. Nameiry, who returned to Israel in August 1949, served in kibbutz affairs until 1960. He later became Director-General of Israel's Ministry of Transportation. He died June 3, 1966, at 58.

* * *

NOTE:
The extent of Samuel Zemurray's role in Aliyah Bet remains unclear. The Encyclopedia Judaica describes Zemurray's activity in the organized Jewish world simply as that of a contributor to Zionist causes and a supporter of the Weizmann Institute; nowhere does this authoritative reference work mention Zemurray's connection with Aliyah Bet. Nor does Zemurray's name appear in Leonard Slater's 1970 book *The Pledge*, an extensively researched account of American Jewish purchasing for Israel before Independence. Slater relied heavily on interviews and acknowledged the cooperation of hundreds of people. Among the sources he acknowledges are Gottlieb Hammer, Rudolph G. Sonneborn, Meyer W. Weisgal, and more than a dozen other persons with connections to Aliyah Bet.

Gottlieb Hammer in his memoirs said Zemurray provided invaluable help. "Danny was always making trips to Boston or New Orleans to see people to whom Zemurray directed him for papers of registry for ships and visas for crews," Hammer recalled.

Hammer described Zemurray as an international mystery man who "made and overturned governments at will according to his business needs. He was one of the richest and most powerful men in the United States, yet Zemurray was able to avoid publicity and keep his name out of the newspapers. The only condition he put on his aid to (Aliyah Bet) was that he never be publicly identified and that the entire relationship be treated with the utmost discretion."

THE PALESTINE POST
LATE Edition
JERUSALEM, THURSDAY, JUNE 27, 1946
PRICE 15 MILS
VOL. XXI, No. 6135

"CARETAKER" RULE FOR INDIA: CRIPPS PLAN IS OUT

NEW DELHI, Wednesday (Reuter). — The British Cabinet Mission in an official statement issued here tonight said:

"It is the intention of the Viceroy to set up a temporary caretaker Government of officials. It is proposed that further negotiations should be adjourned for a short interval during the time elections to the Constituent Assembly will be taking place."

"The British Cabinet Mission propose to leave India on Saturday next, June 29, to report to the British Cabinet and Parliament.

"The Cabinet Mission and the Viceroy regret that it has not so far proved possible to form an Interim Coalition Government, but they are determined that the effort should be renewed in accordance of the terms of Para. 8, of their statement of June 16," the statement declared.

"It is hoped that when discussions are resumed, the leaders of the two major parties, who have all expressed their agreement with the Viceroy and the Cabinet Mission on the need for a speedy formation of a representative Interim Government, will do the utmost to arrive at an accommodation upon the composition of that Government."

Ministers in Touch with Attlee

NEW DELHI, Wednesday (Reuter). — The British Cabinet Mission and the Viceroy were today understood to be in touch with Mr. Attlee and the Cabinet in London on an expected official announcement concerning the interim Government plan for India.

Cabinet Mission quarters said the statement might be expected either late tonight or, at the latest, within the next 24 hours.

Column One, By David Courtney

Glubb: Questions in Commons

"Brigadier Glubb, I am assured, gave no interview.

"The statement by Brigadier Glubb that opinions attributed to him were totally unauthorised has since been published in Middle Eastern papers.

"Brigadier Glubb is not Commandant of the Trans-Jordan Frontier Force and he is not a serving officer in the British Army, but is employed by the Trans-Jordan Government as Commandant of the Arab Legion.

"The second part of the question," therefore, does not arise."

(The statement by Glubb Pasha reportedly repudiating the interview was never received by The Palestine Post, which first drew attention to it. This newspaper is not aware of such repudiation being published in any other newspaper in the Middle East.)

REST OF THE NEWS

A NUMBER of shots were heard in northern Tel Aviv last night and flares were sent up from the P.M.F. Camp at Sarona.... LATER A LORRY load of workers from the Reading Power Station were searched.... TWO PEOPLE were killed in a fire which caused two million dollars damage in New York harbour yesterday.... FULVIO SUVICH, Under-Secretary of Foreign Affairs for Mussolini, has been pardoned after being sentenced to 24 years imprisonment.... A PEASANT WITNESS at the trial of General Mihailovich today declared: "On behalf of my village, I say hang him publicly in Belgrade's Central Square".... ELECTION of the new Provisional Head of the Italian State has been postponed until Friday evening.... THE U.S. NAVY announces tonight that the dropping of the atom bomb on Bikini Atoll has been fixed for 2130 G.M.T. on Sunday.. THE 19-member Medical Committee inquiring into the mysterious death of the young King of Siam has decided by 18 votes to one on either assassination or suicide, ruling out accidents .. TRANS-JORDAN'S new status has been recognized by two more States, Afghanistan and Holland ....

Commons Sit Until Dawn

LONDON, Wednesday (R). — The House of Commons rose just as dawn was breaking at 5.05 this morning after another late sitting on the Finance Bill.

This started only 3½ hours after the longest meeting of the House of Commons for 10 years had ended late yesterday morning.

During the sitting just ended, the Committee stage of the Finance Bill was completed after which the House rejected the Lords' amendment to the Government's Borrowing (Control and Guarantee) Bill, which sought to limit the Government's powers of control of investments to a period of five years.

FRANCE MEETS HER NEW GOVT.

PARIS, Wednesday (Reuter). — M. Bidault, the Premier, this afternoon presented his Government to the National Constituent Assembly.

In his address M. Bidault said that the Government proposed above all, to create conditions in which the Assembly could fulfil its essential mission — to give France a constitution.

It was the Government's duty to end as quickly as possible the uncertainty which at present faced the nation. The Government marked its absolute determination to do everything to ensure that a stable regime might be established by October at the latest.

The Prime Minister continued that within this period the Government did not intend to take measures which would commit future generations.

After a tribute to the Resistance Movement and "its interpreter" Gen. De Gaulle, M. Bidault said that on domestic policy the Government would limit all debates to questions of extreme urgency in order to leave the Assembly the maximum time for the "essential task of constituting the Republic."

Two Killed 420 Slave Children

Swiss to Hand Over Nazi Assets

BERNE, Wednesday, (Reuter). The Swiss National Council — the lower House of Parliament — today ratified the agreement with the Allies on the disposal of German assets in Switzerland by an overwhelming majority.

The settlement obliges the Swiss to hand over to the Allies half of the German assets in Switzerland and to pay 250 million Swiss francs (about £14,700,000) for gold looted by the Germans and transferred to Switzerland.

BEVIN DID NOT OPPOSE

WASHINGTON, Wednesday—(PTA). — The British Ambassador, Lord Inverchapel, has written to Senators Wagner and Mead that Mr. Bevin denies he disagreed with the admission of 100,000 Jews into Palestine and, although he opposes a Jewish National State nevertheless favours a Palestine State of some sort.

$ 465,000,000

WASHINGTON, Wednesday — (UP). — The House Appropriations Committee voted another $465 million for UNRRA today to complete its pledge to the world relief agency.

The Committee praised UNRRA for its "noble work which will serve as a lasting tribute to the readiness, willingness and determination of America to give succour to distressed peoples of other lands."

SPAIN: NEW UNO MOVES

NEW YORK, Wednesday (Reuter). — The Australian delegate to the Uno Security Council, Dr. Herbert Evatt, has prepared a new plan to settle the Spanish question in a last-minute endeavour to break the two-month-old Security Council deadlock, it was learned authoritatively in New York tonight.

The plan has been discussed in a series of closed meetings of the new sub-committee on Spain during the past 24 hours in order to reach agreement before the Polish delegate, Dr. Oscar Lange, leaves for Warsaw tomorrow and M. Trygve Lie, Secretary-General, leaves for Europe.

Dr. Evatt's proposal is that the Security Council should pass a resolution firstly declaring that the Franco question be retained on its agenda; secondly, reiterating the condemnation of the Franco regime contained in last month's report of the sub-committee; and thirdly, stating that this action shall not prejudice the General Assembly's right to discuss the Spanish question.

This morning it was thought that a provisional agreement on Dr. Evatt's plan had been reached by the new sub-committee composed of the Polish, Australian and British delegates.

But later, Dr. Lange, the Polish delegate, after inter-delegation consultations declared that he wanted further discussion of the plan.

The sub-committee was therefore meeting immediately before the Security Council in a last minute attempt to avert renewed split at the Council.

Dr. Lange's action is interpreted here to mean that M. Gromyko, Soviet delegate, has raised objections to the new plan and that he may veto it if it is put before the Council today.

PALESTINIAN PROPERTY

Enquiries concerning the property of Palestinians in Germany and Austria can now be made by the Property Control Branch of the British element of the Control Commission. Such property must have been owned at the outbreak of war by British subjects, British protected persons and Palestinian citizens, according to a notice in the latest Gazette.

The Branch cannot undertake to investigate enquiries in respect of property owned by German subjects and confiscated by the German Government prior to or during the war under discriminatory legislation. No decision has yet been taken regarding compensation of persons dispossessed by discrimination.

EIGHT DIE IN EXPLOSION

LONDON, Wednesday (Reuter) — It is officially announced today that eight soldiers are missing, believed killed, 12 injured are in hospital and six slightly injured, following the explosion of No. 2 Military Fort Cairnyan, Wightownshire, in Scotland on June 25.

A party of men were unloading ammunition from railway wagons to an ammunition dumping craft for dumping at sea. The cause of the explosion is not yet known.

"The Palestine Post"

Delivery of The Palestine Post to Tel Aviv and Haifa is delayed owing to the road curfew in those areas.

Neurath Puts Blame on Frank

NUREMBERG, Wednesday (Reuter). — A large red poster, signed by Constantin von Neurath, announcing the execution of resisters in Czechoslovakia, was shown as an exhibit at the International War Crimes Court today, when von Neurath, former German Foreign Minister, was again under cross-examination.

The poster was signed by von Neurath as "Protector" of Bohemia and Moravia and referred to the shooting of nine Czechs in September, 1939.

Cross-examined by the Soviet Assistant Prosecutor, von Neurath placed the blame on his Deputy, Karl Hermann Frank, who was hanged as a war criminal in Prague a few weeks ago. Von Neurath declared his name had been misused on the poster.

Von Neurath said the arrest of 6,000 and 8,000 Czech hostages was carried out by the Gestapo without his knowledge and the order for closing Czech universities was issued by somebody else, who used his name.

His counsel, Doctor Luedinghausen, told the court today that Neurath is suffering from a "serious disease." The counsel said that yesterday he had formed the impression that the defendant no longer was in a position to do full justice to questions put to him.

"This is not surprising if you consider he is in his 74th year," the counsel added.

I.Z.L. Trial: 31 Guilty Face Sentences Today

The verdict of guilty, was passed by the Jerusalem Military Court yesterday on 31 members of Irgun Zvai Leumi, who had been charged with carrying firearms, bombs and ammunition. One of the accused, Benyamin Kaplan (19), was also convicted of firing at members of H.M. Forces.

The sentences will be pronounced at 9.30 this morning.

Seeming indifference to their fate was shown by all the defendants, (among whom there is one young woman), both to the third day's proceedings and to the verdict.

The Court had made it clear at the beginning of the morning that it would listen only to statements made in defence of the charges, and not to political statements of any kind.

Only two, Binder and Shmukler, were permitted to make their statements in full; all the others were stopped by the President, Lt. Col. Fell, in whose view political speeches were irrelevant to the charge of carrying firearms.

There was a lively interchange between the auburn-bearded spokesman of the prisoners, Haim Luster (28), and the President, and a few tense moments when Luster was stopped and ordered to sit down. The prisoner refused to listen, the guard approached to have him seated, and the other 30 sprang to their feet. At this the police and troops in Court took up positions and aimed their guns at the crowded dock. Luster told his comrades to sit down, they obeyed and order was restored in Court.

A long speech was read by Baruch Shmukler (once detained in Eritrea), in which he accused the British Government and its people on eight counts.

They were guilty, he said, of abuse of confidence, and placing obstacles in the fulfilment of the Balfour Declaration; of violation of international laws

30 GUNMEN ROB DIAMOND PLANT

BNEI BRAK, Wednesday. — Diamonds worth between LP.30,000 and LP.40,000 were stolen by a gang of 30 armed Jews who raided the Naveh Diamond Polishing plant in Pardess Katz just before closing time this afternoon.

The diamond polishers were turning in their stones to the foreman at the control desk at 4 o'clock, when 15 men entered the hall and at revolver point ordered the workers to raise their hands. They then collected the rough and polished diamonds from the table and ordered those workers who had not yet turned theirs in to drop them on the floor.

Meanwhile, the factory itself was surrounded by another party of 15 men armed with sub-machine guns and revolvers. An Arab grocer across the road was kept covered. Telephone lines were cut.

"BIG 4" MEET INFORMALLY

PARIS, Wednesday (Reuter). — The "Big Four" Foreign Ministers are meeting at a special session, informally, tonight, it was authoritatively learned here.

Earlier, the Soviet Deputy Foreign Minister, M. Vyshinsky, had proposed such a meeting to be called to consider vital Italian questions and, above all, Trieste.

This afternoon the Ministers deferred for further study the British compromise proposal that instead of a special clause in the Rumanian treaty, the Big Four should sign a declaration stating their intention that commercial navigation of the Danube and its tributaries would be free and open to all nations.

The declaration would pledge the four Powers to take all necessary steps to secure adherence of the Danubian States to this principle.

Mr. Bevin hoped that his proposal would be a satisfactory compromise between the previous position of the Western Powers and the Russian proposal two days ago that the Big Four should express their confidence that the Balkan States would observe the principle of free navigation.

The United States Secretary of State, Mr. James F. Byrnes, said that he would accept the compromise if Russia and France did so, but would otherwise continue to insist on a special clause in the Rumanian treaty.

M. Molotov said at first glance that he thought that the matter should not be decided by the Big Four without hear-

1,300 Refugees Dock

Allied Warships Mass Off Trieste

Immigration Will Continue

Italy Apologizes

Arabs Want Talks

The Josiah Wedgwood (Beauharnois Colon)

"We survived Hitler. Death is no stranger to us. Nothing can keep us from our Jewish homeland. The blood is on your head if you fire on this unarmed ship."

—Banner flying from the mast of the Wedgwood, June 26, 1946.

The first Aliyah Bet boat to land in Palestine in 1945 brought 35 refugees. Before the end of that year, seven more vessels arrived with a total of barely more than 1,000 passengers. These successes were more than moral victories, but they were not enough. The situation of the Jewish Displaced Persons in Europe was desperate, and the British were stepping up their efforts to seal the shores of Palestine. Larger and faster vessels were needed for Aliyah Bet.

Across the Atlantic in North America, Jewish volunteers went to work in 1945 to meet this need. Operating clandestinely with Haganah emissaries from Palestine, American Jews arranged to buy two war-surplus corvettes of the Royal Canadian Navy. The former warships, in the 650-ton class and capable of 20-knot speeds, represented a dramatic upgrading of the Aliyah Bet fleet. Compared to the little vessels that deposited passengers on the beaches of Palestine in 1945, the corvettes could carry large numbers of refugees. Their speed presented a new challenge to the mounting British blockade. And they would be manned by sailors of a different type — North American volunteers, in place of hired crews.

By December 1945, Zionist activists in the New York area had received word of the purchase of the corvettes Beauharnois and Norsyd. Prospective crew members were recruited and sworn to secrecy. Their first job was to help recondition the newly acquired ships. The task took months; the Beauharnois and Norsyd went to City Island near the Bronx for removal of their gun emplacements, then to Staten Island for provisioning and other refurbishing. Equipment troubles plagued the Beauharnois on a shakedown cruise from City Island. One volunteer later recalled telling a superior that the ship would never make it across the ocean; the response was that the ship had to make it.

In April 1946, during the Jewish holiday of Passover, the Beauharnois and Norsyd departed for Europe with new identities. The Norsyd, renamed the Balboa, headed for Marseilles flying the Panamanian flag. The Beauharnois, now named the Colon, sailed for Italy. There she was to pick up her passengers and sail for Palestine as the Josiah Wedgwood, the first American-manned Aliyah Bet ship to confront the British blockade.

* * *

Josiah Clement Wedgwood was a British statesman who became an outspoken advocate of Zionism. He took up the Jewish cause after meeting volunteers of the Zion Mule Corps commanded by Joseph Trumpeldor at Gallipoli in 1915. A Member of Parliament from 1906 to 1943, Wedgwood participated with great passion in the political efforts that led to the Balfour Declaration in 1917, visited Palestine in 1926 and 1934, and envisaged a Jewish state on both sides of the Jordan as part of the British Commonwealth.

Before he died in 1943, Wedgwood had become close to Vladimir (Ze'ev) Jabotinsky, founder of the militant Revisionist wing of the Zionist movement. Wedgwood called for armed Jewish resistance against British repression. The volunteers manning the ship that bore Wedgwood's name had little to do with Jabotinsky and Revisionism. Some of the volunteers were Zionists from socialist youth movements; these groups bitterly opposed Jabotinsky and his ultra-nationalist views. Two of the ship's American officers had backgrounds in the "Wobblies," the far-left Industrial Workers of the World. Still other volunteers had no Zionist ideological or organizational affiliations. Whatever their viewpoints, the volunteers put into action Wedgwood's call for Jewish immigration in defiance of the British Mandatory authorities.

* * *

A week into her Atlantic voyage, the Wedgwood broke down. Rough seas rendered many of the inexperienced sailors too seasick to keep up their shipboard routines, and the inadequately attended boilers salted up. Engines, steering, and fuel pumps failed. After strenuous efforts, particularly by the engineroom gang, the Wedgwood succeeded in reaching Ponta Delgada in the Azores islands. There, the ship underwent repairs.

In the Azores, the Wedgwood picked up her first refugee passenger, the sexton of the tiny local synagogue. After he met the mostly Jewish crew and began to understand the mission of the ship, he pleaded to be taken along. He explained that he was a Jewish refugee who had wound up in the Azores after fleeing Europe. When the Wedgwood resumed her voyage two weeks later, he was aboard.

The resuscitated Wedgwood now headed for Italy. One day at sea, a British aircraft carrier also sailing eastward signalled to her. The Wedgwood did not return the signal. When the Wedgwood arrived at Gibraltar for refueling, she tied up alongide the same aircraft carrier, whose crew seemed curious about the former Canadian corvette. The Wedgwood, according to her cover story, was in the service of a United Nations refugee agency.

After Gibraltar, the Wedgwood proceeded to Italy, stopping first at Genoa and then at Savona, where Haganah agents from Palestine met her and began the final stage of her reconstruction into a refugee transport. Carpenters rebuilt the insides and superstructure, installing wooden racks to serve as bunks for the refugees. According to the new cover story, these were racks for bananas. The believability of this story depended on ignorance of the banana trade, as bananas were shipped in a hanging position, not lying on racks.

Secrecy was a concern at Savona, where British army jeeps passed frequently. British intelligence agents, aware of Aliyah Bet activities in Europe, had learned of the purchase of the Canadian corvettes. In May, working with the Italian authorities, the British almost prevented the Aliyah Bet vessels Dov Hos and Eliahu Golomb from sailing from the nearby Italian port of La Spezia with more than 1,000 refugees. The refugees conducted a hunger strike in the harbor, and their predicament so stirred anti-British and anti-Italian feelings that

The Wedgwood completes her journey

the British allowed them to enter Palestine in the monthly quota of 1,500 Jews. The La Spezia incident remained in the minds of the Haganah commanders as a warning that the network of British agents might prevent an Aliyah Bet vessel from leaving Europe.

One day at Savona, the Wedgwood began to sink at her mooring in the harbor. But it was not sabotage. One of the volunteers had connected a water hose to the ship's tanks from a street hydrant. Just then, two women passing by attracted his attention. The distracted sailor forgot to turn off the water, which overflowed the tanks and flooded the ship, ruining clothes and bedding in the cabins.

In the third week of June, the Wedgwood was ready for the journey to Palestine. She left Savona the night of June 18 and sailed to a lonely stretch of nearby beach to meet her passengers. They arrived in two convoys of war-surplus American trucks. The refugees were of 14 nationalities. According to a police report prepared after they arrived in Palestine, more than two-thirds were Polish. The others were Rumanian, Hungarian, Lithuanian, Czechoslovak, Greek, Latvian, Russian, Austrian, Italian, Yugoslav, German, Bulgarian, and Dutch.

After the first truck convoy arrived as scheduled, delays of several hours ensued. The second truck convoy was late because of engine trouble. Tension mounted as the Wedgwood remained offshore instead of approaching and dropping her gangplank.

Despite the Wedgwood's precautions to avoid a repetition of the La Spezia incident, British agents and their local collaborators succeeded in pinpointing the time and place of the sailing. As the refugees were boarding, Italian police appeared on the isolated beach and ordered the ship not to leave.

I.F. Stone, an American journalist who had also arrived at the dark, lonely beach in expectation of traveling to Palestine on the Wedgwood, became the vessel's representative to the Italian authorities. With Ada Sereni of the Aliyah Bet network in Italy as his interpreter, Stone displayed his American credentials and began firing questions at the police. Soon he was in the office of the police prefect in Savona, asking permission for the Wedgwood to leave. By this time, it was dawn. The negotiations went nowhere, and Stone threatened to telephone his newspaper in New York with the story of the Italians' efforts to prevent the Wedgwood from sailing with her refugee passengers. The police prefect told Stone he could make no telephone calls until the prefect's superior, the district commissioner, arrived to conduct a hearing.

While Stone diverted the attention of the police officials at the prefecture in Savona, Haganah representatives on the beach made final preparations for the Wedgwood's getaway. First, they persuaded the Italian police to allow the refugees remaining on shore to board the ship to receive food. The second convoy of trucks, now emptied of their passengers, drove off before the police could decide what to do about them. After all the passengers were aboard the Wedgwood, the crew cut the mooring ropes, jettisoned the gangplank, and slipped away into international waters shortly after 9 a.m. on June 19.

Meanwhile, in Savona, the district police commissioner arrived at the prefecture. Stone asked the commissioner to telephone the American Embassy. Before the call went through, a policeman dashed into the room and reported that the Wedgwood had escaped.

Stone feigned anger and demanded to be taken to the Wedgwood to continue his reportorial journey. While the police officials were explaining that this was impossible since the ship was already outside Italian territorial waters, the telephone rang. Instead of the American Embassy, it was a British major in Genoa, demanding that Stone be held for questioning. Stone went into the next room and changed clothing, donning his American military correspondent's uniform. He showed the police his American documents and declined an invitation to meet with British intelligence agents. The Italians decided to

Haifa in view

release him. After signing a statement that he had been courteously treated by the Italian authorities, Stone walked out into the daylight. That night, Stone made his way to an Aliyah Bet station and arranged to catch the next American-manned ship to Palestine.

The Wedgwood, meanwhile, headed out to sea. As a naval vessel, she had carried a crew of about 50 men. Now, she was crammed with more than 1,250 passengers, most of whom were kept below decks on their wooden shelves. For emergencies, the Wedgwood carried two motor launches with room for 25 persons in each and a total of 168 life-jackets. Food and water were in short supply, and sanitation was potentially a problem. But the weather was good and the trip went smoothly. One of the American volunteers had brought his guitar; he strummed "Dark Eyes" and "Tzena, Tzena," and passengers sang.

At 5:10 p.m. on Tuesday, June 25, with the Wedgwood about 75 miles from the coast of Palestine, a British aircraft flew in from the west and began tracking the refugee ship. Haganah commnders briefed the refugees to remain calm and follow all further orders. Concluding that capture was inevitable, the Haganah command decided to offer only token resistance. The passengers sang Hatikvah, and the Wedgwood hoisted the Star of David flag; many of the refugees wept as they cheered.

Royal Navy destroyers moved into position for the pursuit and capture of the Wedgwood. The destroyers Venus and Talybont advanced toward the refugee ship, sighting her at about 8:30 p.m. The destroyer Haydon stationed herself to be present for the Wedgwood's arrival at the three-mile limit of territorial waters, and a fourth destroyer remained in reserve. British intelligence agents in Palestine had reported that the Wedgwood might transfer her passengers to three or four small boats to attempt landings at various widely separated points along the coast; the British also speculated that the Wedgwood crew would leave by small craft outside territorial waters. To thwart a possibility that the passengers might abandon ship outside the three-mile limit, leaving the destroyers to pick up the refugees from the water as the Wedgwood eluded capture, the British ships shadowing the Wedgwood remained at a distance great enough to discourage attempts at swimming.

The destroyers became the refugee ship's constant companions for the final 23 hours of the journey. Early on the evening of June 26, as the Wedgwood approached the three-mile limit near Haifa, the British ships closed in. Emil Reynolds, an American photojournalist invited aboard the Haydon to photograph the capture, was transferred to the Venus so he could have a better view. The Wedgwood lowered a motor launch with 20 men aboard, a ruse to lead the British to think the Wedgwood crew was escaping; the men in the launch were actually refugee volunteers. The crew remained on the Wedgwood to mingle with the passengers and avoid identification by their captors. A banner flying from the Wedgwood's mast proclaimed:

The Wedgwood prepares to meet the Royal Navy

"We survived Hitler. Death is no stranger to us. Nothing can keep us from our Jewish homeland. The blood is on your head if you fire on this unarmed ship."

The Venus fired two warning shots and the Talybont prepared to drop depth charges if the Wedgwood did not stop. Evasive maneuvering by the Wedgwood's captain delayed the capture for almost an hour more, but eventually the Venus came alongside and sent a boarding party to take over the Wedgwood's bridge and engine room. As the British marines pulled down the Star of David flag, the passengers and crew sang Hatikvah again. The Wedgwood, detained on the official charge of having been a "menace to navigation," remained anchored outside the port overnight.

The next morning, the Wedgwood was brought into the harbor. The refugees sang Hatikvah, this time joined by Jews watching from the shore. The passengers and crew filed down to a line of 35 buses waiting to take them to a detention camp. Fifteen trucks to carry the refugees' belongings accompanied the buses. Haganah agents dressed as dock workers escorted the ship's officers onto a bus and took them off at the rear door while a British soldier stood guard at the front door. The officers disappeared from the dock in the confusion, and the crew went with the passengers to detention camp at Athlit, south of Haifa.

The maneuver left the British guessing as to the whereabouts of the captain and crew. A report to British authorities by Haifa Frontier Control Inspector J. Tavory speculated that the captain, rumored by passengers to be an American, "slipped off in one of the ship's boats and may have taken the crew with him."

"In view of the fact that there were several fishermen, ex-seamen and experienced engineers and mechanics among the illegals," the inspector continued, "I am inclined to believe that the refugees themselves attended as crew of the vessel."

The Americans never understood why the British didn't try harder to identify the crew members. An American Morse code operator was seen at work by members of the British boarding party, but they made no attempt to arrest him. Later, in the detention camp at Athlit, he came down with a serious case of dysentery. In the hospital, he confounded the doctors and nurses by refusing to speak. The volunteer was observing the Haganah's warning to the crew to avoid speaking English and to keep their American identity secret.

A few days after their capture, passengers and crew from the Wedgwood were removed from the Athlit camp to an open field to make room for new prisoners. The British had arrested hundreds of Palestinian Jewish leaders on the weekend of June 29 in a surprise roundup which has been recorded in Israeli history as the Black Sabbath.

Within a month, the Wedgwood crew were free again, some to remain in Palestine, some to sail again in Aliyah Bet, and others to return to the United States.

* * *

As the British were capturing the Wedgwood, one of the Palestinian shu-shu boys stole some engine parts vital to the operation of the ship and hid them in his mother's house. In 1948, after the British departed, he looked for the parts to get the ship running again for service in the new Israeli navy. His mother was cleaning house and was in the process of throwing out the critical parts when her son arrived to rescue them.

* * *

A few years after the Wedgwood's voyage, one of the American volunteers was attending medical school in Boston when an Israeli naval flotilla arrived for a visit. Among the visiting ships was the Wedgwood, once again a combat vessel. She was now warship K-20, and her new name was Hashomer. Her commander was one of the Israelis who helped organize her Aliyah Bet voyage, and he invited the former volunteer to dinner with the crew.

"I remember the thrill of seeing the shiny ship with its uniformed crew, guns remounted," the volunteer recalled. "It was *deja vu,* for at City Island we had cut off the guns to make it into a blockade runner. All had come full cycle."

Wedgwood in the Israel navy

Late Edition

JERUSALEM
WEDNESDAY, July 3, 1946

PRICE 15 MILS
VOL. XXI. No. [illegible]

TRUMAN READY TO MOVE 100,000 AT U.S. COST

WASHINGTON, Tuesday (R). — President Truman said tonight that the U.S. Government was prepared to assume technical and financial responsibility for the transport of the 100,000 Jewish immigrants to Palestine.

The President also declared that he hoped that the leaders of the Jewish community recently arrested in the raid by British troops would be "soon released" and that the situation in Palestine would soon return to normal. He expresed his regret at these developments in Palestine.

The statement was issued after the President had had a 15-minute interview with the four American members of the Jewish Agency.

Mr. Truman added that the arrests by the British would not affect his determination to avoid delay in pushing forward with the policy of transferring 100,000 Jewish immigrants into Palestine with all dispatch.

He also expressed his thanks for the workman-like suggestions embodied in the letter which American members of the Jewish Agency Executive sent him on June 14 with respect to technical and financial problems involved in the transfer and re-settlement of 100,000 immigrants.

The four Jewish Agency members who saw the President were Dr. Nahum Goldman, Mr. Louis Lipsky, Rabbi Abba Hillel Silver and Rabbi Stephen S. Wise. After the interview they issued their own statement, saying they had appealed to the President to intervene in Palestine, and accusing the British of perpetrating "acts of brutal aggression."

Palestine, to judge by reports from abroad, appears to be holding the attention of the civilized world, wherever accounts of the events have reached.

Column One

By David Courtney

[illegible]

CABINET v. ATTLEE

[illegible]

HOUSE DEBATES BRITISH SWOOP

WESTMINSTER, Tuesday (R). — Several more members of all parties took part in the debate on Palestine, on Mr. Silverman's motion for adjournment, before Mr. Attlee replied at length in the House of Commons last night. (Mr. Attlee's reply is given in another column.)

[illegible]

A crowd made up of Jewish ex-soldiers, youths, rabbis, workers and intellectuals, picketed the British Consulate in New York on Monday, displaying a placard, "Our patience is exhausted." Other slogans were "Remove the Army of Occupation" and "Is Attlee another Chamberlain?"

The singing of "Hatikva" by [illegible]

"COMMONS RESTRAINED"

By GEORGE LICHTHEIM, Palestine Post Correspondent

LONDON, Tuesday. — The tense, crowded House which last night rose at 10 o'clock after a three-hour Palestine debate, impressed observers with the mingled restraint and earnestness with which the Members reacted to the Government statement.

[illegible]

BIKINI TOLL: 5 SHIPS SUNK

By JOSEPH LAITIN, Reuters Special Correspondent

ABOARD U.S.S. "Appalachian", Bikini Atoll, Tuesday (R). — Vice-Admiral W.H.P. Blandy, Commander of the United States atom bomb test force, today announced that five ships were sunk and six heavily damaged by the fury of the Bikini bomb.

Giving a new summary of the extent of damage, 24 hours after the bomb fell, Admiral Blandy added that the ships sunk were two destroyers, the Japanese light cruiser "Sakawa" and two 1,200 ton transports.

He told newspaper reporters that continued radio activity would prevent them from inspecting the target ships today.

"Crumpled Paper"

As the observer ship "Appalachian" made its way through the lagoon, it was seen that the submarine "Skate" looked like crumpled paper.

A correspondent who accompanied Admiral Blandy and Mr. James Forrestal, United States Navy Secretary, on a tour of inspection quoted Admiral Blandy as saying that the "Skate" could be repaired in [illegible]

[illegible] the bull's-eye target ship stood up well on their tyres, apparently withstanding the heat effectively, the correspondent declared.

As the extent of destruction caused to the "target fleet" became more evident, non-professional observers came to regard the atom bomb with a new awe as the world's [illegible] instrument of destruction.

The first reaction to the test has been one of having been "let down," possibly because of the comparative lack of spectacle at the time of explosion.

One observer said: "Most correspondents expected the atom cloud to bloom into a huge geni and reach out for them with tentacles."

Bikini Reporters Under Censors

NEW YORK, Tuesday (R). — Censorship has clamped down on some atom test correspondents at Bikini, according to the Columbia Broadcasting System correspondent.

He declared today: "I have received written orders which prevent me telling you what [illegible]"

TRIESTE TO BE INTERNATIONAL

PARIS, Tuesday (UP). — The Russian delegate to the Foreign Ministers' conference here last night accepted the French compromise plan for Trieste.

This agreement — reached after weeks of wrangling — provides for the implementing of the original French plan, previously accepted by Britain and France, which makes Trieste an international enclave in Italian territory. The international zone will extend from Duino, near Montfalcone, to Nova Città.

M. Molotov accepted the French plan after making a new proposal which was categorically rejected by Mr. Byrnes, who said that the United States would accept nothing else but the "French line."

PEACE CONFERENCE PLANS

The "Big Four" Ministers agreed to the Line, but failed to agree on the type of government to be established within it, M. Bidault and M. Molotov suggesting a "set-up", which Mr. Byrnes said that he must study. He hoped to give his decision this afternoon.

The agreement will open the way to the Peace Conference which is now expected to meet about July 25, when 21 nations will thrash out the Peace Treaties for Italy, Hungary, Rumania, Bulgaria and Finland.

The Foreign Ministers Conference is now expected to end within 10 days.

Both Italy and Yugoslavia tonight protested against the decision. The Yugoslav Deputy Premier said that M. Molotov's amendment to the French plan was equally unacceptable.

STRIKE AND RIOTS

ROME, Tuesday, (R). — Allied police fired into the air at Trieste during the night to rescue a Venezia Giulia policeman, who was being stoned outside the Slovene Anti-Fascist Headquarters, said a report reaching Rome today.

British and United States soldiers were lined up along the centre of the streets, forming a solid barrier between the two rival factions, one shouting "Long Live Italian Trieste", and the other "Long Live Tito and Stalin."

The strike called by the Italian Committee of National Liberation has now led to an almost general stoppage, with the Slovene Anti-Fascist Union ordering its members to leave their work.

Transport, port facilities and postal and telegraphic services are at a standstill.

Weary police were last night sprawled on the floor of their headquarters, snatching a few hours sleep after nearly two days' continuous duty.

"BIRYA" HAD 1,000 ABOARD

Palestine Post Staff

HAIFA, Tuesday. — The refugee ship s.s. Akbel, renamed Birya, carrying 1,100 immigrants without permits, was escorted to Haifa by the destroyer H.M.S. Virago early this morning and anchored outside the breakwater.

Among those on board are a number of wives of Palestinian servicemen, who met their husbands while these were serving with the Brigade in Belgium and Holland.

Three suspected cases of bubonic plague were reported to the authorities by the captain of the ship, and none of the immigrants have been allowed to land. They have been transferred by launches to the refugee ship "Smyrni" (Max Nordau), which arrived in Haifa with 1,602 persons on board on May 14, which was cleaned and prepared for them. All passengers on the Birya had their clothing sprayed with D.D.T. and were given anti-plague injections.

The immigrants will be held in the Max Nordau in quarantine for a minimum of six days. If further plague cases occur, the period will be extended for a further six days. Those actually infected were taken to the isolation section of the Government Hospital in the morning.

No excitement was in evidence at the ship's arrival, no crowds gathered, nor were any preparatory security measures in evidence. A police launch of the Port Marine Division left to meet the ship at 7.45 a.m.

Sailed from France

The "Akbel", which is registered as Turkish, and was built in 1898, is a 284-ton steamer and sailed from a port in France nine days ago.

Congestion on board was extremely bad, — worse than any previously encountered on similar ships. Food was very scarce, and water even more so, being rationed to half a cup for those in immediate danger from thirst. The initial inspection party was met with cries for water.

The passengers are stated to be mostly young, half of them being girls. There are 60 old people on board, and 15 children under 16. Their countries of origin are Poland, Germany, Holland, Belgium and France. Many are ex-inmates of concentration camps.

The Captain and the crew, totalling 10, all Turkish, have been detained.

COUNTING ARMS AT YAGOUR

Palestine Post Staff

The large caches of arms and ammunition, and the nature of the military operations still in progress at Yagour were shown to foreign and local newspapermen by the Army Public Relations Office, who brought them for this purpose from Jerusalem yesterday afternoon.

Soldiers, of whom there are apparently several hundred in the settlement, were walking about with rifles slung and picks and shovels on their shoulders, and a drill was working.

In a barbed wire enclosure near the kibbutz workshop there was a display of rifles, trench mortars, steel ammunition boxes with thousands of [illegible]

In a grainstore, under a heap of grain, four large cases of American gelignite had been found, and soldiers were still breaking up the floor of the barn with the pickaxes.

The party was shown a cupboard in the children's house, where under a false shelf a few rifles were hidden, and under some tiles in the floor, an ammunition case with 6,000 rounds.

The tour was conducted through the settlement, which presented a scene of great disorder and confusion. Armoured cars, barbed wire enclosures, clothing strewn on verandahs, here and there some shoes in the yard, and furniture from the houses which had been, or were about to be searched, piled up outside. The King's Shropshire Light Infantry have taken [illegible]

[illegible] taken off under arrest. The rest of the women and children were taken to Jalami camp, and most of them were returned to Yagour that evening and the rest on the next morning. Ten men were injured and taken to Government and 22nd General Hospital.

There was no proof as yet of any stores or property being missing, the O.C. said. He thought that the people would find their things later; at present their belongings were scattered all over the place.

On this point the women of the settlement did not see eye to eye with the Officer Commanding, and they also said several children had been injured. They pointed out that the sanitary condition of the kibbutz was bordering on the point of [illegible]

The Remaining

[illegible]

Hundred Men

[illegible]

Commons And Mufti

[illegible]

NO ADVANCE NOTICE

[illegible]

REST OF THE NEWS

34 Killed in India

AHMEDABAD, Tuesday (R). — Two fresh outbursts of violence, bringing the total of casualties up to 33 killed and 250 injured, occurred this morning after the curfew had been lifted in Ahmedabad in the Bombay Presidency.

Hindus and Moslems began pitched battles here yesterday.

The origin of the disturbances was reported to be the stoning of a Hindu religious procession passing through an area of mixed population.

From Patna it is reported that one person was killed and another seriously hurt in a communal clash yesterday at Monghyr.

Cabinet Mission Back

LONDON, Tuesday (UP). — The Cabinet Mission, consisting of Lord Pethick-Lawrence, Sir Stafford Cripps and Mr. A.V. Alexander, arrived back in London last night, bringing with them commitments from both Congress and the Moslem League to agree to the long-term British plan for India, in spite of the failure to secure agreement for the interim plan.

STANSGATE TO HASTEN TREATY

CAIRO, Tuesday (Reuter). — Lord Stansgate, chief British delegate in the negotiations, will be charged with concluding the Anglo-Egyptian Treaty as [illegible]

"Persuasion" [illegible]

[illegible]

Mlle. Bidault Clubbed

[illegible]

Internees Escape

[illegible]

THE PALESTINE POST

JERUSALEM
TUESDAY, JULY 30, 1946

PRICE: 15 MILS
VOL. XXI. No. 6166

Column One

By David Courtney

IT is easier to build an empire than to liquidate it. There comes a time when the notion of imperial rule exercised on the principle of masters and subjects is repugnant even to the rulers. That time has come in India and must come elsewhere. The process of handing India over to the Indians is difficult because throughout the period of British suzerainty Indians have not been encouraged in self-government. There is no question of their taking over a going political concern. The political structure of India is foreign to Indians; its keystone is London; and if that is to be removed a new one must be built in its place. The new Indian nation, as a system of Government, has only just begun; and those who expect it to begin at a point where other national systems have left off, and pretend that because it cannot begin at that point it should not begin at all, know little of logic and overlook the basic principle of nationhood: that the people, as Hartley Bluntness put it the other day, override the State idea; and embody it. The rest is the machinery of State. Fundamentally, it is the machinery of State which just now is causing all the trouble. Even Indians are ambitious for power. Even Indians, like their Western brethren, allow their own progress to be perplexed by inter-sectarian feud. But they, with generations of foreign rule behind them, have some excuse; and that is the explanation of the present crisis affecting the Moslem League on the one side and the Congress Party and British Government on the other. In the long run, only the Indians themselves can resolve their differences; and to them, as their first test under autonomy, it should be left.

■

INDIA, Egypt and Palestine are three problems each as vital as any on the Paris agenda and each is a British problem. On the handling of them the future of Britain herself depends far more than on the handling of the Italian or Finnish Treaties. If the Empire is not to disintegrate, it must liquidate itself in the birth of nations and become greater in its passing away than in its coming into being. For this to happen there must be no shilly-shally and no coming to terms with the powerful and too often uninformed residue of outmoded policy. The latest despatches on the Anglo-Egyptian negotiations are hopeful after a couple of days of doubt and suspicion; and it looks as if the attempt to bargain for extra-territorial and extra-sovereign rights has been dropped. It is a pity the deal has had to be made with a Government devoid of even the pretence of a people's mandate; and it is to be hoped that if Egypt remains within the British sphere of influence the London Government will be at least as much concerned for Egyptian Democracy as it is for Bulgarian and Polish Democracy; but that aside, we have no business in Egypt and will be none the worse for getting out of it.

■

IT is probable that the final solution of the Palestine, India and Egypt questions depends a great deal on the solution of the differences which sunder the Big Three from each other. If Britain, America and Soviet Russia were unified in principle and purpose, and not merely in their reluctance to risk the full consequences of disunity, the fatal calculations of strategy and competitive economics founded on strategical considerations would have a diminishing effect on foreign policies; and every problem would be instantly clarified. In the presence of those calculations the Peace Conference itself looks frail. It met yesterday, in sultry weather, say the reports; and sultriness is the mark of the whole international atmosphere.

Jerusalem, July 30.

BYRNES SMILES, ATTLEE BOWS
BIDAULT OPENS THE CONFERENCE OF PARIS

Palestine Post Staff

The Paris peace conference, of the 21 victorious nations, was formally declared open by the French Head of State, M. Georges Bidault, at a few minutes past 4 o'clock yesterday.

A little earlier, M. Bidault had been elected temporary President of the conference. The proceedings were purely formal and the conference adjourned at 5.20 hours G.M.T. until tomorrow.

M. Georges Bidault

WHAT THEY SAY

M. Bidault: "I foresee numerous difficulties at the peace conference. The feeling of security and promises of stability so far only appears in an uncertain manner."

Mr. James Byrnes: "The U.S. position on the five treaties will be to support the conclusions agreed among the Foreign Ministers. The U.S. Government reserves the right to alter its position in matters not agreed by the 'Big Four.' I will favour giving a full hearing to the ex-enemy nations."

General de Gaulle: "I urge the closest association of France and Britain to restore the balance of power in a world which is tending to split into halves, dominated by the U.S. and Russia."

Dr. Evatt: "A peace settlement must be reached by democratic methods, giving every nation which helped to win the war equal rights to participate in making the peace."

BIDAULT WELCOMES THE DELEGATES

PARIS, Monday (Reuter). — M. Georges Bidault, the French Head of State and host to the 21-nation conference, arrived at Luxembourg Palace this afternoon to receive the heads of the delegations before the formal opening.

He drove into the courtyard of the Palace through a long line of French police, on both sides of the pavement, forming a barrier holding back hundreds of people along the immediate approaches.

As his car entered the courtyard, two lines of gendarmes fanned out and presented swords before the entrance reserved for the delegates.

M. Bidault entered the Palace through a small bodyguard of five members of the Republican Guard, dressed in gold helmets, red plumes, white trousers and long coats folded back in the Napoleonic style.

Unknown to the crowds in the courtyard, armed firemen were stationed at strategic points on the roof of the Palace. From their hiding places they had a clear view of the whole courtyard and some streets in the immediate surroundings.

The first delegates began to arrive shortly before the clock over the main entrance struck three.

Quick Succession

In quick succession, the cars of Mr. MacKenzie King, Canadian Prime Minister, and the representatives of Holland, Abyssinia, Norway and Brazil arrived. Then arrived Dr. Wellington Koo, Chinese delegate and after him came Dr. Herbert Evatt of Australia.

M. Molotov then arrived and was followed a few minutes later by Mr. Byrnes and Mr. Attlee. M. Molotov walked from his car looking straight ahead. Mr. Byrnes was smiling as he climbed up the steps and appeared to be enjoying a joke with one of his staff.

Attlee Bows

As Mr Attlee, in a dark grey suit, stepped down from his car, he gave a slight bow to the crowd.

M. Bidault held his reception, which was private, in the Victor Hugo room, where the "Big Four" Foreign Ministers occasionally held their meetings. After formal exchanges of courtesy, the delegates dispersed into groups to await the opening of the conference.

Bevin Not To Resign

LONDON, Monday (Reuter). — Reports that the Foreign Minister, Mr. Ernest Bevin, is intending to resign were emphatically denied by the Foreign Office in London tonight.

There is no truth whatsoever, it is understood, in the rumour that Mr. Bevin plans to leave the Foreign Office for health or any other reason.

While there have been suggestions over the week-end both that Mr. Bevin is more seriously ill than has been officially admitted and that his illness is purely diplomatic, the fact remains that the Foreign Secretary is suffering from a genuine but slight indisposition.

After two days' rest, he was reported to be much better today and it is confidently expected that he will join the rest of the British delegation to the peace conference in the none too distant future.

Britain Accepts One-Zone Plan

WASHINGTON, Monday (R). — The British Government has accepted "in principle" Mr. Byrnes' offer to join the American zone of Germany with the other zones as an economic entity. This was announced today by the State Department.

It added that this acceptance by Britain was welcomed as a first move towards ending the heavy financial burden resting on the two occupying powers, and the State Department hoped that the other two occupying powers would also respond similarly to Mr. Byrnes' offer.

Cairo Delegates Disagreeing

By Reuters Diplomatic Correspondent

LONDON, Monday. — The Anglo-Egyptian Treaty delegates are disagreeing. The points of disagreement are on the length of time British troops should take in evacuating Egypt and the method of operation of the Joint Defence Board, which the Treaty is supposed to establish.

This was learned from well-informed quarters in London. But a Foreign Office spokesman today denied that the negotiations had broken down adding that the "gap between the two points of view is being continually narrowed."

Wedding Lorry Smash
5 Dead, 17 Injured

Five people lost their lives and seventeen others, including 11 women and four children, were injured when a lorry carrying a wedding party overturned on its way from Jerusalem to Nablus early yesterday afternoon.

The bodies of the dead were brought to the Government Hospital in Jerusalem, but their names were not available last night.

The injured detained in hospital are Rushel Youssef and Ali Kueidi, adults, and Muyhasar Pausik, Rafik Abdul Al, Maimel Rushdi and Ehsen Mahmoud, children.

(Other road fatalities, Page 3)

SPIRIT OF FRIENDLY CO-OPERATION

PARIS, Monday (Reuter). — Opening the Conference of Paris this afternoon, M. Georges Bidault, head of the French State, said: "In the name of the French people, Government and Republic, I welcome from my heart the delegations of the friendly nations, who have come to this Conference to settle the problems of the post-war world.

"I am convinced that our nations will work in common accord and in a spirit of friendly co-operation at the important task which has been submitted to them.

"The French Government appreciates at its full value the honour and confidence paid to France by her partners and friends. It knows that this honour is the result of the fate which for the second time has placed France on the side of the democratic nations against aggression.

"The Allied Conference after the 1914-18 war proposed to the world solutions which did not prevent less than 25 years later a new, longer and more terrible war breaking out.

"It is too easy to put on trial the men and the politics which are responsible for these solutions. History must be the judge.

Two Powers Absent in 1919

"But whatever may be the errors and weaknesses, the basic reason for that failure must be attributed to the fact that two of the great powers, whose armed might had in turn played a decisive part in the battle, remained absent from the peace settlement.

"This cause of weakness, which was doubtless decisive, no longer exists today. All the democratic nations today share in the discussions. An international concept of power is already in existence and the French Government particularly hopes that it will be speedily completed by the admission of all European powers.

Uno's Ideal

"The association of peaceful powers inspired by the same ideal is the basis of the United Nations Organization, whose beginnings were established last year at San Francisco and which in 1946, in the midst of great difficulties, but with confidence and hope, has entered upon its first year of existence. It is this same association of peaceful nations that the Council of Foreign Ministers has summoned to share in the working out of the peace settlement.

"Criticisms have been made of the broad lines of the procedure of the four Foreign Ministers conferences. Complaints have also been heard on the slowness with which our work has been carried on and of the delays which resulted in the necessary consultations with the other nations principally interested.

Basis for Settlements

"As the representative of the Government which you have accepted as your host, I am less than anyone in a position to set myself up as the champion of the methods which are thus under discussion. But the difficulties encountered were enormous, because the interests at stake were difficult to reconcile."

Treaties Out At Midnight

PARIS, Monday (Reuter).— It was announced after today's meeting of the "Big Four" Foreign Ministers' deputies that the complete text of the draft treaties with the satellite powers of Germany would be published at midnight G.M.T. on Tuesday.

2,678 ARRIVE IN 'HAGANAH'

Palestine Post Bureau

HAIFA, Monday. — The largest party of illegal immigrants ever to arrive on one ship was towed into Haifa Port at 10.30 this morning aboard a corvette renamed "Haganah," lashed alongside a destroyer.

The corvette, similar to the "Wedgwood" and of the same tonnage, was crammed to the last inch with 2,678 ragged, weary and thirsty people, over twice the number which arrived on her sister ship, the Wedgwood.

Intercepted at midnight last night 90 miles off the coast of Palestine by H.M.S. Venus, the "Haganah" was in distress. It is stated, having had several breakdowns of her engines, as well as a failure of the electric and ventilating system.

Officials who boarded the ship on her arrival outside the Port stated that conditions on board were appalling, and congestion was such that they could scarcely make their way across the decks to the bridge.

There are 150 expectant mothers on board, and a son was born to one of them last night. There are in addition some 100 children under 10, many of them infants under a year old. Three sick persons were taken to hospital together with the mother and her baby when the ship berthed.

"Mostly Young"

The immigrants are mostly young, with only about 50 old people on board. They include 700 members of the Youth Aliya, and other large groups belonging to pioneering organizations.

The "Haganah" which was originally named s.s. Balboa and is registered in Panama City, left from a port in France and had been at sea since last Monday. She was flying the Zionist colours and the Red Ensign, and carried a banner across her funnel saying: "We will never surrender" in Hebrew and English.

The ship was anchored outside the breakwater this morning, but was brought into Port later in the day.

Some difficulty is foreseen in finding accommodation for the refugees, as Athlit Camp is full up with the "Birya" immigrants who have not yet been released.

Distributed

As an immediate palliative, the new arrivals will be distributed over five other refugee ships, and the first 1,000 will move this evening.

An official statement says that the ship was sighted by air reconnaissance at 3.30 on Sunday afternoon, about 150 miles west of Haifa. A destroyer came up with the ship at 9 o'clock and shadowed it until it reached territorial waters about 8.40 on Monday morning. About five minutes later the destroyer Venus went alongside and a boarding party went aboard the Balbao, which sailed on to Haifa.

WHITE PAPER ON VIOLENCE
FULL, OFFICIAL TEXT
PAGE 2

Agency Members For Paris

Three members of the Jewish Agency Executive — Rabbi Y. L. Fishman, Acting Chairman, Mr Eliahu Dobkin, and Dr. Emil Schmorak, the only ones at liberty in Palestine — left by air for Paris yesterday morning to attend the forthcoming extraordinary session of the Agency Executive on August 4.

Rabbi Fishman was accompanied by his son-in-law, Mr I. Werfel. Prior to their departure, the Executive on Sunday appointed a Provisional Executive to handle all current political affairs, consisting of Mr. J. Suprassky, Rabbi M. Ha'Meiri (Ostrovsky), Mr. Z. Rubashov, and Mr. Levi Skolnik.

Temporary Committee

The Executive also appointed a committee to deal with current administrative matters, comprising Mr. S. Eisenberg, Mr. D. Baharal, Mr. D. Horowitz, and Mr Z. Scherf.

Others going to Paris were Mrs Golda Meyerson, of the Histadruth Executive who left yesterday, and Dr. F. Rosenblueth, Chairman of the "Aliya Hadasha" (New Settlers' Party) who is going in a few days on invitation to attend the meeting to voice his party's views.

Two members of the Vaad Leumi Executive are also to leave within the next few days, according to a decision taken yesterday. It is pointed out that Mr. I. Ben-Zvi, the President, and Mr. David Remez, the Chairman, usually attended meetings of the Agency Executive in Jerusalem; Mr Remez is now interned at Latrun.

Mr. Michael Comay has left for Paris as an observer on behalf of the South African Zionist Federation.

The session in Paris is expected to last three weeks.

"MUFTI NOT A WAR CRIMINAL"—NOEL-BAKER

LONDON, Monday (Reuter). — The Mufti of Jerusalem's position in Egypt was referred to in the House of Commons today, when Major Wilkes (Labour) asked: "Under what conditions and surveillance the Mufti, who is classified a war criminal, is today living in Egypt."

Mr. Philip Noel-Baker, Minister of State, replied that negotiations about the Mufti were proceeding with the Egyptian Government. He said that Major Wilkes was mistaken in thinking that the Mufti was classified as a war criminal.

He was not an enemy national, nor a person who served in the enemy forces.

"NO RESTRICTIONS"

Major Wilkes said that he was officially claimed as a war criminal by the Yugoslav Government. Major Wilkes also referred to a speech in the Egyptian Senate on July 15, in which, he said, the Egyptian Prime Minister stated that no restriction was to be put on the political activities or movements of the Mufti in Egypt.

Mr. Noel Baker said that as the negotiations were going on, he could not say anything further except that the British grievances against the Mufti were more serious than those of Yugoslavia.

In reply to another question, Mr. Noel Baker said that there was certainly no truth whatever in the report that the Mufti has been invited by the Palestine Administration to go to Palestine.

TRUMAN HAS NOT YET ACCEPTED LONDON EXPERTS' PLAN

By H. R. WISHENGRAD—PTA Special Correspondent

PARIS, Monday. — President Truman has not yet accepted the recommendations of the committee of British and American experts on a Federal plan for Palestine, but Mr. Attlee in his talks with Mr. Byrnes is reported to be pressing for quick American acceptance.

The admission of 100,000 Jews into Palestine would not be permitted under these proposals until a decision is taken to put the constitutional scheme into effect, it is learned. Similarly, the discriminatory Land Transfer Regulations imposed under the 1939 White Paper will not be rescinded until the new Constitution is adopted.

Further disclosures of the plan show that the presiding officers of the provincial legislature will for the first five years be appointed by the High Commissioner, having an absolute veto right over any legislation passed by the provinces. There is no appeal from his veto.

The High Commissioner will appoint a provincial executive consisting of the Chief Minister and other Ministers, and may supersede the provincial government whenever he deems necessary.

The plan further specifies the disarming and dissolution of all illegal forces.

General Problem

One of the recommendations deals with the general problem of European Jews, proposing that the problem can be solved by the following means:

(1) settling as many D.P.s as possible in the American and British zones of Germany;

(2) stipulating in the Italian-Danubian peace treaties that the D.P.s should be settled in those countries;

(3) appealing to the Uno Assembly for the settlement of D.P.s in all countries, the possibility of Brazil being emphasized.

A quick survey of Jewish opinion in Paris indicated that the plan has not the ghost of a chance of being accepted. It is pointed out:

(1) the plan resembles the proposals submitted to Britain several years ago by a leading Arab politician in the Middle East;

(2) it "freezes" the Jewish population and bars immigration and settlement in 85 per cent of Western Palestine;

(3) the provisions for autonomy are a mockery, since the most vital issue of immigration will be controlled by the High Commissioner.

A Jewish Agency spokesman, when apprised of the details of the plan, caustically commented: "This Anglo-Arab League scheme for the liquidation of Zionism will have the support of at least one Jew — the gentleman who voted for the White Paper in 1939."

Adverse Reaction

Reuter's diplomatic correspondent adds that the adverse Arab and Jewish reaction to the federal plan is reliably believed to have been among the questions discussed in Paris last night.

The Colonial Secretary, who was also present at the meeting, has now returned to London to consult about the local situation with Sir John Shaw.

While the main purpose of last night's talk was to discover the official U.S. attitude to the proposals, the whole problem has been given a new twist by the indications that the existing scheme is likely to be rejected by both Jews and Arabs.

Before either the Palestine Jews or Arabs have received invitations to discuss the plan, it has become plain that the federal scheme, as reported in the press, is unlikely to be accepted as the basis for discussion by the interested parties themselves.

Byrnes Silent On Paris Talk

Although the British Prime Minister and the American Secretary of State conferred together in Paris on Sunday night for an hour and a half, mainly, if not solely, about Palestine, Mr. Byrnes declined to comment on the conversation.

The three American experts had been called to Paris from London to advise him regarding the proposals worked out by them and their British colleagues as the document was long and complicated, he said.

He pointed out that as the Anglo-American experts did not constitute a joint committee their report was not a joint document. The American members would simply report to their Government.

It is reported from Washington that Zionist circles there are concerned over the administration's attitude to the experts' recommendations regarding Partition. A spokesman described Sunday's meeting between the President and Senators Mead and Wagner and Mr. James MacDonald as "disappointing."

The attitude of President Truman and Mr. Byrnes is not clear to Zionist leaders, who feel that if the President is standing by the demand for the immigration of the 100,000 he should disapprove of the experts' plan publicly and inform the British Government accordingly before the question is discussed in Parliament.

"Trodden Down"

On the other hand, a "New York Times" despatch from London states that "London sources in close touch with Washington say that the whole Federal plan is likely to be trodden down by the American Government."

The despatch adds: "It is learned that the whole scheme for a new Palestine constitution is based on a British paper, the final draft of which is dated July 13. The plan does not reflect British resentment over the King David Hotel explosion, since the principles had been finally accepted by both British and American representatives before that date."

At the mass demonstration in London (reported in yesterday's issue of The Palestine Post), Mr. Berl Locker said that if the world were divided into accusers and accused, it is doubtful who would be the accusers. Hitler's downfall had not ended Jewish troubles. Instead of accusing the Jews, people should be surprised that the vast majority of the surviving Jews remained sane.

Crimes had been committed in Palestine and those responsible should be punished, but the British people and British Labour must ask themselves whether they had not sinned against the Jewish people.

Stressing the question of immigration to Palestine as cardinal, Mr. Locker said that the Yishuv was not prepared to buy peace at the expense of other Jews. The Middle East presented the sad picture of Socialist states appearing not the Arab peoples but their exploiters.

(PTA, Palcor & UP)

AFTER MIDNIGHT

The British Embassy in Cairo has denied that an attempt was made on Lord Stansgate's life.. Mr. Attlee will not return from Paris for the Palestine debate on Wednesday and Thursday. Mr. Morrison, Sir Stafford Cripps and Mr. Hall, the Colonial Secretary, will speak for the Government.. A one-day general strike was called in Calcutta yesterday in sympathy with the 60,000 postal workers who struck 19 days ago. Anti-British slogans were shouted in front of the Government offices. ... Dr. Weizmann, although not fully recovered from his illness, went to the House of Commons last night to attend a meeting in the committee room of M.P.'s of all parties.

Sir John In London

LONDON, Monday. — Sir John Shaw, Chief Secretary to the Palestine Government, arrived by air at a London airport this afternoon from Palestine. He told Reuter:

I am here on a special mission to the Colonial Office and shall be returning to Palestine as soon as possible.

The new round-up of Jews in Palestine is a purely precautionary measure as a result of evidence that the Palestine Police has obtained.

King David 84 DEAD

The casualty list last night was: —

84 dead;
46 injured, detained in hospital;
20 missing.

Only one more body has been extracted from the wreckage since Sunday's casualty figure was published. It was that of Edvokia Pereletor, a woman previously reported missing. Khalil Dajani, previously reported to be missing, is now stated to be safe.

Zero Hour Was 2 p.m.

Palestine Post Staff

Sappers of the Sixth Airborne Division yesterday afternoon blew up the central pillar still standing in the ruins of the south-west corner of the King David and during the remainder of the afternoon and evening removed the demolished sections which had constituted a danger to rescue operations.

The half-wrecked roof of the top floor and the ceilings of the next two floors were still suspended, held up by the steel rods anchored in the concrete.

People in the vicinity were evacuated at about 1.30, and armed troops stood at the edge of the field between the hotels and King George Avenue, and further along Julian's Way towards the railway-station.

Exactly at 2 o'clock there was a flash of flame, followed by falling masonry and the crash of the explosives.

The thud of the blast was felt as far as two miles off in south-eastern Jerusalem. A cloud of dust was carried over the half-masted Union Jack over the hotel, and was blown by a westerly wind across the Old City wall to the east.

2ND DIVISION REASSURED

Following representations made by the Second Division Civil Service Association concerning the safety of Government offices, the Chief Secretary has replied to the Association assuring them that this is a matter of "the utmost concern and importance to Government."

The safety of offices and the protection of the lives of officers was receiving the most urgent and careful attention, and all possible measures would be taken to ensure their safety.

Minute's Silence

One minute's silence was observed at the Tel Aviv Magistrates Court yesterday morning and court proceedings were suspended for 15 minutes in tribute to Messrs. E. Many, M. Rosin and Dr. Z. Goldschmidt, the three Jewish members of the Judicial branch of Government who lost their lives in last week's bomb outrage.

Haganah (Norsyd/Balboa) and Biryah (Akbel II)

The efforts of the Royal Navy at preventing the illegal traffic will be largely frustrated if ships of this speed are allowed to fall into the hands of the Jews.
—*September 14, 1946, letter from the Admiralty to the Dominions Office.*

The only American-manned vessel to make two Aliyah Bet voyages from Europe was the Haganah, sister ship of the Wedgwood. On her first voyage, in June 1946, she departed from France. More than a month later, she sailed again, this time from Yugoslavia. Both contingents of passengers came perilously close to disaster in the Mediterranean.

Formerly a Royal Canadian Navy corvette known as the Norsyd, the Haganah went through the same initial routine as her sister ship. Stripped of her guns at City Island in New York and then transferred to Staten Island for further work and provisioning, she sailed for Europe during the Jewish holiday of Passover in April 1946.

Crossing the Atlantic with Panamanian registry under the name Balboa, she made for Marseilles to be prepared for passengers. Her crew consisted mainly of young Americans recruited through Hashomer Hatzair and Habonim, two Zionist youth movements.

In Marseilles the former warship was refitted with wooden shelves, which were said to be bins for bananas; they were actually bunks to accommodate about 1,250 refugees. Security precautions were in effect, but British agents were aware of her movements and presented a constant threat to her leaving Europe. After many weeks, the preparations were complete, and the crew received orders to sail. On June 21, 1946, a Friday, the Haganah left Marseilles and put into the smaller and less-conspicuous port of Sete, about 30 miles away, arriving at 8 p.m. on the sabbath eve. More than 1,000 refugees boarded. By 6:30 a.m. the next day, they were sailing for Palestine.

First voyage of the Haganah

I. F. Stone, an American journalist writing for the New York City newspaper *PM*, was among the participants in this first voyage.

Originally scheduled to travel with the Haganah's sister ship, the Wedgwood, Stone was left behind in Italy when the Wedgwood slipped out to sea while he interceded on shore with Italian officials. The Jewish underground in Europe arranged for him to continue his reporting on the next ship out, the Haganah. Stone's book *Underground to Palestine* recounted the Haganah's first voyage. Stone described the departure from Sete:

> We saw a line of ten trucks heading for the freight terminal. They were open trucks jammed tight with refugees.... Crew members waved from the deck and shouted, *Shalom.*
>
> Every section of the ship in which there was emergency sleeping space had been given a letter of the alphabet, and every bunk a number. One member of the crew was assigned to each section and instructed to act as usher for the refugees.
>
> On the pier each refugee was given a slip of paper with the letter of his section and the number of his bunk.... A group of former Partisans was given the honor of being the first to come aboard ....
>
> The embarkation was complicated by the fact that it had to take place on a Saturday morning, and many of the passengers were Orthodox Jews. One of the underground workers said there had been considerable discussion as to whether it was permissible for such a purpose to travel and to carry bags on the Sabbath, which begins at sundown Friday evening.
>
> The majority decided that it was a *Mitzvah* (a pious deed) for a Jew to go to Palestine and that they would therefore be forgiven for what would ordinarily be a sin. But two members of the Agudath Israel stayed behind. They felt that even for such a purpose it was not proper to violate the Sabbath and that they would rather take their chances and wait for another ship....
>
> Among our refugees were five Gentiles who intended to settle in Palestine, four for religious, one for idealistic reasons.
>
> Two thirds of the refugees were men.... Most of our passengers were 30 years of age or younger.... Our oldest passenger was 78; our youngest, 10....
>
> There were Jews from 16 different countries on board, including one rather lonely Egyptian Jew who spoke only his native Arabic and a smattering of French.... There were 585 refugees from Poland. The next largest national group, 109, were Czechoslovakian Jews, most of them from Slovakia and Carpatho-Russia. There were 84 immigrants from Holland, all young people.... There were 59 Jews from Hungary, 51 from Rumania, 44 from Germany. Twenty-four were from Lithuania. Twenty were from France, 12 from Belgium, and 11 from Austria. There were six Russian Jews, three Latvians, two Swiss, two Turkish, two Greek, and the Egyptian.... Linguistically, the ship was a floating Babel....
>
> One hundred and thirty-eight persons on board had no party affiliation. The rest belonged to 17 different Zionist parties, the largest group being orthodox. There were 195 members of Agudath Israel and 90 of Poale Mizrachi (orthodox labor.) Next were 140 Revisionists, chauvinistic and right wing. There were 82 Chalutzim from the Hashomer Hatzair, a left-wing socialist group which advocates a binationalist Arab-Jewish Palestine rather than a Jewish state.
>
> Of the 1,015 passengers, 568 were chalutzim who intended to spend their lives in collective settlements in Palestine. All of them were socialists of one kind or another.

A voyage from Sete to Palestine could have been made in four days; instead, the trip took almost three times as long. The first eight days at sea were uneventful, although there were moments of excitement for passengers and crew. For the refugees, conditions were far from comfortable. Their quarters were crowded and poorly ventilated, and the ever-present threat of discovery by the British required a rule that the passengers go below decks whenever another ship was sighted. At night, an 11 p.m. curfew confined the refugees to the stale air below decks until morning. For the first two days, stormy seas kept the sanitation crew busy mopping up after cases of seasickness. A group of two dozen young refugees who had been given a first aid course tended to the sick. Serious cases were sent to an infirmary set up in the officers' mess and presided over by a refugee doctor. Calm weather returned after two days, and the skies were again sunny by day and star-filled by night. For most of the refugees, this was their first chance for peaceful relaxation in years, and they passed time on deck telling stories, singing or listening to songs, and taking the sun. Meals were served on deck three times a day; typically, the food consisted of vegetable soup or an egg for those who observed the religious dietary laws, soup with meat for those not keeping kosher, and an abundance of bread prepared by four refugee bakers. The leisurely pace of the voyage gave passengers and crew opportunities to meet and talk. For the Americans, this was a chance to hear first-hand about the Jews' experiences in Nazi Europe. Some of the refugees had fought the Nazis; among these were followers of Aba Kovner, the Vilna partisan leader who later would become a poet in Israel. Kovner's wife, Vitka, was among the group on board, and she told American volunteers about ambushes in the forests and the final struggles of the Vilna ghetto.

On the second day at sea, a dramatic reunion occurred when a 20-year-old Hashomer Hatzair woman talking with one of the Americans suddenly spotted a massive man almost three times her age among the refugees on deck and threw herself in his arms. He had saved her from execution in Auschwitz, and neither had seen the other since.

The man was a former circus strongman whose exploits in saving Jewish lives in the death camps made him a legendary figure among the refugees. Orphaned at age eight in Poland, he had gone to Cuba before the first World War, served time in a U.S. federal penitentiary for rum-running, became a professional wrestler, and was on a circus tour in Europe in 1939 when the war trapped him in Poland. In Auschwitz he organized a black market based on gold and jewels salvaged from gas-chamber victims. Eventually he bribed the camp commander, from whom he purchased the lives of Jews including the young woman travelling on the Haganah.

On the fourth day, the steering gear broke down. The engines had to be stopped, and the ship began rolling heavily. Soon, many passengers were seasick. The problem was repaired by 10 p.m., and the Haganah had no further mechanical trouble on this first voyage.

One afternoon, a religious betrothal ceremony was held on the foredeck for a couple who had met at a refugee training center. Afterwards, passengers celebrated by dancing a hora, and the dancing and singing went on for hours.

On the sixth day, all passengers were summoned to the foredeck at 4:30 p.m. The commander addressed them from the bridge, instructing them how to behave if captured and questioned by the British. He cautioned that they might see barbed wire again, in Palestine. He told them that, whatever the English might say, the passengers were now citizens of the Land of Israel. This was underscored as the passengers were instructed to line up and go to the captain's cabin to receive their immigration permits. Each was given a blue "Permit to Enter Palestine," issued in the name of "the Jewish Community of Palestine." The next morning, smoke was sighted to the east, and the passengers were sent below. When they came back on deck, a ship was on the horizon, and the Haganah appeared to be following it. Word spread that the stranger was a Turkish ship.

At sundown of the seventh day, Sabbath candles were lit and the foredeck was turned into a synagogue. Some of the Americans took part in the service, and others watched from the bridge. The next morning, Sabbath services were held on the foredeck, and the captain and commander were invited to read from the Bible. The captain's portion included a prophecy, from Isaiah 66:13, that "you shall be comforted in Jerusalem." That night, the passengers were instructed to pack their belongings and have them ready for the morning. Understanding the order to mean that they would land in Palestine the next day, the passengers reacted with excitement. Dancing began on the foredeck. In the mess, the crew were invited to a surprise party; only Hebrew songs were sung at this party, and a request for Yiddish songs was turned down with an explanation that the old sad songs were the songs of exile. The galley crew was ordered to pack a sandwich lunch and water for each passenger for the next day.

On the morning of the ninth day, crewmen and passengers coming on deck saw that the ship they had been following the day before was now only a few hundred yards from the Haganah. The other ship was the Akbel II, an old, 250-ton wooden freighter from Istanbul. She flew the Turkish flag. Word spread that the passengers were to transfer to the Akbel for the final part of the trip to Palestine. The Akbel was less than half the size of the crowded Haganah, and it was clear that conditions aboard the Turkish vessel would be difficult.

Until then, the American crewmen had not known of the plans to transfer the passengers to another vessel. Some of the officers aboard the Haganah were also unaware of the decision to transfer the passengers. The transfer had been ordered at a higher level, by Aliyah Bet leaders aware that the movement had already lost one of its two prized Canadian ships. With the Wedgwood captured by the British, the Haganah was needed all the more to continue the voyages. Since the Haganah's chances of reaching Palestine in the face of the British blockade were slim, the Mossad decided to free the Haganah for another voyage by transferring her passengers to the Akbel for the short trip into the British-patrolled waters off Palestine. This also involved risk, since the transfer point was within the range of British air and sea patrols. A transfer would immobilize both vessels for some time, increasing the chances of detection by the British.

Explaining the situtiongas to the youth-movement leaders aboard the Haganah, the commanders said the rendezvous was taking place at a predesignated site about 100 miles from Haifa. This was less than a day's sailing from Palestine, even at the slow speed of the Akbel. The commanders apologized for the poor condition of the Turkish vessel but emphasized that it was seaworthy. Most important, they said, was the need to release the Haganah to return to Europe to pick up some of the thousands of refugees waiting there.

The transfer began badly. The two vessels maneuvered around each other but failed to tie up together. The water became choppy, and the empty Akbel rode high in the water, rolling heavily. With a crash, the impact of the heavier Haganah damaged the port side of the wooden Akbel as the two craft collided. The captain of the Akbel shouted to the Haganah to back away, and further communication through interpreters made it clear that he wanted to call off the transfer because of the damage to his vessel. The Turkish craft sounded three blasts on her whistle, as if to signal her departure. Nine husky men from the Haganah, led by one of the commanders, jumped into a motor launch and boarded the Akbel. The boarders carried sidearms. Surrounding the captain and his first mate, they ordered the transfer to proceed.

The refugees boarded the Akbel, crossing 30 at a time in two motor launches from the Haganah. The order of transfer was men first, women and the sick later, and the doctor last. Aboard the Haganah, an argument flared over what to do with the refugees' belongings, which remained in a heap on deck. Because the transfer had taken so long, the commanders wanted to leave immediately to avoid detection. Some Americans pleaded that the refugees should not be deprived of their bundles containing photographs and other keepsakes that had accompanied them across Europe as their only link to their past lives. The transfer of the belongings was ordered.

Ninety minutes later, as the last of the bags was being put aboard the Akbel, the smoke of a warship appeared on the horizon. The Haganah pulled away, leaving one of her two motor launches behind. With the Haganah and Akbel moving in opposite directions, an attacker could not pursue both. The Haganah's next destination: Mylos, Greece, for provisions and fuel.

* * *

Voyage of the Biryah (Akbel II)

As the Haganah steamed westward at 23 knots, the creaking Turkish vessel went due east, straining for her top speed of seven knots. The Akbel raised a Star of David flag to draw attention to herself, and the approaching warship bore down on her. To the relief of all aboard, the warship was flying the French flag. The refugees on deck broke into a cheer, and some of the French sailors waved back. The French ship resumed course and disappeared to the south.

The Jewish flag was not the only symbol of the Akbel's mission. The Turkish freighter also took on a new name for this voyage. She became the Biryah, named in honor of a Galilee settlement seized by the British earlier in the year.

Even for a trip of less than a day, conditions aboard the Biryah were intolerable. The passengers were crammed into hot, stuffy quarters. The air below deck quickly turned foul, and people were jammed together, unable to move; some fainted without being able to fall down. The weight of a thousand bodies pushed the old freighter lower and lower into the water; the Biryah began to list, and passengers on the deck dangled their feet in the sea. Fist fights broke out among below-deck passengers competing for the privilege of standing nearer to the ladders leading upwards to breathable air.

More than three-and-a-half hours after embarkation passed before the crates containing food and water could be opened. Each lunch was in its own paper bag, a jelly sandwich on hardtack biscuits for the religiously observant, a slice of bologna in place of the jelly for the non-kosher. There was also a large chocolate bar and some currants. This was the only food the travelers would have for two days.

The Biryah's situation worsened. As the food was being consumed, the commander ordered the radio operator to send an SOS signal informing the British of the refugee vessel's plight and position. The old freighter appeared in danger of capsizing and sinking. Distress flags were hoisted. Shortly before 5 p.m. a twin-engined British aircraft appeared from the east and circled the Biryah several times, flying so low that it created a breeze on board the Biryah. Later, a four-engined aircraft repeated the maneuver. After sunset, patrol planes dropped flares.

But the British made no other contact that night. Without water, and suffering from the stench of the overloaded Biryah, the passengers were sustained by the knowledge that the voyage to Haifa should end by morning. During the night, a major problem was to persuade the male passengers to take turns in the fetid hold, so that others could go above to breathe cleaner air. Some went below voluntarily, while others resisted with physical force. The former circus strongman from Auschwitz, now head of the security staff on the ship, fought his way around the deck. Naked to the waist, blowing a whistle and shouting commands, he supervised the transfer of unwilling passengers to the hold.

At dawn on the 10th day after leaving France, the travelers had two surprises. Mountains appeared on the port side of the ship. The Turkish captain had taken them to Cyprus; starting the day before 100 miles from Palestine, they were now 180 miles away. The second surprise was to starboard: the British destroyer Virago, waiting about one mile away.

From the bridge of the destroyer, the British commander could see that the refugee vessel was heavily loaded. He noticed that about 100 people on the Biryah's deck were dangling their legs over the side. In a report the next day to a superior officer, he wrote, "The thought of using them as fenders, although tempting, was filed for future reference."

The commander of the Birya sent a message to the British vessel, asking for a tow to Haifa. The British responded by sending an ensign and six sailors to board the Biryah and investigate. The Biryah commander agreed to surrender his vessel in return for food, water, and a tow to Haifa. As the Jews cleared portions of the foredeck to accommodate a tow cable, the boarding party returned to the British destroyer. Shortly after 7 a.m., the destroyer steamed away, leaving the Biryah without food or water.

The refugees on the deck of the Biryah were puzzled by the British destroyer's abrupt departure. According to a confidential report filed a week later by the Royal Navy's officer in charge at Haifa, the British did not take seriously the request for food and water. They regarded the Biryah's appeal for help as a ruse. The British report said the refugee vessel's predicament was "therefore immediately recognized as a new attempt to trick the destroyer patrol into taking action which might subsequently prejudice the chances of impounding the illegal immigrant carrier by order of the Palestinian law courts." Because of possible legal implications, the destroyer was ordered not to make an arrest in Cypriot waters. "It might also have led to an awkward situation if some immigrants had tried to land to avoid arrest," the report continued.

Aboard the Biryah, the Haganah commander ordered the Turkish captain to make for Haifa. As the sun moved higher in the sky, the heat became intense. The passengers became too miserable to fight. The voyage proceeded.

That night, the barometer began to fall and the sea became perfectly calm, as if a storm were near. At 11 p.m. the captain said he was alarmed that the Biryah might sink. Panic developed as the passengers were moved below deck and word spread that bad weather was on the way. SOS signals went out again.

Another disheartening contact with the Royal Navy followed. At 2 a.m., as the sea grew rougher, the British destroyer Virago approached again. Floodlights from the Virago illuminated the Biryah. Three appeals for a tow to Haifa went out from the Biryah, but they were met by silence. The only response from the British ship was in answer to a question as to the distance from Haifa: 35 miles. For about 15 minutes, the Biryah lay still in the sea, her engines shut down, as a further word from the Virago was awaited. No response came, and the Biryah resumed her voyage.

As the sun rose on the 11th day, July 2, 1946, the Palestine coast was in view. The Biryah's passengers could see Haifa and Mount Carmel. They cheered and sang Hatikvah. In the Haifa port, British ships were waiting. They ordered the Biryah to stop her engines. The destroyer Haydon dropped a depth charge in front of the refugee vessel. The Biryah lowered her Turkish flag and hoisted the Star of David and the Union Jack, side by side. The Virago, the same destroyer that twice had ignored the Birya's appeals for help, escorted her into the harbor. An ensign from the Virago, preceded by Palestinian Arab policemen, boarded the Birya at 8 a.m. and took possession of her. He ordered the Union Jack pulled down but allowed the Star of David to remain flying. The first drinking water was brought aboard at 10 a.m.; it was noon before an adequate water supply was provided to the passengers. The refugees were told that they would be kept in the harbor, since British arrests of Jewish leaders in Palestine had filled the Athlit detention camp in which Aliyah Bet passengers were normally interned. Later, the refugees were told that the British suspected bubonic plague on the Biryah and would quarantine the passengers in the harbor for ten days to two weeks. They were placed aboard two of the eight Aliyah Bet ships interned in the harbor.

* * *

Second voyage of the Haganah

On July 23, 1946, British authorities received a report predicting that the arrival of the Haganah in the Adriatic Sea "may make this a busy area in the near future."

The British report, submitted by the Commander-in-Chief for the Mediterranean, speculated that Aliyah Bet tactics had changed with the arrival of the American-manned ships:

> The recent appearance of two ex-Royal Canadian Navy corvettes NORSYD (or BALBOA) and BEAUHARNOIS (or JOSIAH WEDGWOOD) ... is a new departure and appears to mark a change in the tactics of illegal immigration in an attempt to avoid the capture of expensive ships. The NORSYD, having transferred 1100 immigrants at sea to a small and slow ship, the AKBEL, has now entered the Adriatic.... This suggests a policy of transport by the fast and seaworthy corvettes to a point outside territorial waters where the immigrants are transferred to smaller or less valuable ships....

The night after that report was sent, the Haganah took on her second load of refugees and made final preparations to sail from the Adriatic for Palestine.

* * *

After her June 30 rendezvous with the Akbel 100 miles from Palestine, the Haganah had headed for Mylos, Greece, to take on fuel and provisions. There, a doctor was waiting. Because the British had spread a report of plague aboard the Biryah passengers, the Mossad sent the doctor to inoculate the crew of the Haganah at Mylos.

A few days later, the Haganah proceeded to Yugoslavia. She stopped at Split and picked up a local pilot to guide her through mined waters. The crew were ordered to remain aboard ship in Split, where British agents were active. Then she proceeded north to Baka, not far from Fiume. At Baka, the crew had some leisure time while the Haganah underwent more renovations. Carpenters came aboard and built more banana bins. Crew members wondered how the commanders intended to cram the ship with more refugees than the Haganah carried on her first, overcrowded voyage. Food and water were brought aboard; the food was mostly war-surplus American K-rations. Word circulated that an agreement had been struck with the Yugoslavs: in return for local cooperation, the Haganah would evacuate all Jewish Displaced Persons in the country.

On July 24, 1946, the Haganah prepared to leave Baka with more than 2,700 refugees. This was more than twice the number she carried on her first voyage. The plan was that the refugees would board at night, and the ship would be out of the harbor before dawn.

Crew members looking up to the surrounding mountains could see a chain of railroad cars winding down to the harbor. The refugees arrived and lined up on the wharf. They were mainly from Transylvania and included more older people and families than the Haganah's first passengers, and a smaller proportion of youth organizations. The passengers filled the below-decks spaces and overflowed onto the deck.

As the departure routine went forward, there was bad news from below: the boiler had broken for the second time since docking in Baka. The engine crew labored to repair the trouble, and the Haganah pulled out of the harbor at 6 a.m. on July 25, two hours behind schedule.

The schedule called for four to five days of travel, with strict allotments of food and water. Passengers were allowed to come up on deck in turns. They were warned against any large movement of people from one side of the deck to the other; the overloaded ship was already listing. The first two days passed uncomfortably, but without incident in calm seas.

On the third day, the ship slowed down off the coast of Greece, and crew members noticed that the heat below decks was increasing. The engines were failing again, 36 hours from Palestine. Suddenly, the ship went dark below deck. (More than 25 years later, a Haganah passenger met one of the American sailors in Tel Aviv and asked what happened when the lights went out. At the time, there had been no explanation to the passengers—only darkness and confusion.) The engines had ceased to function. As the Haganah stopped dead in the water, the ship's electrical generators halted and the ventilation system shut down, turning the below-deck area into a chamber of hot, suffocating air permeated with the stench of sweating bodies.

The incline of the listing ship grew perilously steeper. It reached 27 degrees, approaching the point at which the Haganah might capsize and take its human cargo to the bottom. The engine crew struggled unsuccessfully to restore power. No one was certain of the cause, which could have been water leaking into the fuel lines, or perhaps doctored fuel.

The radio operator was ordered to send an SOS. After some time, a British ship answered, requesting location and a description of the problem. The stricken vessel identified herself as the Haganah, carrying Jews to Palestine and in danger of capsizing. As in the first voyage, the British response was to break off radio contact.

Crew and passengers responded with determination to this indication that the British were leaving them to drown. A desperate solution was improvised: dismantle the banana bins and burn the wood for fuel to get the engines going. Passengers mobilized around this decision. Ripping out planking, refugees formed a human chain to pass the wood down to the engine room. There, the heat was so intense that no one could endure it for more than a few minutes, and crew members took turns making the fire. They worked through the day and into the night to get up enough steam to move the ship. Slowly, the Haganah resumed her course to Palestine.

As the fourth day dawned on July 28, 1947, the first light revealed two British destroyers alongside. Apparently, they had been nearby throughout the ordeal. Through a bullhorn, the Haganah requested to be towed to Haifa. Again, there was no reply from the British. The word from the engine room was reassuring, and the Haganah put on full steam to close the distance to Haifa.

Fifteen miles from Haifa, the British ordered the Haganah to stop. Still outside territorial waters, the Haganah ignored the order. Refugees were instructed to arm themselves with bottles and sticks and resist the British if they attempted to board. The Haganah hoisted the Star of David flag, and the passengers stood to sing Hatikvah.

During the singing of the Jewish anthem, a shot was fired across the Haganah's bow. This was followed by another British order to stop the engines. The Haganah's response was full steam ahead.

Suddenly, one of the British warships rammed the Haganah, damaging the propeller. The impact injured passengers inside the remaining wooden bins. As the British ships maneuvered into boarding positions on either side of the Haganah, the order went out to the refugees to resist.

A hand-to-hand battle followed. British marines boarded and were thrown overboard. Both sides suffered injuries. During the fighting, the crew were instructed to remove all indications of their status and mingle with the passengers. After more than an hour of battling the boarders, the refugee vessel surrendered to overwhelming force.

The British boarded and hoisted the Admiralty ensign in place of the Star of David flag. As the Haganah entered Haifa harbor, an American crew member and the commander staged a fist fight on the foredeck, in the course of which the commander dropped the ship's papers to the Jewish captain of a tugboat below. As the Haganah stopped moving, the passengers sang Hatikvah again.

* * *

A few days later, a British naval captain reporting to higher authority on the Haganah's interception wrote that the destroyer Venus had handled the situation well. The officer commented disdainfully on the actions of the Haganah:

> It will be noticed again that the "shot across the bows" was treated with a certain contempt and it may be necessary shortly to put a burst of Lewis gun fire into the wheelhouse....There was nothing of particular interest in the actual sighting and interception, only one new complaint being added to the S.O.S. tale of woe—that of suffocation.

More than a month later, though, other British officials were worrying about the implications of the Haganah interception. A September 14 letter from the Admiralty pointed out:

> The S.S. BALBOA was a corvette and is capable of 15 knots. As it is possible to intercept ships carrying illegal immigrants only inside Palestine territorial waters, the task of coming alongside and boarding them at this speed becomes one of great difficulty. On this occasion the operation was successful owing to a combination of good luck and superlative seamanship by the Commanding Officer of His Majesty's Ship VENUS. In the view of My Lords, however, it may not in the future be possible to guarantee such success and, indeed, such boarding operations are likely to lead to serious damage to His Majesty's Ships or to Jewish ships or to both....the efforts of the Royal Navy at preventing the illegal traffic will be largely frustrated if ships of this speed are allowed to fall into the hands of the Jews.

The letter asked the Dominions Office to impress on the Canadian government "the vital need of preventing the acquisition by Jewish interests of any ships and particularly ships of this size and speed."

* * *

As in the case of the Akbel passengers, the travelers on the Haganah were detained in the harbor and later went to Athlit detention camp. The crew members who had mingled with the passengers were eventually released and began new lives in Israel or returned to North America.

The Haganah carried the largest number of refugees to arrive on an Aliyah Bet ship to date. The record would stand for almost a year, until the American-manned Exodus 1947 was captured in July 1947 with more than 4,500 refugees aboard. For almost two years, the Haganah remained moored in Haifa alongside her sister ship, the Wedgwood. After independence came in May 1948, the Haganah became the warship K-18 of Israel's new navy.

THE PALESTINE POST
JERUSALEM
SUNDAY, MARCH 2, 1947
PRICE 15 MILS
VOL. XXII. No. 6344

WIDESPREAD TERRORIST ATTACKS: CURFEWS UNTIL FURTHER NOTICE

20 KILLED, 30 WOUNDED IN TEN OUTRAGES

Palestine Post Staff

In a week-end wave of terror, 20 people — army, police, and civilians — were killed and about 30 wounded in a series of ten outrages that began in Haifa on Friday afternoon; continued yesterday with a devastating explosion that wrecked the Goldsmith Officers' Club in Jerusalem, and later in the day with attacks on Army camps and a number of explosions in Haifa and elsewhere. A curfew was imposed on a large area of Jerusalem at 7 o'clock last night until further notice, while Tel Aviv, Ramat Gan and Petah Tikva were placed under curfew at midnight.

The crowded streets of Rehavia and King George Avenue suddenly emptied yesterday afternoon when staccato bursts of Bren gun-fire were directed at the Goldsmith Officers' Club in King George Avenue, opposite the Yeshurun Synagogue, on a peninsula jutting past the northern gate to Security Zone B.

According to an official statement, a truck loaded with explosives rammed the barbed-wire barrier at 3.15 and stopped outside the lounge of the building. Simultaneously, a party of terrorists rushed towards the building, plucked one or two suitcases out of the truck and hurled them into the lounge of the building. Shortly afterwards the charge exploded, wrecking the three stories of the building and blowing out the corner diagonally across the road from the Jewish Agency. A covering party of terrorists is believed to have opened fire at the same time as the explosion, killing two policemen and a civilian. Troops immediately returned the fire, and in the exchange of shots a number of passing civilians were wounded as they scrambled for shelter.

Almost simultaneously with the explosion, the sirens sounded, bringing all wheeled traffic to a standstill till the All Clear was blown three hours later.

Fifteen people are feared to be dead, including a British Army Captain, a British police officer, a soldier, a Polish girl telephonist (Olga Padovraczynski), three other NAAFI civilian employees (including Mr. M Mattouti, an Italian, the manager of the club) and five unidentified persons.

At a late hour in the evening rescue squads were still at work on the debris under which three are believed to be buried.

A British police officer was killed as the truck in which he was driving came into the line of fire. Other officers in the vehicle engaged the attackers until their ammunition was expended, when they took shelter behind their vehicle.

Twelve persons were wounded, including a British officer and a British soldier seriously injured, and five officers, a British policeman and a soldier less dangerously hurt, and three civilians.

Lawyer Wounded

Among the civilians wounded were Mr. S. Horowitz, well-known Jerusalem lawyer, who was one of a party of four caught in the cross-fire.

He was wounded in the face and arm by ricocheting bullets and was taken to the Hadassah Hospital. A woman in the party was struck in the back.

Ovadiah Mizrahi (7) was burned by a flaming petrol tin.

A number of civilians passing in a car on their way to Rehavia were badly shaken by the explosion. King George Garden was crowded with children at the time, and the shots which preceded the explosion sent the parents and children, many in prams, rushing away from the scene.

In a few minutes the whole area was covered with troops in search parties combing the Rehavia Quarter and the Mamillah cemetery.

Rescue and salvage work was still proceeding at a late hour last night, with acetylene flares and emergency electric lamps lighting the heaped rubble.

A bulldozer was used to pull down tottering walls.

Officers and privates, padres and police constables, toiled to rescue the staff and residents who were trapped in the building. A platoon of British soldiers and a company of Mauritian pioneers joined in the rescue work, using their hands as well as picks to clear away the rubble. By the side of the building, half over-turned, lay the 15-cwt Fordson truck which, it is believed, was used in the outrage.

Three Hit

Troops who opened fire on the terrorists believe that at least three of the attackers were wounded, but were dragged off by their comrades.

The first casualties were being brought out of the debris when a reporter of *The Palestine Post* arrived shortly after the explosion. Troops and police — some of whom, in football kit, had been on their way to play a match — carried the wounded out to ambulances.

An Intelligence Officer, Capt. M. Gibbs, who was sunbathing on the roof, said when he had been rescued that he heard bursts of machine-gun fire that appeared to be coming from some distance down King George Avenue north of the club.

"Almost immediately afterwards," Capt. Gibbs said, "there was a commotion at the front of the club and machine-gun fire below us at the main entrance. I looked out and saw a body lying in the roadway in a pool of blood. I do not know whether it was one of our guards or not. From where we stood we couldn't see what followed but half of the building fell away in front of us. We were horrified to see three friends who were sun-bathing with us disappear with the debris."

(Continued on Page 3 Col. 1)

PALESTINE NOT YET BEFORE U.N.

By ERNST ASCHNER

LAKE SUCCESS, Saturday. — The Palestine case has not so far been put before the United Nations, stated the Secretary-General, Trygve Lie, in an exclusive interview with *The Palestine Post* this morning.

Mr. Lie said that his knowledge of the matter stemmed mainly from newspaper reports and from a confidential talk with Sir Alexander Cadogan, the permanent British representative on the Security Council. He said he had not been requested to call a special General Assembly session, and all reports discussing this were mere guesswork. Should he get such a request for a special session he would have to circularize 55 members for their consent.

Asked if the Jewish Agency would be able to state the Jewish case through its own representatives, Mr. Lie replied that this was entirely in the hands of the General Assembly. "The only precedent, though totally different, is the Corfu Straits mining case at present before the Security Council, where the Albanian representatives were admitted to state their own case although Albania is not a member of the Council."

While U.N. is the legal successor to the League of Nations, there is no provision in its charter which would allow the revocation of Britain's Mandate for Palestine or censure of the White Paper policy.

There will be ample scope for discussing the case if and when it is brought before the General Assembly, but the Assembly cannot take — though it can recommend — action for implementing any definite policy.

ERITREAN DETAINEES FOR KENYA

Palestine Post Staff

The Jewish detainees now held in the Eritrean camps are to be transferred to Kenya, it was officially announced in Jerusalem on Friday.

According to an official statement, the transfer has been decided upon in view of the uncertainty of maintaining the camp when the future of the country comes to be decided under the peace settlement.

The new camp has been placed at the authorities' disposal by the Government of Kenya.

STOP PRESS 9 a.m.

MARTIAL LAW

STATUTORY MARTIAL LAW IS TO BE IMPOSED IN CERTAIN AREAS OF PALESTINE AT 8 O'CLOCK THIS MORNING, IT WAS REPORTED IN JERUSALEM LATE LAST NIGHT.

AN ANNOUNCEMENT TO THIS EFFECT IS EXPECTED TO BE MADE SIMULTANEOUSLY IN JERUSALEM AND IN LONDON.

Troops in Tel Aviv

TEL AVIV, Saturday. — A number of violent explosions were heard at 11.30 tonight, followed by bursts of firing.

Mr. I. Rokach, the Mayor of Tel Aviv, was called to Army headquarters at Citrus House for a midnight conference with the Army Commander.

Troops entered the town shortly after curfew had been imposed and shooting was heard in the direction of the Tel-Aviv-Jaffa boundary.

One man, Mr. Walter Neuhut (36) was wounded.

About two hours earlier, the water pumping station was attacked.

FOUR KILLED IN HAIFA

HAIFA, Saturday. — In a series of explosions yesterday and today four people were killed — two soldiers and two civilians — and six other people wounded.

The latest incident occurred about 10 o'clock tonight, on Mountain Road, when a military jeep was blown up by a mine. Two soldiers were killed and two others injured.

Two explosions were heard on the road just below a building which is in the process of construction. The jeep went up in flames, which spread to a wooden hut and trees nearby.

About an hour earlier, five bombs exploded in the Naval Car Park in Harbour Street, damaging 15 vehicles. A fire that broke out was quickly extinguished. There were no casualties.

According to an eye-witness, half-a-dozen armed men in uniform were seen approaching the car-park, shortly before the explosions occurred.

At 2.45 p.m. yesterday, as the 1,400 immigrants began to be transferred from the ss. Haim Arlosoroff to the landing craft, a bomb exploded in Barclays Bank building in Kingsway. Two people were fatally injured and four others wounded, two of them soldiers who were on guard duty.

Third Floor

The explosion occurred on the third floor of the building in which were located the office of the Haifa Shipping Agency, which moved a fortnight ago from the corner of Kingsway and Carmel Gate, the Movements office for Central Haifa Port Area, and the Army Area Cashier's Office.

The dead are Yehuda Melul (36), who leaves a wife and two children, and Yaacov Fogelstein. Both were employed by the Shipping Agency. The injured are Mr. Blair, a British Naval employee; Pte. Ellis, of the R.A.P.C.; Pte. Abdul Razzik Kassan, Arab Legion; and Chief Petty Officer Pollock, R.N.

Streets were strewn with broken glass and sheets of paper, among them applications for permission to remain in Palestine. Little damage to the building could be seen after the explosion, except for shattered windows and twisted shutters, but extensive damage had been done to offices inside.

Barclays were opened to the public this morning.

HADERA CAMP ATTACKED

HADERA, Saturday. — At 8.10 this evening mortar and machine-gun fire was directed upon Army Camp No. 80, on the Pardess Hanna - Affula road.

No details of the attack were available late this evening.

2 INJURED IN RISHON

RISHON-LE-ZION, Saturday. — Two soldiers were injured about 8.30 this evening when the vehicle in which they were travelling was damaged by a mine on the Beit Dajan-Rishon Le-Zion road.

Police and troops who searched cars on the Tel Aviv-Rehovot road warned drivers of the danger of mines.

Officer Killed Near Nathanya

NATHANYA, Saturday.— A British officer was killed and four soldiers wounded about 7 o'clock this evening in two terrorist attacks near here.

In a short attack against No. 22 Army camp south of Khirbet Beit Lid, terrorists used machine-guns and mortars, killing the officer and wounding two other ranks.

A few minutes earlier, a patrolling armoured car was blown up by a land-mine near the Beit Lid road junction on the Haifa-Tel Aviv road. Two of the soldiers in the vehicle were wounded.

Later Camp No. 21, on Kfar Yona, east of Beit Lidd, was attacked by mortar fire.

Last night a suspect was detained by military and police forces who searched the industrial quarter "B" here.

Mystery Explosion In Rehovot

REHOVOT, Saturday. — A mysterious explosion which vibrated throughout a wide area near here and shattered windows in a number of villages and settlements at 8 o'clock this evening was still unexplained at a late hour tonight.

Police and military parties scoured the countryside in an attempt to find the source of the explosion, but were unable to discover any clue.

A few minutes later, a bomb exploded near the police station here, shattering more windows. Police personnel inside the station opened fire, but no casualties were reported.

At 9.45, a third explosion was heard, but caused no damage except to windows still unbroken by the two earlier explosions.

The electricity current failed throughout the area at 8.45.

REFUGEE SHIP AGROUND NEAR HAIFA; 1,400 ON BOARD

Palestine Post Reporter

HAIFA, Saturday — Apparently determined not to come into Haifa port as a prize under her own power, the ss. Haim Arlosoroff (formerly the s.s. Ulua), carrying 1,400 immigrants, eluded her naval escort yesterday morning and ran herself aground at Bat Galim, at the foot of the Peninsular Barracks.

The third refugee ship to arrive in February since the severe Mediterranean weather cleared, she had left a North European port five weeks ago with about 700 passengers, the others embarking at a Mediterranean port last week.

The official account speaks of her "stubborn resistance to interception." She had dodged British warships on Thursday, but yesterday morning, encircled by five destroyers, she was boarded after an unsuccessful attempt.

Several of the first boarders were thrown into the sea by the immigrants, but were picked up by a destroyer. Then, according to the official report, although the ship took "violent evasive action," almost colliding with a minesweeper, a second party managed to get aboard, following "a severe struggle," gaining control of the vessel only after she had beached herself.

Shots and Tear-Gas

Shots were fired and tear-gas was used during the operation. Thirty of the immigrants were injured, three seriously, as well as 11 naval personnel, two seriously. None of the injuries were from firearms, it was stated officially.

As the ship ran into the sand, 12 men and two women jumped overboard. A few were picked up by a naval launch, while the others were caught by soldiers when they reached the shore. One, a young girl, swam as far as the Casino pool before she was overtaken and picked up.

> ### SELF-IMPOSED CURFEW
>
> A self-imposed curfew will be observed by the Jewish community throughout Palestine from 7 o'clock to 11 o'clock this evening.
>
> The curfew was announced last night in a statement issued by the Executive of the Vaad Leumi, which read:
>
> The refugee vessel named Haim Arlosoroff is anchored at the gates of Haifa. The Yishuv and its institutions are taking legal and political steps in order to secure their remaining in Palestine. The Yishuv will demonstrate its identification with the fate of the refugees by a self-imposed curfew from 7 o'clock to 11 o'clock tonight. Between these hours all places of entertainment, cafes and cinemas will be closed and all dances and theatre programmes will be cancelled. Urban and inter-urban traffic will stop between 7.30 and 11 o'clock.

Leaving 10 men, presumably the crew, under arrest here, and six persons in hospital at the Athlit Detention Camp, the military transferred the refugees to the s.s. Ocean Vigour and two other liberty vessels new in the deportation shuttle, named the Empire Comfort and the Empire Lifeguard. The first took on 418 men, 367 women, including 20 stretcher cases, and 53 children; the second 237 women and 18 men; and the third 196 men, 76 women and 13 children.

Sang and Cheered

The following are in Athlit Hospital: David Blum (21), Joseph Scherter (21), Malla Greenberg, Joseph Hirskovitch (21), Haim Cofmitski (15), Ivor Goldwitch.

The deportation vessels will remain inside Palestinian waters until the High Court decides the fate of the refugees on Tuesday.

From 10 o'clock in the morning until 1 o'clock in the afternoon, in a sudden stifling heat, the immigrants crowded the deck of the ship, which listed to starboard. Their songs and cheers were answered by the children of Bat Galim, who perched on the fences of houses along the beach.

Residents of the quarter sent food and clothing to the refugees, and 400 students of the Hebrew Technical College came down to see if they could help.

After several unsuccessful attempts were made to tow the stranded vessel, while some 20 naval craft and tugs stood by, two military landing barges were brought alongside. With no resistance or incident, the immigrants were brought by these to Haifa Port and there transhipped.

Efforts to tow the vessel off the beach were abandoned in the afternoon when the engine-room was reported to be flooding as a result of a hole knocked in the bottom of the ship, according to an official statement.

There was a spontaneous strike in the Hadar Hacarmel Quarter in the morning, and shops were re-opened again from 3 to 4.30 to allow shoppers to prepare for the Sabbath.

At a mass meeting in the afternoon one of the speakers, Mrs Rachel Kagan, appealed to the women of England to influence their Government to stop deportation.

The ship was renamed for Haim Arlosoroff, Mr. Shertok's predecessor as Head of the Jewish Agency's Political Department. An outstanding labour leader, Arlosoroff was murdered in 1933 while walking along the beach in Tel Aviv.

AFTER MIDNIGHT

"Since accommodation on the Empire Comfort and Empire Lifeguard is inadequate for the detention of the 840 persons on board pending the determination of the habeas corpus proceedings and since there is no other Government accommodation available for them in Palestine, it has been decided to transfer them to Cyprus," stated an official announcement last night, which added: *"Effect will be given to any decision of the Supreme Court in relation to the persons at present on board these two ships no less than it will be in relation to the 838 persons on board the Ocean Vigour."*

Anglo-French Pact TO BE SIGNED IN DUNKIRK

LONDON, Saturday (Reuter). — Agreement has been reached between the British and French Governments on the terms of the Treaty of Alliance, Mr. Bevin told Parliament in a brief statement last night. There were loud and prolonged cheers.

The Treaty is scheduled to be signed by the French Foreign Minister and Mr. Bevin on Tuesday next at Dunkirk, and the text will be laid before the House of Commons as soon as possible afterwards. The Dominions have been kept fully informed, he added.

Opposition Approves

On behalf of the Opposition, Mr. Anthony Eden warmly welcomed the statement and congratulated him upon his part in the negotiations.

"The British and French peoples have been through so much together through ordeal on to final victory, and any expression of this true feeling of friendship in the Treaty must be as welcome in Britain as I have no doubt it is in France."

Bidault Cheered

A storm of cheers lasting five minutes greeted M. Georges Bidault, the French Foreign Minister, when he told the French National Assembly last night that the Anglo-French Alliance would be signed next Tuesday.

Rarely since the approval of the new Constitution last September has the Assembly shown such enthusiasm.

FIRST STEP TOWARDS CLOSER HARMONY

By JON KIMCHE, Palestine Post Cable

LONDON, Saturday. — The formal signature of the new Anglo-French alliance at Dunkirk next Tuesday is considered here only the first step towards closer harmonizing Anglo-French political and economic interests in international relations.

A strong pro-French group in Parliament and the Government is pressing for mutual orientation on three main issues: the first is international trade; the second is the coordination of British and French policies on international bodies, particularly in the U.N.; and the third is the settlement of British and French differences about policy in the Middle East and North Africa.

The last point in particular has considerable urgency, in the view of diplomatic circles here. With the increasing likelihood that the Egyptian Treaty is being submitted to the U.N. and the Palestine issue follows next, the attitude of the other great powers must be ascertained.

It is felt here that the French view on a central German administration is already nearer the British policy than the Russian, and that French support on the Egyptian and Palestine issues would be sufficient to ensure at least that no decision will be taken against Britain, even if the British case does not succeed.

Arab States' Dilemma

Last week's mediation attempt in the Anglo-Egyptian dispute has clearly further confirmed the Foreign Office view that the Arab States do not want this matter brought before the U.N. It is thought here that if Egypt proceeds, then the Arab States must either side against Egypt or against Britain on an issue where Britain appears to defend the right of self-determination, and that by siding against Britain, the Arab States may prejudice their case on Palestine.

A Foreign Office spokesman again emphasized yesterday that Britain is not committed to take the Palestine case to the U.N. before the next Assembly in September, even if the Americans or the U.N. Secretariat evolve a method by which this could be done.

EGYPT REFUSES TO PAY

CAIRO, Saturday (AFP). — The Egyptian Government has rejected the British demand for compensation payments for British subjects killed or wounded during the disturbances in Cairo and Alexandria last year.

Egypt maintains that these disturbances were caused by "British provocation," and that the number of Egyptian victims was greater than that of the British. It is possible that Britain will submit this matter to the International Court at The Hague.

The British Military Mission with the Egyptian army will be dissolved as the Egyptian Government has decided not to renew the contracts of the members of that mission established by formal stipulation of the Anglo-Egyptian Treaty signed in 1936.

U.S. Asks Britain to Remain in Greece

AMERICA READY TO GIVE FINANCIAL AID

WASHINGTON, Saturday.— Following Britain's request to the United States for aid in bearing the economic burden of Allied policy in Greece, it was authoritatively stated here today that the United States has asked the British Government to maintain her security forces there after March 31.

In a note handed to Lord Inverchapel, British Ambassador, by Mr. Dean Acheson, United States Under-Secretary of State, making known this request, Britain has been assured regarding her proposals for economic assistance.

The State Department has prepared plans for an allocation for this purpose for submission to Congress.

No detailed information is available regarding the contents of the note, but discussions have centred on the following points:

(1) Proposals for United States' financial assistance up to 250,000,000 dollars for this year.

(2) Expansion of the Greek Army.

(3) Guarantees to be given by the Greek Government regarding the non-partisan nature of their government and policy.

According to British sources, Britain considers about 100 million pounds and 50 Liberty ships necessary, as well as a declaration by the United States in support of a moderate Greek Government.

It was pointed out there was no question of asking American troops to be sent to Greece. It was added that unless American aid was forthcoming, the present Government would not last a month.

Britain is reported to be anxious for action by Congress before General Marshall goes to Moscow to counter Russia's plans for a greater Balkan Federation under Tito.

Some U.S. officials and Congressmen are alarmed at the possibility of the Greek Government falling as a result of the withdrawal of British military and economic assistance.

This, they consider, would firstly precipitate civil war in Greece, in which the Communists, assisted by arms and eventually men from Greece's northern neighbours, would be able to seize control. Secondly, they believe that this would set up a political chain of reaction, which would at least weaken the influence of the United States and Britain in Turkey and the Eastern Mediterranean, Italy and ultimately France, and might even lead to a clean sweep, bringing all these countries under Communist and pro-Soviet control.

(Reuter and U.P.)

RUSSIAN CHARGES REFUTED

BERLIN, Saturday (Reuter).— Britain and the United States, in vigorously worded statements from their military chiefs in Germany, replied last night to Soviet allegations that they had turned their backs on the Potsdam agreement and were planning the political fusion of their zones in Germany.

The first statement from Lt.-Gen. Lucius D. Clay, the U.S. Military Governor-Designate, was followed within a few hours by a British reply equally uncompromising in tone from Marshal of the R.A.F. Sir Sholto Douglas, British C.-in-C. in Germany.

Both flatly contradicted the assertion of Marshal Vassily Sokolovsky, the Soviet C.-in-C. in Germany that the economic fusion of the British and American zones in Germany meant the subjection of German economy to "Anglo-American Monopolism."

General Clay made the counter-charge that large sections of industry in eastern Germany had been transferred to Soviet ownership. Both General Clay and Marshal Douglas reiterated that agreement for economic fusion of the two zones was still open to Soviet adherence.

EMIR SAUD LEAVES BRITAIN FOR HOME

POOLE, Hampshire, Saturday (Reuter). — Before leaving England for Cairo today in a B.O.A.C. flying boat, Prince Saud, the Crown-Prince of Saudi Arabia, said his visit to Britain had been very pleasant and satisfactory from all points of view.

"I hope," he added, "that the relations between our two countries will always be most friendly."

Truman to Visit Mexico

WASHINGTON, Saturday — (Reuter). — President Truman is leaving for Mexico City tomorrow, where he will make a speech on Thursday at a banquet given in his honour by President Miguel Aleman.

His address will, according to Mr. Charles Ross, the Presidential Press Secretary, be a "major one, dealing both with foreign and domestic affairs," and lasting about 25 minutes.

After his return to Washington, the President will leave for a 15-day tour of the Caribbean Sea area on March 8.

STORM TROOPERS STOPPED

LONDON, Saturday (Reuter). — Former Storm Troopers of Hitler's army were stopped at the last moment from returning home with 450 German P.o.W.'s who left Hull last night on compassionate grounds, according to the "Daily Graphic" correspondent.

54 GENDARMES KILLED IN GREEK AMBUSH

ATHENS, Saturday (Reuter). — Fifty-four Greek police were killed in a guerrilla ambush yesterday, when a party of 66 gendarmes and an officer were proceeding to Domokos in Central Thessaly, which a U.N. Inquiry Commission team was expected to visit tomorrow.

Britain Accepts, Egypt Rejects Levant Offer

LONDON, Saturday (Reuter). — Britain has replied to the Levant States accepting their offer of mediation in the matter of the revision of the Anglo-Egyptian Treaty, according to a Foreign Office spokesman.

Britain has asked Syria and the Lebanon to outline the procedure which they propose. Despite Britain's acceptance, mediation is unlikely in view of Egypt's determination to lay the issue before the U.N.

The Egyptian reply to the Levant States' offer has now been received in London. Official quarters say that it holds out little encouragement for a renewal of the Treaty negotiations.

Haim Arlosoroff (Ulua)

> With the ... Arlosoroff, the route of Aliyah Bet gained a new dimension of danger. The British and the Jews now knew that each arrival off the coast of Palestine could bring a virtual battle at sea — a battle in the classic mode, complete with boarding parties and hand-to-hand fighting.
>
> *David C. Holly, Exodus 1947*

A young British officer watched the battle that raged on the deck of the refugee ship. Jews were hurling bolts, cans of preserves, whatever makeshift weapons they had been able to stockpile, at the boarding party. In the wheelhouse, the Haim Arlosoroff's volunteer helmsman from Canada was shouting curses at the British and steering closer and closer to the Bat Galim beach. The British officer, white-faced, raised his pistol and fired in the air, in what appeared to be an effort to quiet the situation. The shot struck an American sailor who had climbed a mast to protect the ship's blue-and-white Star of David flag against the boarders. The sailor survived the wound; within the year, he would sail again on an Aliyah Bet ship.

The din on deck continued, and the embattled ship proceeded toward shore. Thousands of Jewish residents of Haifa watched as the Haim Arlosoroff came to rest on the reefs of Bat Galim, 34 days after leaving Sweden on the longest voyage of Aliyah Bet.

As recently as five months before her battle with the British at Bat Galim, the Haim Arlosoroff was an obsolete vessel with an obscure past and no evident future. Built in 1912, she served during the Prohibition era as a revenue cutter protecting the American coast against the illegal entry of alcoholic beverages. In World War II she was a weather ship.

Her new life as a blockade runner began on October 17, 1946, when the Weston Trading Company bought her for Aliyah Bet. At that time she was known as the Unalga; her name was changed to the Ulua, the name of a river in Honduras, appropriate to the Honduran registry her new owners acquired for her.

A crew of American volunteers joined her in Baltimore. Her captain was a Palestinian Jew who had served in the American merchant marine and was on Okinawa when he received a telegram to come home. He went to New York and was given his command at Baltimore, where Aliyah Bet officials came aboard for a visit before the Ulua sailed. Three other Palestinians came to Baltimore to join the crew; after seeing the ship, one stayed on the pier at Baltimore, and a second got off at Marseilles.

The Ulua arrived at Marseilles after 21 days. On the way, she stopped at the Azores, where three American crew members went ashore in a little town and dutifully asked for the local synagogue. To their surprise, they were led to an ordinary house inside which was a beautifully appointed synagogue that looked as if it had been used for prayer only a short while before. No Jews had lived in the town for many generations, but a local family maintained the synagogue as the town's common property. The sailors guessed that they had met a group of Marranos, descendants of Jews who had been forcibly converted to Catholicism at the end of the 15th century.

At Marseilles, French authorities were waiting for the ship; they took custody of one of the American volunteers, a religious student whose parents had reported him as an under-age runaway. British agents also became aware of the Ulua in Marseilles; as early as December 6, 1946, a British report noted that work was being done on the vessel.

The Ulua stayed in Marseilles for about a month, undergoing extensive refitting to accommodate 2,500 passengers. Some of these changes would later present problems at sea. An upper deck, whose weight shifted the ship's stability in the direction of top-heaviness, was added. To increase the Ulua's sailing range, three large fuel tanks were installed on the foredeck, and 500 barrels of fuel were stored in the holds. Six Spanish sailors joined the crew in Marseilles; the Aliyah Bet leadership decided to bring the experienced Spaniards aboard as a reserve, in case the American volunteers proved inadequate to the task.

A few days before the work in Marseilles was scheduled to be completed, the Ulua received orders to prepare to leave for Sweden, where winter weather had prevented three less-seaworthy Aliyah Bet vessels from sailing. The plan was that the Ulua would pick up a group of refugees in Sweden, transfer these passengers in the Mediterranean to another Aliyah Bet vessel bound for Palestine, and then pick up a new complement of immigrants from Europe. The Ulua left Marseilles on January 1, 1947, passed Gibraltar again, and sailed north to Le Havre, where she took on fuel and water and received further instructions from Paris-based Aliyah Bet representatives.

She put into Copenhagen on January 21, 1947, after receiving word that Swedish harbors were closed by ice. During the three days the Ulua sat at Copenhagen, Danish officials came aboard and asked questions. A friendly Dane drank French brandy with the Ulua officers and confided that Lloyd's, the British maritime intelligence service, had informed his government that the Ulua was suspected of transporting prostitutes to Latin America. Later, the port commandant came aboard; after listening to the Ulua's cover-story claim that she was involved in fish experimentation, he asked: "How much are the Jews of New York paying for this fishing expedition?" The commandant went on to explain that he had been one of the coordinators of the Danish underground's wartime evacuation of thousands of Jews to Sweden, and he wished the Ulua well. He warned the Jews to stay aboard ship to avoid further problems with the British ashore, and he offered his help until the Ulua could proceed to Sweden.

Early on the morning of Friday, January 24, 1947, the Ulua arrived at the Swedish port of Trelleborg, east of Malmo. She took aboard 664 passengers, each of whom had an entry visa for Cuba. More than 500 were teenaged Jewish girls who had been rescued from Nazi concentration camps in a secret deal between Swedish officials and Heinrich Himmler, the Gestapo chief, who was trying to bargain for his post-war future. To attend to these refugees, 61 emissaries of various movements in Palestine had come to Sweden.

Earlier, the passengers had been scheduled to sail from Göteborg, a larger Swedish port. The Jewish community and social service agencies arranged to see them off. But Göteborg was a busy port, and the Haganah representative in Sweden feared that British intervention might prevent the Ulua's departing from there. With the help of Gunther Cohen, a leader of the Jewish community in Sweden, the Haganah man arranged for the railroad train carrying the passengers to be switched to Trelleborg. The last-minute change left the Jewish community waiting in Göteborg with food, music, and flowers for the passengers, who failed to apppear. The change of plan also caught port officials in Trelleborg by surprise. Without approval from higher authority, the Trelleborg port commander was reluctant to permit the Ulua to sail. To overcome his objections, the Haganah brought in a Jewish community elder. He explained that the sailing had to take place before sundown, when the Jewish sabbath would begin. The port commander accepted this explanation. After inspecting the Ulua's safety facilities, the Swedish authorities issued a permit for a short voyage to Le Havre and provided a Swedish Royal Navy pilot to guide the Ulua out to sea.

The Ulua's activities were now public knowledge, and the cover stories were beginning to peel away. The New York Times reported:

> STOCKHOLM, Sweden, Jan. 24—Six hundred and sixty Jews who took refuge in Sweden during the war left today aboard the small Honduran ship Ulua for Cuba. The ship is so small that Sweden was unwilling to let her sail, and said she would not have been allowed to leave if the passengers had been Swedish. Most were men from 13 to 30.
>
> Persistent rumors here say the Jews are not going to Cuba and that this is merely a camouflaged journey to Palestine. Swedish newspapers agree there is something "mysterious" about the trip.
>
> A British naval vessel has been cruising

> in Oresund between Sweden and Denmark, and the Swedes are convinced the British Government is making sure she keeps contact with Ulua until the latter's destination is known definitely.

Traveling southward, the Ulua stopped again at the French port of Le Havre to refuel. There, British intervention again threatened the voyage. Tugboats came alongside to trap the Ulua in the harbor, and two truckloads of armed police deployed on the dockside. Port officials said the ship could not proceed with so many people on board and would have to put some of its passengers ashore. The Ulua's representatives displayed Swedish and French documents, to no avail.

Then followed several days of telephone calls to the Haganah office in Paris, and negotiations at Le Havre. Finally, the Ulua was allowed to leave, taking with her a new document which said that French officials approved her carrying as many as 1,000 passengers.

A United Press dispatch in The New York Times misspelled the ship's name; it reported:

> LE HAVRE, France, Jan. 31—The little tramp steamer, Ulna, packed with 600 Jewish refugees, about ten times the number she can comfortably carry, finally was allowed to sail for Palestine today. Port authorities, appalled by the lack of lifeboats and life-rafts, by the overcrowding and by the filth on the 170-foot 208-ton vessel, had refused clearance since Monday, when the Ulna arrived from Sweden.

At Le Havre, the Ulua received further instructions: After transferring her passengers to another Aliyah Bet ship in the Mediterranean, she would proceed to Yugoslavia and pick up 2,500 immigrants.

If there had appeared to be trouble on shore at Le Havre, worse awaited the Ulua at sea. At midnight she arrived at the Bay of Biscay and encountered a storm. The weather became so severe that, at one point, a volunteer noticed one of the ship's few experienced sailors weeping for fear the ship was doomed. Almost everyone aboard became seasick; a detail of crew members cleaned away the vomit twice daily. One of the commanders reported that it was impossible to imagine the filth on the ship. By the second day, the wind was at 72 miles an hour, and the 15-ton fuel tanks on the foredeck tore loose from their moorings, threatening to slide across the deck and take with them the superstructure. Unable to tie the tanks down, the crew took the risky choice of cutting them loose and trying to slide them into the sea. The effort succeeded, after two hours of struggle on a deck covered with thick, black oil that congealed in the salt water washing over it from the churning sea.

As the Ulua fought the storm, the grey shape of a British vessel appeared. The Royal family, including King George VI, Queen Mary, and Princesses Elizabeth and Margaret Rose, were on their way to South Africa for an official visit. In the poor visibility of the storm, the Royal family's ship overtook and passed the refugee vessel, and the Ulua hoisted the Star of David flag.

The Haim Arlosoroff (Ulua)

British ships in port, intending to sail out for a salute, were forced by the storm to turn back to harbor, and the Ulua went forward.

After the weather calmed, the Ulua passed through the Straits of Gibraltar for the third time and received a message that her transfer ship had sailed and would be waiting for her at their rendezvous point north of Crete. The next day came a further message: the transfer ship had engine trouble, and no replacement was available. The Ulua was instructed to await further orders.

Meanwhile, in Britain, Foreign Secretary Ernest Bevin made known on February 7 his government's intention to turn the Palestine question over to the United Nations.

For several weeks, the Ulua and her passengers laid low on the Mediterranean coast of North Africa. At Algiers, she stopped for fuel, which was obtained through a member of the local Jewish community. He brought aboard a non-Jewish port official who greeted the refugees, showed them a photo of his son killed two years previously in the anti-Nazi French underground, and added his seal to the Le Havre document certifying the Ulua for the remainder of her trip. The Ulua left Algiers and proceeded to a secluded anchorage near Phillipeville for repairs, then to Sousse, Tunisia, for water.

When her sailing orders came through, the Ulua headed first for the southern Italian port of Gallipoli, in the Gulf of Taranto. There, Aliyah Bet representatives were waiting with detailed instructions.

On the way to Gallipoli, the Ulua prepared for more passengers. The 500 barrels of fuel in holds had to be removed, and passengers joined crewmen in the arduous work of transferring the fuel to bigger tanks and throwing the barrels overboard.

There was also luggage to be disposed of. This was the only Aliyah Bet voyage from northern Europe, and, unlike the passengers who traveled from the southern ports, the girls who boarded the Ulua had brought aboard more belongings than the typical Aliyah Bet immigrant's knapsack contained. The word went out to the passengers to reduce their personal belongings to 20 kilograms (44 pounds) per person and jettison the rest. Some had brought suitcases containing 50, 75, even 100 kilograms. The extra things, clothing and keepsakes, went overboard.

At Gallipoli, the Ulua received her final instructions and proceeded the same night to a beach code-named "Alaska" at Metaponte, near Taranto, to pick up almost 700 more passengers. They boarded in the dark on rubber rafts. The Ulua shot a metal cable ashore, and the rafts were then attached to the cable. Each raft trip to the Ulua took 15 minutes, and the boarding operation took all night. At the last moment, Ada Sereni and Yehuda Arazi, the Haganah's top representatives in Italy, asked a favor: Could the Ulua take a few dozen extra passengers? They were children who had been left behind from every voyage in the past two months. The crew gave up their bunks, and the children came aboard. A month after leaving Sweden, the Ulua pulled anchor from Italy and began to organize hundreds of able-bodied passengers to defend the ship against the Royal Navy.

In an effort to avoid identification of the ship, the commanders sent all passengers below decks.

Shortly after leaving Italy, the Ulua entered a storm. The newly embarked passengers became violently seasick. Then, the weather calmed and the Ulua headed toward Port Said, with the intention of unloading her passengers at the beach at Nitzanim on the southern coast of Palestine.

When the Ulua was about 150 miles from Port Said, a British aircraft appeared, and the ship was never without surveillance for the remainder of the journey. After a few hours, a destroyer arrived and asked the Ulua to identify herself. The refugee vessel replied that she was the Ulua, sailing with passengers and freight to Cuba, plus 750 shipwrecked Palestine-bound passengers whom she would drop at Tel Aviv. The Ulua notified the Haganah in Palestine that she had been discovered. With deception no longer possible, the passengers were allowed on deck. Night fell. By radio, the Ulua and commanders on shore weighed a plan to bring thousands of people to the beach at Tel Aviv at midnight and attempt a landing there. The Mossad had used this tactic successfully in the past. If enough people were waiting on the beach with dry clothing and identity documents, the passengers could escape arrest by losing themselves in the crowd and exchanging clothes and papers. After an hour, the Tel Aviv plan was abandoned as too risky.

More British warships arrived, until there were six. The British ships escorted the Ulua through the night. From time to time, a British ship approached the Ulua as if to interfere with her passage; the Ulua warned the British that they were endangering shipping on the open seas, and they pulled back.

That night, the Ulua changed her name to the Haim Arlosoroff and received orders to proceed to Haifa. The choice of a new name reflected infighting among the Zionists on shore. Earlier, the plan had been to rename the Ulua in memory of the Struma, a refugee boat that sank in the Black Sea with all but one of its 766 passengers on February 24, 1942. Virtually everyone blamed the British for the death of the Struma's passengers. The fifth anniversary of her sinking on the Jewish calendar was February 27, 1947, the date of the Ulua's name change. The political problem was that the Haganah leaders feared that their arch rivals, the Revisionist Zionists, would exploit this symbolic gesture. Revisionists had sailed the Struma. Even now, a new Revisionist immigrant ship was waiting in France to pick up passengers for Palestine. A Haganah order went out to rename the Ulua in memory of Haim Arlosoroff, a Labor Zionist leader. This was a sardonic twist, since the Labor Zionists blamed the Revisionists for Arlosoroff's unsolved 1933 murder. The argument over the name triggered some sharp exchanges aboard the Ulua. But the seafarers could not dwell on Zionist politics; they painted the name Haim Arlosoroff on her sides and prepared for a naval engagement with the British.

Commanders divided the Arlosoroff's deck into three sections and assigned a fighting force of passengers and crew members to each section. The fighters stacked bolts, wooden clubs, and cans of food to be used as weapons. Fifty of the deck force were bolt throwers; 300 formed behind them with sticks and iron pipes to resist boarding parties. Fifteen men were assigned to spray a water hose at boarding parties, and 50 were detailed to defend the bridge. Another group manned a hose to shoot hot oil at boarders. A reserve fighting group of 80 sturdy young men was kept below deck.

In the morning, with the shores of Palestine in sight, the Arlosoroff headed toward Haifa. She notified the British warships of her course. The British commander, seeing the battle preparations on board the refugee ship, warned the passengers in English and German that the Arlosoroff would not make it:

"You are approaching the territorial waters of Palestine. When you reach it we shall send a boarding party. We advise you to be reasonable and act wisely. You know our strength is greater than yours. We shall treat you well on condition you do not oppose us."

The Arlosoroff passengers shouted their response: "We know you. You are no better than the Germans. You are the fathers of the concentration camps."

As they neared the three-mile limit, the passengers aboard the Arlosoroff sang Hatikvah, and the blue-and-white flag was unfurled. A British destroyer drew near, within 20 yards of the Arlosoroff, and hailed her by loudspeaker. Again warning that the Arlosoroff's actions were endangering the lives of the passengers, the British asked the captain to identify himself. After no reply from the Arlosoroff, the British demanded again that the captain who had taken the passengers' fate in his hands come forward and identify himself.

A Haganah commander aboard the Arlosoroff put a gold-braided officer's cap on the head of a 10-year-old boy and sent him to the bridge. The boy stood alone on the bridge, smiling, as a voice from the deck shouted: "This is our captain. For his sake, and in his name, we are going to fight you."

The destroyer pulled back to about 100 yards and fired a warning shot. On the Arlosoroff, all non-combatants were ordered below.

The Arlosoroff began her final run, zigzagging in an effort to evade her pursuers. If she could reach water too shallow for the British ships, the bathtub-shaped Arlosoroff stood a chance of beaching herself and putting her passengers ashore. At the three-mile limit, the British tried to drop boarding rafts onto her deck. The first round went to the refugees, who hurled their makeshift missiles at armed boarders wearing steel helmets, gas masks, and rubber clothes. A second destroyer moved into position, and the Arlosoroff dropped her booms to ward off the boarders. Again, the British were repulsed. Stung by their initial setbacks, the British sent alongside another ship which sprayed gas at the Jews. Soon, the defenders on deck were helpless from the gas, and another boarding party tried to swarm the Arlosoroff. Eight British soldiers got aboard before the Arlosoroff made another sharp turn, ramming a British destroyer. The maneuver trapped the eight boarders on the Arlosoroff's deck. Reserve Jewish fighters from below deck, unaffected by the gas, attacked the boarding party. The Jews threw two overboard and captured the others; one British soldier was injured and was taken to the sick bay.

As the Arlosoroff steered closer to the shore, the British returned to the battle with stronger measures, opening fire with automatic weapons above the Jews' heads, spraying more gas over the ship, and smashing her booms. With only minutes left before the Arlosoroff could reach the beach, 50 British soldiers fought their way onto a deck strewn with bodies of the injured and then to the bridge. The engine-room held out; by the time the attackers reached it with the help of gas bombs, it was too late. The Arlosoroff bumped onto the Bat Galim reefs.

Some of the Arlosoroff's people tried to escape by jumping into the surf, but they were surrounded. A British army camp was opposite the point where the ship went aground, and barbed wire surrounded the beach.

Time magazine described the aftermath in its next issue, dated March 10:

> Behind the barbed wire on the beach, hundreds of Jews waved handkerchiefs at the immigrants.... The news spread to Haifa. Thousands stopped work and swarmed angrily toward Bat Galim. They passed Barclay's Bank Building, shattered by a bomb soon after the ship's interception (two Jews were killed). Then they ran into tough, maroon-bereted British paratroopers, who barred their way. Jews and soldiers traded insults. Then the Jews went away into the dusk of Sabbath eve.

The next day, on the Jewish Sabbath, an explosion killed 16 people at a British officer's club in Jerusalem's King George Street, a British soldier was killed by mortar fire on a regimental camp, three British soldiers died on mined roads, and the British imposed martial law. The British high command reported that the Irgun Zva'i Leumi, the Revisionists' fighting arm, had taken credit for the bombing of the officers' club in retaliation for attacks "on our brothers (on the Arlosoroff)."

On Sunday, to "demonstrate its identification with the fate of the refugees," the Jewish community announced a self-imposed curfew throughout Palestine. For that night, all traffic would cease, cinemas and cafes would be closed, and all dances and theater programs would be cancelled.

Only a few of those aboard the Arlosoroff escaped. The British arrested five refugees and five crew members and interned them at Athlit; six additional Jews were taken to the prison camp's hospital. The others, 632 men, 680 women, and 66 children, were taken to Cyprus. Twenty of the deportees to Cyprus were stretcher cases.

The Arlosoroff lay abandoned on the Bat Galim reefs. After Israel became independent, the wreck was sold for scrap.

THE PALESTINE POST

JERUSALEM
MONDAY, MARCH 10, 1947

PRICE: 15 MILS
VOL. XXII No. [illegible]

BIG 3 ARRIVE IN MOSCOW FOR BIG 4 TALKS

GERMAN PEACE TO BE DECIDED

MOSCOW, Sunday (Reuter). — Following Mr. Bevin's arrival in Moscow yesterday for the Big Four Conference on the German Peace Treaty which opens tomorrow, M. Andrei Vyshinsky, the Soviet Deputy Foreign Commissar, today welcomed Mr. George Marshall, the U.S. Secretary of State, who arrived here by plane from Berlin in the afternoon, and M. Georges Bidault, who made the journey to the Soviet capital by train.

Sir William Strang, Mr. Bevin's adviser, and the remainder of the British Delegation, who took off from Berlin early this morning, were forced to return due to bad flying weather, and are not expected in Moscow until tomorrow afternoon.

Not one of Moscow's morning papers carried a word about the conference on Germany, and the radio, usually prolific in its world-wide emissions of news and comment on the future of Germany, also gave the conference a complete miss.

From yesterday's newspapers readers would never know that a conference was contemplated, let alone almost upon them. There was no reference to the city's magnificent preparations for the delegations. During the past week, little or nothing has been published about the job of playing host. What is for Moscow a gigantic influx of foreign visitors has left the local press blandly aloof.

"I am very happy to have arrived in Moscow," said Mr. Marshall at the airport. "I am very much gratified at the reception given me. This has been my first real view of Russia and the Russian people."

Referring to the Conference, the Secretary of State said he was aware of the fact that there had been many difficulties in the past, but they had all been successfully overcome. "I am confident," he added, "that we shall reach an agreement which will greatly advance the cause of peace."

M. Bidault, upon his arrival referred to his earlier visit to Moscow when he signed the Franco-Soviet Treaty of Friendship and Military Aid. "Now I have come in peacetime," he said, "so that the enemy against whom our alliance was directed can never rise again. I have made this pleasant trip with complete faith in the successful course of our conference and agreement of the Great Powers in the cause of peace."

GERMANS PRAY FOR PEACE

BERLIN, Sunday (Reuter). Berliners have been called to offer special prayers for peace in connection with the Moscow talks. A Pastoral letter read in all Catholic churches in Berlin this morning said that "as there will be no Germans admitted to the Peace Conference, we can pray to God, our Lord alone, to hold his protective hand over our people."

Special prayers will be said every Sunday for the duration of the talks in Moscow.

ON EVE OF TALKS

NO OPTIMISM IN LONDON

By Reuters Diplomatic Correspondent

LONDON, Sunday. — With the Conference expected to prove the most important since Potsdam more than 18 months ago, the atmosphere in London is marked by the absence of easy optimism. This is not only because the public has now learnt from experience that negotiations between Great Powers rarely go smoothly. It is because no-one here can see a simple solution to the ultimate problem which the conference has to face — the problem of into whose sphere of influence future Germany will be fitted.

The issue of the control of Germany will be thrashed out in the discussion of a number of administrative and constitutional questions. The most difficult of all these is believed to be the question of Germany's political and economic unity both in terms of the present system of control and of the eventual German peace settlement.

The first item on the agenda when the conference opens will be the consideration of the report prepared with as much dispute and difficulty by the four Allied representatives on the Control Council in Berlin. Although this is a combined document, it discloses wide divergencies on a number of points.

Any attempt to find a solution of such problems will have to begin with a reconsideration of the Potsdam decisions, particularly the economic decisions over which a wide difference of interpretation has arisen. Somehow the Foreign Ministers will have to clarify and re-interpret this basic Big Four agreement.

To judge by the recent trend of Soviet propaganda, one of the thorniest individual questions will be the economic merger of the British and U.S. occupation zones, alleged by Soviet sources to be an attempt to incorporate these zones economically and financially in the Western "Dollar and Sterling" system and split them off from Eastern Germany.

It remains to be seen whether the Big Four will be able to solve this question in terms of an extension of the merger to the Soviet Zone as Britain and America had originally proposed, or whether despite Soviet pressure for economic unity there may be some insuperable Soviet objection.

Economic Unity

German economic unity will inevitably be linked with the question of political unity or decentralization, both during the control period and in the peace settlement. When the Foreign Ministers' Special Deputies heard the views of the smaller Allies in London, Soviet Russian and the other [illegible] states all pressed for the political unity of Germany; Britain, the U.S. and France, the British Dominions and smaller Western European states favour decentralization, whether in the form of federation, confederation or some other arrangement of self-governing units.

There will also be such special questions as Poland's western frontiers, which have not yet been accepted as permanent by Britain and America, and the ultimate disposal of the Ruhr, the Saar and the Rhineland, over which France may find herself at odds with the other Allies.

But before any detailed discussion can begin on the principles of the German settlement, the Big Four will presumably have to tackle the awkward problem of the part which the smaller Allies should play in preparing the Treaty.

France Demands Ruhr Coal

PARIS, Sunday (Reuter). — The French Communist Vice-Premier, M. Maurice Thorez, today criticized unnamed Allies of France for planning to restore Germany rather than help France.

Speaking at St. Maurice, he declared: "In Germany Nazism is raising its head. We are alarmed to see certain of our allies planning to restore Germany rather than help our country. We want justice and we ask that the German people, who followed Hitler, now work to make amends.

"We demand that Germany be disarmed and demilitarized, that their heavy industry must be controlled. We ask that the Ruhr be internationalized, so that it cannot be used for rearming but only for the restoration of the peoples who were victims of Germany. Our miners dig 203 [illegible] more than before the war, but that is not sufficient for our consumption, and therefore we need Ruhr coal."

U.S. Price Control To Go On

WASHINGTON, Sunday (Reuter). — The US Senate Banking Committee has recommended a year's extension of sugar rationing and price controls. This means that the supporters of continued adherence to the international allocation system have won the first battle in Congress.

If rationing legislation is enacted, the Department of Agriculture will automatically be permitted at its discretion to continue for another year its participation in the international emergency food council allocations.

11 Death Sentences In Yugoslavia

BELGRADE, Sunday (Reuter). — Lieut.-General Harold Turner, former Nazi Government chief in Serbia, and 10 members of his administration were today sentenced to death by a Belgrade military Tribunal, found guilty of mass executions and looting during the occupation. Three other Nazis received sentences of hard labour, ranging from 20 to 8 years.

This was the third important trial of German war-time officials in Yugoslavia. During the trial Turner admitted that he had collaborated with Mihailovitch's Chetniks as early as 1941/42.

Russia Replies U.S. PROTEST REJECTED

MOSCOW, Sunday (Reuter). — The Soviet Government has now replied to and rejected the recent American note protesting against Russian interference in Hungarian affairs, according to "Tass".

The State Department had proposed a joint investigation of the present situation in Hungary, where the Russian Chairman of the Allied Control Commission was allegedly interfering with the non-Communist Hungarian Government.

Lieut.-General Sviridov said in his reply that he could not agree to a joint investigation, because "this would constitute direct intervention in the internal affairs of the Hungarian republic and a gross violation of the lawful rights of the Hungarian Peoples' Court."

JEWISH CLAIMS ON GERMANY

LONDON, Sunday (JTA). — The Foreign Ministers Conference in Moscow is not expected to include Jewish affairs in their discussions of the German peace Treaty, and no Jewish organizations have representatives on the spot.

Interest in the Jewish aspects of the Austrian Treaty is more practical, however, since there appears to be some difference of opinion among the Big Powers as to the necessity for continued supervision over the manner of its implementation, for which Jewish organizations are asking.

The Americans are most inclined to give the Austrian Government full internal sovereignty and therefore least inclined to maintain controls. The British might be more inclined to the Jewish point of view that such matters as the safeguarding of human rights and the restitution of property should be supervised.

RUSSIAN DELEGATION ON VISIT TO BRITAIN

LONDON, Sunday (AFP). — Led by M. Vassiliev Kuznetsov, Chairman of the Trade Union Council, a delegation of the Supreme Soviet is expected here tomorrow.

The delegation includes writers, scientists, teachers and trade union leaders, and will remain in England as guests of the Government for about a month.

MORE ARRESTS IN HUNGARY

By AUREL VARANNAI, Reuters Correspondent

BUDAPEST, Sunday. — Arrests continue in connection with the alleged plot to overthrow the Hungarian Republic and establish a regime similar to that of Admiral Horthy, the Regent of Hungary during and before the war.

Many officers, civil servants and industrialists have been detained. Somkos Szentivanyi, a former official of the Hungarian Foreign Office and one of 13 Hungarians being tried by the Peoples' Court here on charges of complicity in the alleged plot, told the Court today that Horthy sent him to Moscow to try and negotiate an armistice in October, 1944, three months before the armistice was actually signed by the new Government of Liberation, headed by Bela Miklos.

He said the conspirators tried to gain positions in the Army, Police and Administration through Bela Kovacs, General Secretary of the Smallholders Party, whose recent arrest by the Russians drew protests from Britain and the U.S.A.

Szentivanyi declared the plotters had no definite and clear ideas about the future form of the state, but wanted to enforce their will through political parties, and that one reason for the movement was that the smallholders were unable to use the majority they won in Parliament in last November's elections.

Riots and Arson Disorder In Punjab

By NOEL BUCKLEY, Reuters Special Correspondent

LAHORE, Sunday. — Taxila, an ancient Indian university town 260 kilometres north-west of Lahore, was reported tonight to be in flames — the eighth town to be drawn into the week-old Punjab rioting in which Hindus and Sikhs are grappling with Moslems.

Sir Evan Jenkins, the Punjab Governor, left Lahore by train today for Rawalpindi where rioting and arson continue. He has resumed special emergency powers until the formation of the Punjab Provincial Government to succeed the Coalition Ministry which resigned in face of the Moslem League attacks.

The overall picture of the Punjab situation was:

Lahore — calm, but further trouble feared. British troops and armed police to keep order.

Amritsar — British troops and armed police on patrol.

Multan — travellers from Multan today reported over 100 killed and 150 injured in disturbances.

Rawalpindi — rioting reported, troops ordered to shoot at sight at people breaking orders.

Murree — huge fires still burning, half the town in ruins.

In Lahore itself dense clouds of flies alone disturbed the Sunday calm of the streets in the old walled section, where fire-blackened skeletons and balconies of charred wood showed how near the heart of the city came to destruction in the riots.

Two airborne battalions have been sent to Multan, third largest city of the Punjab. A brigade of troops from Southern India will arrive in the capital, Lahore, in a day or two, it was learned here tonight.

The Anti-Pakistan Council today issued a statement urging Hindus and Sikhs throughout the Punjab to observe "Anti-Pakistan Day" on Tuesday.

NEHRU APPEALS FOR TOLERANCE

LONDON, Sunday (Reuter). — Pandit Nehru, the Vice-President of the Indian Interim Government, appealed for tolerance and cooperation in a message to the youth of India, broadcast today by New Delhi radio.

They might belong to one religion or another, but the first thing they had to learn was that they were all human beings and Indians — with the honour of India in their keeping, he said.

Hippo: 8th Day SCHOOLS OPEN FOR 3 HOURS

Palestine Post Staff

After a week's unwanted holiday, 2,000 children living in Jerusalem's Martial Law area went back to school yesterday — on a three-hour schedule with volunteer teachers and in makeshift classrooms.

While the 17-hour curfew still required to maintain control in the closely wired area was continued, two school principals from outside the area have been allowed to enter, and are organizing the Martial Law school system. Classes will have to be restricted to three out of the seven "free" hours daily, to give children a chance of exercise.

Three of the schools in the zone have been re-opened, and a number of retired teachers have again gone back into harness to take the places of the teachers unable to re-enter the area. In addition, a number of people have put their enforced idleness to use by volunteering to teach classes at home without pay.

Mr. D.G. Stewart, the new Financial Secretary, accompanied by Mr. M. Brown, Principal Assistant Secretary, called upon the Chief Rabbi, Dr. Herzog, and Chief Rabbi Uziel yesterday.

In the meantime, Brigadier Davies assured journalists yesterday that "every effort was being made to allow schooling to proceed as normally as possible."

Arrangements to supply the area with newspapers were also under consideration.

No Movements

A decision was expected, he said on the applications for certain residents for passes to leave the area, but it must be realized, he added, that Martial Law meant that no movement into or from the area was allowed.

Twenty-two truckloads of foodstuffs were admitted into the area yesterday, and supplies are now sufficient. Because most workers in the area are cut off from their employment, however, and have no way of maintaining themselves, about 6,000 persons are on relief.

Persons outside the area with relatives or friends inside the zone, who may need assistance, were asked by the Jew-

(Continued on Page 2)

LIGHT OF DAY ON T.A. ATTACKS SCOPE OF ACTION EXAGGERATED

Palestine Post Bureau

TEL AVIV, Sunday. — The echoing shooting which held the Military-Law bound city in alarmed suspense for over an hour last night was re-examined in the light of day this morning, and a number of new facts have now emerged.

'Step Back'

TEL AVIV, Sunday.— Martial Law was a step back to the Ottoman regime, and history would not forget that 300,000 persons had been punished for the crimes of a handful, said Mr. Rokach, the Mayor, at a meeting of the Municipal Council here this evening.

The closing of the Tel Aviv Port, which could by no means be considered a security measure, had deprived hundreds of workers, most of them ex-servicemen, of their livelihood, he said.

Mr. Rokach condemned the terrorist groups which consisted of "madmen, uncaring for life or property."

The toll, as given officially this morning, is:

One Guardsman killed; British constable seriously injured; TAC slightly injured; three Jews dead; eleven Jews seriously injured; three Jews slightly injured.

Of the four civilian dead whose bodies are at the Hadassah Hospital morgue, two died of heart failure; one, a girl, was shot in the Caucasian Quarter, and one, the fourth, a man, was shot while on his way home.

In addition to Shoshana (Rd. as) Rachimov, 18, killed in Shehunat Hatikva, Itzhak Pierer, 35, a worker at the cold storage plant here, died of his wounds during the night. Pierer is believed to have been walking to his home in Shchunat Harakevet when he was hit by bullets near Citrus House. He was taken by the military into the Security Area, where first aid proved unavailing.

This evening, Zeev Lustig, injured last night, succumbed at the Hadassah Hospital, bringing the number of ascertainable Jewish deaths to five.

A 17-year-old girl, Esther Tusah, was fired upon and dangerously wounded, allegedly by a T.J.F.F. patrol, in Rehov Kalisher this afternoon. It is believed that she was going along Kalisher Street towards Jaffa, though the spot where she was fired on is some distance from the boundary.

Later this evening, a 16-year-old boy, Shabetai Makowsky, was admitted to hospital suffering from bullet wounds. He had been fired upon while returning to his home in Hatikva Quarter.

At a press conference this afternoon, Lt.-Col. Sheffield confirmed last night's statement that several Jewish attackers had been killed, though the number was now given at three, not four. No other details were available.

In the meantime, one of four Arab women who were injured near the Tel Aviv-Jaffa border died today of her wounds.

Attack Exaggerated

Reports from units involved in the action seem to lead to the conclusion that the scope of the attack had been exaggerated in the darkness and confusion. Troops have replied very little firing on their part, and said that most of the firing seemed to come from police patrols which, for many hours after the shooting ended, raced through the streets on the alert.

It now appears doubtful whether any attack at all was carried out against Jaffa Police Headquarters, while Citrus House this morning showed few bullet marks. On the other hand, houses in the vicinity were severely scarred by bullet holes, and many shop and flat windows were pierced.

A bren-carrier which was despatched to Rehov Yehuda Halevi after the Department of Survey building was attacked had a narrow escape when a road mine exploded directly in front of it. Another mine, constructed to look like a milestone and filled with iron nuts, bolts and explosives, was found in the vicinity this morning.

Several bursts of Bren-gun fire from Citrus House hit a Shell Company lorry loaded with Butagas balloons, setting it on fire. The balloons exploded, increasing confusion and alarm and scattering metal fragments in all directions.

A match store of the Nur Company was also hit by the fragments and burst into flames which the Fire Brigade fought until after midnight. Total damage by fire to workshops, houses and shops is estimated at about LP10,000. Three other lorries parked on the same lot, loaded with vegetables, and an empty lorry parked near the Central Bus Station also caught fire and were completely destroyed.

Most of the vehicles and other property destroyed by the fires were insured, but it is not yet clear whether the insurance companies will be required to compensate the losses.

Electric wires in the neighbourhood of Citrus House were severed by bullets, which also cut off the power from the printing-press of the "Yedioth

(Continued on Page 2)

SHOTS AND HAND-GRENADE

NATHANYA, Sunday. — A police vehicle was shot at from both sides of the road on the Tel Aviv-Haifa highway near Even Yehuda at 7 o'clock this evening.

No one was injured.

A civilian vehicle was stolen at 8 o'clock this morning at Beit Lidd near here.

In Jerusalem, a Jew was arrested in possession of a hand grenade last night at the corner of Tahkemoni and Rashi Streets, it was officially stated. He was later reported to have been indentified as Moshe Baraznni (21).

UNNECESSARY

Writing on the series of attacks in Tel Aviv on Saturday, "Hadashot Haerev" yesterday said: "What was the purpose of the great play staged by the terrorists in and around Tel Aviv? If it was to prove that the Yishuv is not despondent it was entirely unnecessary. Acts such as these can only be used to try to prove what is not true— that the Yishuv has been seized of despair and madness. Neither despairing nor senseless, the Yishuv stands on its self-respect and its constructive tasks. No criminal acts will turn it from its course."

ABRIL REFUGEES DEPORTED

Palestine Post Bureau

HAIFA, Sunday. — While Haifa slept this morning, the latest arrivals in Palestine, 600 immigrants who were intercepted yesterday noon were transferred to deportation vessels. The trim and sturdy looking 700 ton black and white yacht, the s.s. Abril, which had brought them, was manoeuvred by tugs alongside the cargo jetty shortly after one o'clock in the morning.

The vessel had no banners, no Hebrew name. When it was caught, the Honduras flag under which it had sailed was brought down, and the Jewish colours run up the mast.

Twenty men, said to be Americans, and suspected of being the crew, were arrested and are being held under strong guard in the Haifa lock-up.

Admitted as Citizens

One new detail was added to the now almost mechanical procedure of shipping off again the tired and bewildered people. At the entrance to the first tent, where the immigrants were searched, a C.I.D. official stood and asked each one whether he had a passport or visa. Many of the men handed over blue documents, with particulars and photographs. The one shown to the press party, dated Paris February 28, carried the insignia of the Shield of David, with the Lion of Judah. It was printed in Hebrew, English and French.

Rest and Shelter

The 384 men, 195 women and 20 children were put on two vessels, with reassuring names — the Empire Rest and Empire Shelter — "Liberty" ships just brought into the deportation business and on their first run, with brand new wire cages, painted bright orange.

As in other recent transhipments, the newspapermen could only watch the scene on the jetty, glaringly bright in the light of the moon and searchlights, but were strictly forbidden to talk to the people, to ask them where they came from, what manner of life they had left. Some of the young people looked almost confident, the middle-aged wan and confused. One noticed a bandaged head here and there, heard an occasional half-suppressed cry from a frightened woman. There were a few brief scuffles between the soldiers and men who fought to hold on to their belongings, which were being taken away for further inspection, but there was no actual resistance.

The least suspicion that the ban on speaking to the refugees was being broken brought an immediate reprimand, making pressmen wonder what the people had to tell that was being covered by such strict incommunicado orders.

It was noticed that many documents other than the "visas" were collected from the immigrants and a small black box was carried away in great secrecy.

The Liberty vessels started out for Cyprus shortly after dawn.

A 17-year-old girl, Irene Boednia, and her husband, were allowed to stay behind, as she is expecting a child almost immediately.

It is also reported though not officially confirmed that another two men and a woman were being held, all thought to be journalists.

Cyprus Quota Full

By SHAHE GUEBENLIAN, Palestine Post Correspondent

NICOSIA, Sunday. — The Empire Shelter and the Empire Rest are expected in Famagusta at 7.30 tomorrow (Monday) morning, it was stated officially here.

The total number of deportees in Cyprus, after the deduction of those who have left for Palestine and the addition of new arrivals is 9,782 in both camps, to which must be added a number of births that have occurred on the island.

The Cyprus Government official gazette last August provided for a maximum of 10,000 to be detained on the island. Another batch of 750 — already overdue — is expected to leave for Palestine as soon as possible, in order not to exceed the official Cyprus quota.

The fact that the 10,000 quota can be increased, should not be overlooked, however.

Capt. F.G. Wainwright, in charge of the disembarkation of deportees from Liberty ships, left for Lydda yesterday for consultations with Palestine H.Q.

RABBI GOLD IN JERUSALEM

Rabbi W. Gold, of the Jewish Agency Executive, has arrived in Palestine from America.

Rabbi Abba Hillel Silver, Mr. Berl Locker and Dr. N. Goldman are expected tomorrow, and a plenary session of the Executive is likely to be held on Wednesday.

Mr. Daniel Frisch, Chairman of the Zionist Organization of America Administrative Council and member of the Actions Committee was on the plane which arrived at Lydda airport late Saturday night.

GREECE, OIL AND PALESTINE INCREASED U.S. INTEREST IN M.E.

By JON KIMCHE

LONDON, Sunday. — Evidence of the formidable growth of American Middle East interests is now piling up daily. Following the United States intervention about the future of Greece, has come the Americans turning down of the British plan for a special Assembly appointing a Fact Finding Committee on Palestine to report to the U.N. Assembly by September.

This latest step is interpreted here that the United States is unwilling to leave the policy decision for the future of Palestine entirely in the hands of the U.N. It is apparently the view of the State Department that Britain should submit definite proposals to the U.N. and this is understood here to mean that the United States want to be consulted about these proposals before they are submitted officially to the Assembly.

The view now is that the future steps concerning Palestine are more likely to be taken in Moscow than in New York, and that it is one of the first topics for discussion between Mr. Bevin and Mr. Marshall, when they meet for the first time, somewhat ironically, at the Kremlin.

New Pipeline

How pressing American interests are in the Middle East can be seen here in the speed with which the Americans have been conducting negotiations for a new oil agreement with the Anglo-Iranian Company. After dealings concluded in record time, it has been announced by Sir William Fraser, Chairman of the Anglo-Iranian Company, that a contract has been placed for a second 1000 mile pipeline through Arabia independent of that controlled by the American Trans-Arabian Pipeline Company, which is to carry oil from Saudi-Arabia to the Mediterranean seaboard.

No secret is made here that the British Government, which is in control of the Anglo-Iranian Company, is interested in this development, though it has, officially, not taken part in the negotiations.

In military quarters here the view is expressed that this new line which will start from Abadan and also from Kuwait will have to run much the same course as the other lines from Saudi-Arabia and Iraq, as otherwise the security demands would become uneconomically large. This question and that of the terminal are now being discussed with the Arab States concerned, and particularly the Americans are anxious to make a watertight arrangement for securing the safety of the lines. It is understood that the American Navy in particular is pressing the view that the only way for ensuring this is the establishment of an American base, preferably in the Persian Gulf. Whether this comes about or not, there is no doubt that during the next 12 months American influence in the Middle East will grow beyond all previous expectation, and for the first time there appears some uneasy speculation about Britain's position as a result.

Sterling Balances

Meanwhile the Eady Mission, which has been discussing the future of the Sterling balances, is expected back shortly. A powerful Conservative Committee has been formed, which has already received assurances from Dr. Dalton, the Chancellor of the Exchequer, that Britain's counter-claims must be considered by the Middle East countries.

The Committee has now submitted a proposal to Dr. Dalton, pointing out that India is drawing on the Sterling balance at a rate of £100 million annually, in the form of goods and securities, and that this endangers the whole settlement. They demand that Britain should block all Sterling accounts accumulated between 1939 and 1945.

London Surprised By U.S. Attitude

The American objection to the proposed United Nations fact-finding commission on Palestine owing to the absence of concrete formulation by the British of the issues involved has caused considerable surprise in political quarters in London.

Defending the proposed commission, British political observers point out that it was being explored by Britain, (another source says that it was actually put forward by Britain in the first instance) in connection with the well-known wish of the U.S. Government that the next six months should not be wasted.

The same observers say that Mr. Bevin has made it clear that Britain intends to explain to the General Assembly of the U.N. that further administration of Palestine by the Mandatory Power has become impossible without a decision on the ultimate constitutional future, which Britain under the Mandate is not empowered to take.

Commenting on the American objection to the proposed commission, the "New York Times" notes that the U.S. Government examines the Palestine problem with the utmost care. It adds that it is believed that at the U.N. the United States will support a general solution acceptable to the Zionists. Whether South America will follow the United States is problematical, however. *(Reuter, PTA & Palcor).*

ARAB LEAGUE TO MEET NEXT WEEK

BAGHDAD, Sunday (Reuter). — The Premier, Nuri Pasha es Said, will lead the Iraqi Delegation to the next meeting of the Arab League to be held on March 17, informed political quarters here said today.

Jamal eff. Husseini, Deputy-Chairman of the Palestine Arab Higher Committee, now visiting Baghdad, said here today: "Palestine is not affiliated to the United Nations and will oppose any decision of the United Nations which may not ensure Arab rights."

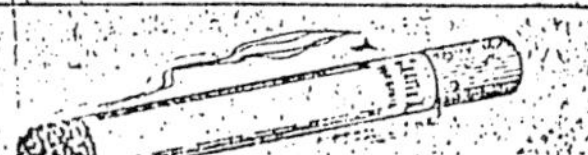

Ben Hecht (Abril)

We felt that by conducting the repatriation of the Hebrew people in a secret manner as a smuggling operation and by refusing to assume public responsibility for this activity, the Jewish Agency and its Zionist affiliates were strengthening the British claim as to the "illegality" of Hebrew immigration into Palestine. We determined to challenge this claim of "illegality" by publicly announcing our intention to repatriate the Hebrew people to Palestine and by assuming responsibility for this action....

I need not point out to you the immense difference between such a program and the secret activities of the Haganah....

—Will Rogers, Jr., Board Member of the American League for a Free Palestine, in a letter to Bartley C. Crum, August 14, 1946.

In the sultry late-summer days of 1946, a musical pageant opened at New York's Alvin Theatre. The producers eagerly scanned the early editions of the morning papers for favorable comments from the reviewers.

Like other Broadway entertainments, "A Flag is Born" had stars, scenery, a script, professional management, and an advertising budget. But this production was different in one major respect; the show was frankly polemic in nature, intended to promote a cause.

The producers explained: "It was not written to amuse or beguile. 'A Flag is Born' was written to make money—to make money to provide ships to get Hebrews to Palestine. The play will net thousands of dollars for the repatriation drive and, in addition, arouse American public opinion to support the fight for freedom and independence now being waged by the resistance in Palestine."

After the show opened, a press release further spelled out its aims: "The play was written as a propaganda vehicle for unlimited immigration of stateless European Jews to Palestine and the withdrawal of British rule in the Holy Land."

"A Flag is Born" was produced by the American League for a Free Palestine, which in May had announced a campaign to bring refugees to Palestine in defiance of the British blockade. The American League for a Free Palestine was one of those phenomena of American public life, a public organization that does not neatly fit established categories. Its President,

United States Senator Guy M. Gillette of Iowa, and some of its other non-Jewish members were Americans who supported a militant stand against the British on behalf of Jewish nationalism. Its Jewish members came from a variety of backgrounds; the driving force was provided by adherents of the Revisionist Zionist movement founded by the late Vladimir (Ze'ev) Jabotinsky. Before World War II, the Revisionists as well as the Haganah had conducted many of the early voyages bringing refugees to Palestine against British opposition. In 1946, the Revisionists were led in Palestine by Menachem Begin, head of the underground Irgun Zvai Leumi.

The leading character of "A Flag is Born" was a Jew named Tevya, played by the veteran actor Paul Muni, who as Muni Weisenfreund began his career at age 12 in the Yiddish theater of Maurice Schwartz. Muni had achieved stardom in gangster movies, but he was more than a Hollywood tough guy. He won an Academy Award for a sensitive performance in a 1935 film on the life of Louis Pasteur and became known for playing characters who achieved greatness not by physical force but through heroism of spirit.

Muni's supporting cast in "A Flag is Born" included Quentin Reynolds, Celia Adler, and Marlon Brando. The musical score was contributed by Kurt Weill, a cantor's son who had become a leading Broadway and Hollywood composer after fleeing the Nazis; Weill had written "The Threepenny Opera" with the leftist playwright Bertolt Brecht in pre-Hitler Germany.

The controversial author and initiator of the pageant was Ben Hecht, a screenwriter with a publicist's flair for advocacy and invective. A former Chicago newspaperman, Hecht co-authored the stage hit "The Front Page" with Charles McArthur in 1928 and went on to establish himself in Hollywood. At the time he wrote "A Flag is Born," Hecht was perhaps the most successful Jewish writer in the movie capital.

What made Hecht a controversial figure was his penchant for a scrap, and his readiness to argue Zionist issues in front of the whole world. In his early years, Hecht had been openly unsympathetic to his fellow Jews. As the Nazi menace grew, his attitude changed. He wrote an anti-fascist novel in 1937 and took up Jewish nationalism in 1941 as an American advocate of the Irgun Zva'i Leumi. Hecht passionately championed the Revisionist cause through the American League for a Free Palestine and the Hebrew Committee of National Liberation. Scathingly, he criticized those who took a less militant stance. He was biting in his denunciations of the Jewish establishment, and he encouraged non-Jews to take his side in these debates. The targets of his criticism included leaders of Jewish organizations in the United States, and the Jewish Agency and the Haganah in Palestine.

The activities of the Broadway-Hollywood combine caused consternation to the secrecy-minded Haganah shu-shu boys.

Not only were Hecht and his circle unprepared to keep quiet about Jewish immigration to Palestine. More than that, Hecht and the American League for a Free

Palestine wanted to tell the world about it.

Opening night of "A Flag is Born" was September 5, 1946. The producers clipped the newspapers and distributed excerpts of 15 reviews to the mailing list of the American League for a Free Palestine. The League's newsletter quoted Brooks Atkinson of The New York Times, dean of American drama critics:

> Mr. Hecht manages to show that the Jews have a noble heritage, that Europe has persecuted them with a savage violence unprecedented in the whole dark history of the world, that post war politics is continuing the inhuman race war and that something decisive ought to be done about it....Mr. Muni is giving one of the great performances of his career.

John Chapman, of the New York Daily News, the nation's largest-circulation daily paper, wrote that the play was "more than just a plea for a homeland, for a Jewish nation; it is a demand."

> Mr. Hecht is against the British and wholeheartedly with the Jews who are fighting the British with guns....Mr. Hecht and all those who have worked with him have reminded a rather sleepy commercial theater that the stage can still be a forum, a pulpit and a platform.

On September 30, a few weeks after the show opened, the American League for a Free Palestine held a testimonial dinner in Paul Muni's honor. Senator Guy M. Gillette, President of the American League for a Free Palestine, referred to Muni's character of Tevya as a "Hebrew Abraham Lincoln." The American League for a Free Palestine announced that $74,000 had been raised at the dinner and would be used to buy ships for Jewish immigration to Palestine. Muni concluded his speech at the dinner by delivering some of Tevya's lines from "A Flag is Born:"

> Remember, Englishmen, that you have never won a war against a people that wanted to be free! So why make such another war and lose it? And lose your own honor, also. Lose all the fine things that Englishmen fought for—when they were defending themselves—and called the world to help them by crying that everybody should be allowed to live on earth without fear of oppression....
>
> Listen to me, Americans, my people were killed in Europe by the Germans —and Tevya is left with a handful. Let them into Palestine or they die—all that are left. Why did you fight the Germans—so you could take over their work of killing the rest of the Jews? You have conferences. You have more conferences. How many conferences do you need to hold before one of the Freedoms—for which your soldiers fought and died—can exist? Tevya says, open one little door for the Jews who have opened so many big doors for everybody else. Open one little door to Palestine.

Scheduled to play for four weeks, the show extended its Broadway run to 10 weeks and then went on the road. Before opening in Boston on February 18, 1947, "A Flag is Born" was scheduled to play in Washington, D.C. But racial segregation was the rule at the time in the nation's capital, and the American League for a Free Palestine announced that it would not allow the play to be performed at the National Theatre if Blacks were barred from the better seats. The producers obtained a commitment for unsegregated seating from the Maryland Theatre in Baltimore and organized a special railroad car to bring members of Congress to the performance as their guests. The American League for a Free Palestine announced in a press release:

"For the first time in the history of the State of Maryland negroes were permitted to attend the legitimate theatre without discrimination. Negro segregation at the theatre was broken Tuesday, February 11th, when the Maryland Theatre sold orchestra and box seats to 'A Flag is Born' to anyone who asked for them without reference to race or color. About ten negroes witnessed the performance from choice seats."

Ben Hecht sent a telegram from Hollywood expressing satisfaction that his play served as "the instrument to break down one of the most un-American and undemocratic practices that has disgraced our country."

"The incident," Hecht said, "is forceful testimony to the proposition that to fight discrimination and injustice to one group of human beings affords protection to every other group."

* * *

Meanwhile, the Tyre Shipping Company of New York came into existence. Will Rogers, Jr., a leader of the American League for a Free Palestine, referred to this company, in his August 14 letter cited at the beginning of this chapter, as the agency through which the League would put its immigration program into effect.

With funds supplied by the American League for a Free Palestine, the Tyre Shipping Company bought the 400-ton, 150-foot former yacht Cytheria. Built in 1923 at the Krupp works in Kiel, Germany, the Cytheria had an interesting history. She had been a private yacht; during the Spanish Civil War she engaged in smuggling operations. Taken over by the U.S. Navy in World War II, she served on coastal patrols as the radar picket vessel PY-31.

The former yacht was towed to a dock in the Gowanus Canal, Brooklyn. Through the late summer and fall of 1946, during the stage run of "A Flag is Born," the vessel underwent repairs and provisioning. One factor in holding down the costs was advice from Morris Ginsberg of the American Foreign Steamship Corporation. Already a key volunteer in the Aliyah Bet operations of the Haganah, Ginsberg checked with Danny Schind before providing his expertise to the Revisionists. Volunteer crew members, recruited by word of mouth, came aboard, one by one, during this period. They received Honduran seamen's papers, in keeping with the vessel's new Honduran registry. In late December the yacht was ready and moved to Staten Island for sea trials. There, she took aboard a ton of salami, thousands of vitamin pills, and a supply of canned grapefruit juice.

Under charter to the Hebrew Committee of National Liberation, the yacht sailed from New York on December 27, 1946, with the name Abril. After a stormy voyage across the Atlantic, she arrived at the Azores and took on more fuel. On her way past Gibraltar to Port de Bouc, the Abril encountered worse weather. She arrived January 10, 1947, at Port de Bouc, where she remained throughout January and February while crew members repaired sea damage, ripped out her insides and built sleeping racks for passengers.

On February 28 and March 1, more than 600 passengers for the Abril arrived at Port de Bouc by train and bus from Grenoble. This operation involved cooperation with Haganah officials, who again laid aside ideological differences in the interest of the refugee voyage. The Abril sailed from Port de Bouc on March 1. No pilot or tugboat was available to the Abril, and the vessel ran aground leaving the harbor. Tugs arrived to pull her free.

For the next week, as she followed the coast of France and Italy and then headed toward Palestine, the Abril had one problem after another. One of her two diesel engines failed to operate most of the time. One of her two main tanks for fresh water leaked most of its contents overboard. Three days of bad weather made passengers seasick. And the underground radio in Palestine did not respond.

After about a week at sea, British patrol aircraft sighted the Abril, buzzed her, and flew away. On March 8, three British destroyers appeared. The destroyers converged on the little vessel and followed her, sending messages notifying her that she was nearing Palestinian waters. She replied that she was sailing to Chile and asked for food and water; the request was refused. Later the same afternoon, 10.6 miles from the Palestine coast, the Abril was boarded by British marines and towed to Haifa.

The Palestine Post reported: "The vessel had no banners, no Hebrew name. When it was caught, the Honduras flag under which it sailed was brought down and the Jewish colors run up the mast."

"Twenty men, said to be Americans, and suspected of being the crew, were arrested and are being held under strong guard in the Haifa lock-up."

The newspaper reported that some of the passengers presented blue documents bearing their identification photographs and imprinted with the Star of David and the Lion of Judah. The passengers of the Abril were transferred to British prison ships and taken to Cyprus.

Back in New York, the American League for a Free Palestine began issuing statements. The League identified the Abril as "the mercy ship Ben Hecht" and announced on March 10 it had engaged lawyers to defend the crew members. The League said it had also been in touch with American consular officials about the legal rights of the crew. This was different from the practice followed on Haganah-run voyages, whose crew members hid out, took false names, and tried to conceal their Aliyah Bet activity from American officials if they were returning to the United States.

On March 11, the American League for a Free Palestine distributed an announcement in the name of the American Sea and Air Volunteers for Hebrew Repatriation, which identified itself as the organization that had recruited the volunteer crew of the Ben Hecht. The announcement said that enough men to provide crews for five more ships had offered to volunteer in response to the British arrest of the Ben Hecht crew. The announcement said the volunteer group was founded on September 2, 1946, and 20 per cent of its first group of 186 volunteers were non-Jews. Appended to the announcement was a list of the Ben Hecht sailors arrested by the British.

Also on March 11, the Hebrew Committee of National Liberation announced it would provide displaced persons in Germany and Austria with thousands of passports of the type carried by passengers on the Ben Hecht. The Committee said it had issued the passports on its own, basing its action on a legal interpretation of the League of Nations Mandate under which the British governed Palestine.

The American volunteer crew, except for one member who went to Cyprus in the guise of a passenger, were held in jail at Haifa for two days and then imprisoned at Acre. They were tried and convicted of aiding and abetting illegal immigration and were given 17-year prison sentences.

While in Acre, a member of the crew helped Irgun leaders with a critical detail of preparations for a soon-to-be-famous jailbreak. The story was told by Jan Gitlin in *The Conquest of Acre Fortress* (Hadar Publishing House Ltd., Tel Aviv, 1982.) The Ben Hecht sailor had with him a camera, which supplied the answer to the problem of providing new identity documents for the men who would escape from the fortress prison. While at Acre, the sailor took photographs of all the men to be included in the escape. The Irgun sent the film outside the prison, and the photos were used to manufacture false documents which were waiting for the escapees when they broke out on May 4. The escape from the fortress shocked the British and made headlines around the world. By that time the Ben Hecht crewmen were back in the United States.

On March 24, the Hebrew Committee of National Liberation announced that the British would deport the volunteers. The League credited press coverage, speeches in Congress, and its own newspaper advertisements with influencing the British decision to release the men.

On March 30, less than a month after their arrival in Palestine, the volunteers were deported to the United States. They reached New York by ship on April 16. Two days after their arrival in New York, the volunteers were welcomed at City Hall by Acting Mayor Vincent R. Impellitteri, who said: "As a war veteran myself, I can understand how you, war veterans, volunteered for this hazardous voyage with no reward for yourselves except the satisfaction of helping to attain American war aims including justice and freedom for all deserving peoples."

The American League for a Free Palestine announced a series of public rallies for the crew, including an April 21 dinner at the Hotel Astor with guests including Ben Hecht, actor Milton Berle, and actress Rosalind Russell.

* * *

In Haifa, the Ben Hecht remained captive in port after Israel proclaimed her independence. Aliyah Bet ships purchased for the Haganah went immediately into the service of the new State as warships or passenger vessels. But the Ben Hecht was not Haganah property. The former yacht belonged to an American affiliate of the Irgun, a virtually autonomous rival of the Haganah.

The Altalena affair resolved the status of the little refugee vessel. On June 22, 1948, Ben-Gurion ordered Israeli forces to open fire on the Altalena, an Irgun ship that was trying to land at Tel Aviv with a cargo of weapons. The Altalena was destroyed. In the ensuing tension, with an evident possibility of civil war, Irgun Commander Begin broadcast an appeal to his followers to lay down their weapons. The Irgun submitted itself to the discipline of the new government. Not long after that, the Ben Hecht became warship K-24 of the new Israeli navy. A mother ship for seaborne commandos was needed, and the former yacht filled that role. Her new name was the Maoz, a Hebrew word signifying protection.

* * *

While controversy over the Altalena affair has never been put to rest, some facts in connection with American volunteer efforts are not in dispute. The Altalena was a war-surplus American LST purchased in the United States; Harry Louis Selden, chairman of the Executive Committee of the American League for a Free Palestine, signed the necessary papers. Her captain and crew were American volunteers. The Israeli naval vessel that had the lead role in cornering the Altalena at Tel Aviv was the K-20, formerly the Wedgwood, the first American-manned Aliyah Bet ship. Her captain was a Canadian volunteer. And the Commanding Officer of the Israeli Navy at the time was Paul Shulman, a former American naval officer who served Aliyah Bet as a volunteer in several key capacities.

* * *

Despite the intensity of their ideological disagreements with the Revisionists, Haganah officials facilitated the refugee voyage of the Ben Hecht on at least two occasions. Danny Schind gave Morris Ginsberg a go-ahead to help with refitting the vessel, and Haganah representatives in Europe cooperated in the dispatch of refugees.

Some members of the Ben Hecht crew later served as volunteers on Aliyah Bet voyages conducted by the Haganah.

THE PALESTINE POST

JERUSALEM
SUNDAY, MAY 18, [illegible]

PRICE: 15 MILS
VOL. XXII. No. 6109

TWO MEMBERS OF U.N. COMMISSION ALREADY NAMED

CZECHS, YUGOSLAVS TO DEMAND D.P. TOUR

United Nations Delegates scattored to their homes this week-end with a feeling of satisfaction at a great accomplishment, cables our U.N. Correspondent. It is their common belief that one of the thorniest problems of this generation will be solved by the September General Assembly and that the fledgling international organization will be greatly strengthened thereby.

United Nations circles feel that the Inquiry would be ineffective if it failed to clarify the position of Britain, the United States and Russia in good time for the September Assembly. Meanwhile Czechoslovakia and Yugoslavia, both members of the Inquiry Commission, have indicated that they will demand a tour of European D.P. camps.

The first two members of the Palestine Fact-Finding Commission to be named are Mr. N.S. Blom, former Director of Justice in the Netherlands East Indies, for Holland, and M. Emile Papenek, for Czechoslovakia.

Sir Alexander Cadogan, leader of the British delegation, ...

"MASTER PLAN"

WASHINGTON, Saturday (Reuter). — *The U.S. plans to have a stockpile of strategic war materials worth 1,000 million dollars, as part of her "Master Plan" for all out industrial mobilization in the event of another war.*

THOUSAND REFUGEES ARRIVE IN "HATIKVA"

Palestine Post Bureau

HAIFA, Saturday. — From a small antiquated one-time American coastal cargo vessel whose commercial name Trade Winds was changed to Hatikvah (Hope), about 1,000 immigrants disembarked here tonight, the first batch of visa-less immigrants to arrive in three weeks. The vessel steamed in slowly with two watchful destroyers at her side, and at eight p.m. was moored at the cargo jetty, where the four deportation ships Empire Comfort, Lifeguard, Rest and Shelter were waiting.

Her flimsy hull was ripped open in several places where the warships had rammed against her. On a funnel was painted a Shield of David and "Eretz (The Land), 1947." Underneath was a shamrock and "Eire, 1922."

When intercepted by four warships, which fired warning shots into the air ...

INDIAN RIOTS

46 DEAD IN THREE DAYS

By DOON CAMPBELL,
Reuters Special Correspondent

NEW DELHI, Saturday (Reuter). — British troops were today rushed to the Punjab capital, Lahore, where arson and stabbing were reported during the four-hour relaxation of the curfew imposed after the serious outbreak of communal rioting.

Lahore, where the latest communal outbreak began three days ago, was still ablaze this afternoon with fire brigades desperately fighting the fires started by the rioters.

Casualties in the three days are unofficially reported to be 46 dead and 71 injured. Before the arrival of British troops today two people were killed when police opened fire on crowds fighting a pitched battle with stones. ...

Foreign Affairs Debate Closes

HOPES FOR BIG FOUR AGREEMENT

LONDON, Saturday (Reuter). — Winding up the two-day foreign affairs debate in the House of Commons yesterday, Mr. Bevin, Foreign Secretary, declared he had seen many 11th hour 59th minute settlements, and he hoped there would still be a settlement of the major differences between the Big Four.

"But if I have to come to you eventually and say it cannot be done, then in the light of that, the Government will have to review its entire policy," he declared.

The Government did not accept the view that Britain had ceased to play the role of a great power. "We still have our historic part to play," he said.

Dealing with the Middle East and Egypt and the Sudan in particular, and the charge that Britain had been inclined to give in to the Arabs' demands, Mr. Bevin said he wanted to make it clear that in Britain's negotiations with Egypt there had been no attempt at appeasement ...

... visit the former Italian colonies, and that commission should be in a position to start its work as soon as the Italian Treaty comes into Force," Mr. Bevin declared.

"Some weeks ago, Britain invited the other powers to nominate their representatives to meet in London as soon as possible." U.S. and French Governments had accepted the invitation, and he was now awaiting the Soviet reply.

On the question of the Senussi, the British Government had in the past expressed its sympathy with their drive to independence and made it clear they were bound by a pledge, to which the British Government was a party, given to the Senussi not to return them to Italian rule.

Ben Gurion Returning On Tuesday

NEW YORK, Saturday (Palcor). — Mr. David Ben Gurion is leaving New York tomorrow on his way back to Palestine. He is expected to arrive on Tuesday.

POLICE DRIVER KILLED

Palestine Post Bureau

HAIFA, Saturday. — In an attempt on the life of a Police ...

Assembly's Sudden End Came as Surprise

By ALISTAIR COOKE, "Manchester Guardian" Correspondent

FLUSHING MEADOW, Saturday. — The special session of the General Assembly on Palestine came to a swift and rather dazed end at 2 o'clock on Thursday afternoon. ...

LIKELIEST CANDIDATES

Gromyko Put U.S. At Disadvantage

MILITARY FUNERAL

Refugees Stranded in New No-Man's Land

Hearings On U.S. D.P. Bill

Saudi Arabia Seeks U.S. Loan

BEVIN'S HINTS TO U.N.

AGENCY ECHOES PEACE PLEA

Two Bombs Found In Cairo

'Britain First' To Defend Jews

Mock Air Raid Over New York

SYRIAN GOVERNMENT WORKERS ON STRIKE

30 DEAD IN TRAIN

Urges U.S. to Share Palestine Burden

Congress Agrees on Post-UNRRA Relief

EGYPTIAN MILITARY MISSION IN U.S.

GRAIN ARRIVES IN GERMANY

ITALY TAKES OVER

NO CHANGE IN FRENCH POLICY

I.R.O.'s MEMBERSHIP GROWS STEADILY

ZIONIST COUNCIL

AFTER MIDNIGHT

Hatikvah (Tradewinds)

"Boys, don't go getting involved in any of them foreign wars in the Middle East."
—Farewell remark of a Chesapeake Bay pilot to American volunteer crewmen of the Aliyah Bet ship Hatikvah as they sailed from Baltimore.

An American volunteer, a sailor known as Sonny, walked with a pronounced limp up the gangway to the Empire Lifeguard, a British prison ship about to depart from Cyprus. The cause of his limp was a bomb detonator. Concealed in his anus, the pencil-shaped bomb part made a normal gait painfully difficult.

It was July 1947, and the American was about to leave Cyprus after more than two months of internment by the British. With him were Max, Ketzelleh, and Greenie, three of his American volunteer shipmates from the captured Aliyah Bet vessel Hatikvah. They also carried elements of a bomb, which they had prepared under Haganah supervision in the internment camp, using materials smuggled into Cyprus by the Haganah.

The Hatikvah crew had arrived in Cyprus in May, also aboard a British prison ship. When the British captured the Hatikvah and transported her passengers to Cyprus, the American crew members had eluded arrest by pretending to be refugees and using false names. Now, the Americans were being spirited out of Cyprus. The Haganah arranged their release by including them in a shipment of refugees entering Palestine under the monthly Jewish immigration quota allowed by the British.

The Empire Lifeguard sailed for Palestine with the Hatikvah crew aboard. When she arrived at Haifa, the passengers filed off the prison ship and got on buses to be driven to a British transfer camp. The Americans left the bomb aboard the Empire Lifeguard, hidden in a deep hold.

As the Empire Lifeguard sat in the heavily guarded Haifa port on the morning of July 23, 1947, with the transfer buses still waiting to pull out of their parking area, the bomb exploded below the waterline. Water poured into the hole made by the explosion, and the Empire Lifeguard began to settle slowly in the harbor.

The Hatikvah crew members who had carried out the bombing sat in their bus seats and observed the commotion. Later that day, in the British camp at Athlit, they learned that the ship had sunk in the harbor.

* * *

The voyage of the Hatikvah began half a year earlier, in Miami, Florida.

Her name was the Tradewinds in February 1947 when members of her volunteer crew arrived in Miami and took a disbelieving look at the grey hulk they were to sail across the Atlantic.

Not designed for such a voyage, and much the worse for wear, the Canadian-built Tradewinds was a former icebreaker on the St. Lawrence River. Her name had once been the Gresham. In World War II she served as a Coast Guard cutter, patrolling the Atlantic coast against submarines. The captain, a non-Jew hired to take the Tradewinds to Europe, was also in for a surprise: He had expected a fully professional crew, not the motley group awaiting him in Miami. Some were qualified as professional mariners, and some were Navy veterans who at least had been to sea, but others had no knowledge of shipboard routines and would have to learn their jobs at sea. Crew members who understood something about ships were dubious about the condition of the Tradewinds, but, after reminding themselves why they were there, they told one another: "The hell with it; let's go."

The Tradewinds sailed north from Miami, running into bad weather and mechanical trouble en route. Her evaporators failed, and she put into port at Charleston, where crew members showered in turns at the local YMCA to avoid calling attention to the large number of Jews suddenly inhabiting the Young Men's Christian Association. The stop at Charleston brought an unscheduled day of hard work and repair. It was not an auspicious beginning for a vessel intended to cross the Atlantic.

At Baltimore, where the Tradewinds next put into port, to prepare for her Atlantic crossing, the volunteers caught a glimpse of another future Aliyah Bet ship, the excursion liner President Warfield, soon to be the Exodus 1947. The Warfield sailed from her snow-covered Baltimore pier on February 25, 1947, and the next day ran into a gale that nearly caused her to sink off Cape Hatteras; she succeeded in returning to Norfolk for repairs.

More volunteers joined the Tradewinds in Baltimore, and the crew took aboard supplies such as canned food and boxes of women's sanitary napkins to be delivered in Europe for Jewish refugees. A former Navy officer was assigned to load the hold, a job he knew nothing about. He drew a map of the hold and set about arranging the boxes so the load would not shift at sea. At night, some of the volunteers explored the bars near Baltimore's waterfront. One night, although they had been warned to be discreet and avoid any activity that could compromise the secrecy of their voyage, four volunteers exchanged sharp words in a bar with a group of local youths. One insult led to another, and the volunteers accepted a challenge to step out into the alley and

fight. The confrontation ended abruptly when one of the locals slipped on the way down the stairs and knocked himself unconscious. The volunteers departed in the confusion.

After about a week, the Tradewinds was ready to sail for Europe. A Chesapeake Bay pilot who came aboard to guide the ship to the open sea surmised correctly that the crew was almost entirely Jewish. He mentioned this to one of the ship's officers whom he had heard addressed as "Mr. Carruthers." This was not the real name of the volunteer; he was in fact a rabbi's son, and his pseudonym was part of a running joke with a shipboard buddy. The pilot evidently took "Mr. Carruthers" for a fellow non-Jew and spoke to him confidentially when they were alone on the bridge:

"You know, Mr. Carruthers, I've been noticing things, and I think this must be one of them Jew ships. You can make yourself a bundle of money on this one."

The pilot displayed friendship to the Jews as well; as he departed, he warned crew members:

"Boys, don't go getting involved in any of them foreign wars in the Middle East."

By the time the Tradewinds was in Baltimore, the secret of American participation had become public knowledge, and the local press had been carrying stories about the already-departed President Warfield and other Aliyah Bet ships.

* * *

At sea, attitudes clashed. The hard-bitten irreverence of the veteran sailors offended the volunteers from Zionist youth movements, who in turn seemed tediously partisan and a bit stuffy to the veterans. The veterans played jokes on the landlubbers, telling them that the ship would soon be passing the mail buoy, into which they could deposit letters. The Zionists sat up at night writing letters, and the veterans laughed. Another time, with Zionists in earshot, veterans amused themselves by loudly pretending they would make money for themselves by removing the forecastle head and selling it; the veterans had a further laugh when the Zionists went to an officer to report this impossible scheme. Disagreements over authority arose; youth-group members who thought the ship should be democratically run argued with professional sailors who had been taught that the captain and officers gave the orders. A youth-group member who refused an order was confined under guard, by command of a Jewish volunteer accustomed to the traditional ways of running a ship.

The Tradewinds crossed the Atlantic and stopped briefly in the Azores before reaching her first berth at Lisbon. Waiting for the ship at the dock at Lisbon was the Haganah's local representative, "Captain Diamond," a kibbutznik who was in the Portuguese capital with a Canadian passport and false identity. The Palestinian's real name was Yehoshua Baharav, and not many weeks earlier he had been in Sweden helping arrange the sailing of the American-manned Aliyah Bet ship Haim Arlosoroff. Earlier, he had commanded the

Haganah, the second American-manned Aliyah Bet ship. In Lisbon, his cover story was that he was Captain Diamond of the United Fruit Company. One of his first actions when the Tradewinds arrived was to appropriate a U.S. Navy officer's overcoat worn by one of the American volunteers. The bogus sea captain attired himself in the American officer's coat constantly after that. For the next few weeks, the Tradewinds underwent renovations to prepare her for transporting refugees. Carpenters built sleeping racks, which, according to the cover story, were for bananas. A volunteer was assigned to build toilets on deck; they consisted of a metal trough, with crude seats made from wood slats arranged in a repeating v-pattern.

While the Tradewinds was in Lisbon, the Jewish holiday of Passover took place. The crew held a Seder dinner aboard ship, complete with traditional songs and food. Aside from the crew, the only guests were a Portuguese Jewish banker who was helping them with commercial dealings in town, the banker's wife, and "Captain Diamond," who contributed a healthy singing voice. Traditional holiday foods were prepared by one of the ship's two non-Jewish volunteers, a Polish-American ex-Merchant Mariner who had learned the recipes while working in a Jewish-owned bakery. His fondness for his former employers was one of the reasons he was on the Tradewinds as a volunteer. Fearing that the Portuguese soldier stationed aboard the ship as a guard might become suspicious about the Passover festivities, the crew sent food and wine up to him and explained the commotion by telling him they were celebrating the captain's birthday.

One night, some of the Americans got into a fight with British subjects in a bar. Captain Diamond made arrangements to pay for the damage, but the police launched an investigation. The crew from the Tradewinds had attracted the interest of the police, who said they were on the lookout for Communists and terrorists. Captain Diamond offered an explanation for the presence of the Tradewinds in Lisbon: It was cheaper to refit ships in Portugal.

The police were not persuaded by Captain Diamond's explanation. When the Tradewinds was ready to depart from Lisbon, the head of the secret police came aboard with a group of his men. Captain Diamond tried offering Brazilian cigars and telling about his activities for the United Fruit Company. But the police insisted that he step ashore with them. The Palestinian sensed tension among the crew members watching the confrontation. In Hebrew, which some of the volunteers understood, he instructed the Americans to take the ship out without a pilot, and to send the Portuguese police guards aboard the Tradewinds back to shore in one of her small boats.

Captain Diamond descended to the dock in the company of the police, and the Tradewinds crew hurried to set sail. The anchor could not be pulled up properly because it was fouled in a metal hawser. An

American volunteer grabbed a hacksaw and stood on the anchor to cut the hawser. This risky maneuver succeeded, and the Tradewinds pulled away from the dock.

When the chief of the secret police saw the ship pulling out, he grabbed Captain Diamond so hard that he tore the Palestinian's jacket. Policemen ran up to surround Captain Diamond and began hitting him. As the Tradewinds moved out to sea, Captain Diamond negotiated himself out of his predicament. His goal was to regain his false passport, which the police had seized. To get the passport back, he once again took up his cover story and said his company wanted to send many more ships to Lisbon for work. But first, he said, he needed to return to his office in Paris. The negotiation ended in his being released. (Later that year, when a British-owned fuel company in Portugal refused to sell fuel to two Aliyah Bet ships stopping there, Captain Diamond was able to arrange for fueling by telephoning his old friend, the Portuguese secret police chief, and offering to pay him a fee for taking care of the matter.)

The Tradewinds headed into the Mediterranean, passing Gibraltar at night and docking at Marseilles. There, one of the Americans lent a pair of khaki shorts to a volunteer on the Aliyah Bet ship Geula; 20 years later, at a reunion in the United States, the Tradewinds volunteer met his friend from the Geula and was handed a box containing the borrowed pants. From Marseilles, the Tradewinds went to the nearby harbor of Port de Bouc, where she dropped her cargo and her professional American captain. She also turned over to the Haganah a disaffected sailor who had threatened to betray the Tradewinds to the British. At a farewell dinner, the non-Jewish captain became sentimental and told the volunteers: "On the next trip, I'm going to go all the way with you." One of the American Jewish volunteers with Merchant Marine experience took over as captain.

At Port de Bouc, the Tradewinds picked up a hitchhiker, the Reverend John Stanley Grauel, a Methodist minister who was a volunteer in the crew of the Aliyah Bet ship Exodus. Grauel had gone ashore at Marseilles to acquire a British visa to enter Palestine legally, as a correspondent for a church publication, and the Exodus had gone on without him. The Tradewinds would drop him at its next stop, in Italy, where he could rejoin his ship. Although discomforts were common on the Exodus, which had almost sunk on her first attempt to cross the Atlantic, Grauel was not prepared for the conditions aboard the smaller Tradewinds. One night, Grauel stood at the rail of the Tradewinds and said: "When this is over, I'm going to write a book about it and call it the Via Dolorosa." A volunteer heard Grauel's remark and remembered it for many years, because he disagreed so strongly with it. To the Jewish volunteer, the essence of Aliyah Bet was not a story of hardship and suffering, but rather one of rescue and redemption.

At Portovenere, on the northwest coast of Italy, the Tradewinds tied up alongside the Exodus and received two visitors, Ada Sereni and Avraham Zakkai of the Haganah's Italian organization. Plans were made to embark the Tradewinds' passengers for the journey to Palestine.

The passengers boarded on two separate nights on the Italian Riviera. At Bogliasco, the Tradewinds anchored in a cove and the refugees came out to her on rubber rafts in carefully maintained silence. An American volunteer felt as if he were watching a movie with the sound track turned off. The second night, at another secluded anchorage at the mouth of the Magre River, the passengers came to the Tradewinds in small boats.

Seasickness began almost immediately after the Tradewinds started for Palestine with more than 1,400 passengers. As in other Aliyah Bet voyages, the refugees were kept below decks and took turns going above for fresh air in small groups. American crew members brewed strong tea which they gave to the passengers as a tonic for seasickness. One volunteer distributed vitamin pills of various colors, and this remedy seemed to help, too.

When the weather improved, children visited the bridge, where they sang songs and accepted chewing gum from the Americans. One of the Americans with officer's status had a cabin with a washbasin; women with babies were organized in shifts to bathe their infants in the basin.

After more than a week at sea, an airplane with British markings buzzed the

Hatikvah (Tradewinds)

Tradewinds twice and flew off. As soon as the aircraft was gone, the Tradewinds' crew tore down whatever parts of the superstructure they could dismantle, in an effort to change the appearance of the ship.

Not long after that, British warships began to appear. With nothing further to be gained from trying to conceal the identity of the Tradewinds, the commanders allowed the passengers on deck and prepared the ship to resist capture. Decks were cleared of lifeboats, and the davits from which the lifeboats had been suspended were raised and tied to the smokestacks. Fire axes were thrown overboard. The commanders did not want any defenders of the Tradewinds to provoke British fire. The aim was to offer resistance without giving cause for anyone's being killed.

The refugee ship proclaimed her new identity. Earlier in the voyage she had taken the name Balfour, after the British Foreign Minister whose 1917 proclamation promised a Jewish national home in Palestine; one of the two babies born aboard ship was given the name David Balfour Friedman. Now the Aliyah Bet vessel took yet another name, Hatikvah, for her confrontation with the Royal Navy. Her name, which is also the title of the Jewish national hymn, in Hebrew means "the hope."

A British destroyer pulled alongside and hailed the Hatikvah. A voice from the destroyer conveyed the standard message Aliyah Bet ships had been receiving: "Your voyage is illegal, your ship is unseaworthy. In the name of humanity, surrender."

The British destroyer asked the Hatikvah's captain to identify himself. Commanders on the Hatikvah brought a boy of about 10 to the bridge, put a cap on his head, and instructed him to say in English: "I am the captain."

The British destroyer made a sharp turn, creating waves which rocked the Hatikvah. Passengers on deck panicked for a moment and began running to one side of the ship. Their movement, which could have capsized the small vessel, was halted by a command for everyone to sit down.

The destroyer wheeled and approached the Hatikvah in an attempt to board her. The Americans dropped a lifeboat davit, striking the British ship. She veered away. On the next pass, British marines in battle gear fought their way aboard the Hatikvah. Canned goods hurled by the defenders flew through the air. Then came tear gas, fired by the British. Hand-to-hand fighting followed as the boarders began taking over the deck and heading for the bridge. Shots were fired in the air. The defenders tried to cut the steering apparatus from the wheelhouse so that the ship could be steered from the engineroom; the plan failed when the British shot tear gas into the engineroom, forcing the Americans to come out.

The victory inevitably went to the British. The Hatikvah was towed into Haifa harbor on Saturday evening, May 17, 1947. Although there had been spirited fighting, press reports about the capture of the Hatikvah quoted refugees as saying they had offered little resistance because so many children and pregnant women were aboard. News stories noted that on the funnel was painted a Star of David and "Eretz 1947." Below this Hebrew reference to the Land of Israel appeared a shamrock and "Eire 1922;" an American volunteer of Irish-Catholic extraction had drawn this connection between the Zionists' and Irish nationalists' struggles for independence from the British. During the journey, an artist among the refugees had drawn sketches of the American crew members; now, to avoid identification of the volunteers by the British, his work had to be destroyed. The refugee continued to use his skills, as a forger for the Haganah in Cyprus, and later as a successful artist in Israel.

Most of the 27 Americans were taken to Cyprus among the refugees. Six Americans were arrested at Haifa. One American went free by swimming ashore and claiming to be his brother, who was studying at the Technion Institute in Haifa; representatives of the school vouched for him. A British patrol boat picked up an American who tried to escape by swimming from the Hatikvah to the wreck of the Aliyah Bet ship Haim Arlosoroff on the Bat Galim reefs. After trying unsuccessfully to determine if he spoke English, the British placed him in the hold of a Cyprus-bound ship; there, a woman refugee gave him dry clothing, and he vanished into the crowd and joined his shipmates in Cyprus.

The Americans stayed 14 weeks in Cyprus. Originally, the plan was for the Americans to disperse two-by-two into larger groups of refugees, but this did not happen. The British allowed the Jews in Cyprus to organize themselves, and each political movement made its own living arrangements. Most of the Americans wound up in their own little colony. They lived together and cooked together. Some learned Irish revolutionary songs from the volunteer who had painted the shamrock on the Hatikvah's smokestack. Morale was high in the camps, where 16,000 Jews then lived; the Haganah was evident throughout the camps, and the Jews had a sense that they were on their way to Palestine. The story of the volunteers spread among the refugees, many of whom let the Americans know they admired them for what they had done. One American met his future wife in the Cyprus camps. Shipmates taught English and presented lectures on American Jewish life. One night a wedding took place; a singer entertained, making up lyrics about the wedding guests, and the Haganah provided one-half orange for each guest.

The Haganah decided to dig an escape tunnel. Three Americans took part in this project. Working with two refugees and a Palestinian commander, they started the excavation in the floor of a large tent at the edge of the camp. Their goal was a clump of trees some 150 feet away, beyond the fence. For a groundbreaking ceremony, the Palestinian poured wine onto the earth floor and attacked it with a pickaxe. They dug a shaft about 10 feet deep and then tunneled toward the fence. Every night, they dug inside their tent, using water from the camp supply to moisten the soil and hold down the dust. After the excavated soil piled high in the tent, they began removing the excess earth in gunnysacks and dumping it into the camp's latrines. After about two weeks, the tunnel was about 30 feet long and extended beyond the fence. At that point, the American volunteers were given a new assignment. Others completed the tunnel, which the Haganah later used for escapes.

The new task of the American tunnel-diggers was to prepare a bomb capable of sinking a British prison ship. The bomb would have to be smuggled aboard ship and detonated at the proper time. Cyprus was a logical base for such an operation, since British prison ships called there frequently to pick up refugees permitted to enter Palestine under the quota maintained by the British. In each shipment of refugees leaving Cyprus for Palestine were individuals designated by the Haganah. For them to bring a bomb aboard would not be easy, but it could be done.

To make the bomb, the Haganah sent explosives (gelignite, detonators, and other materials) to Cyprus. One night, the Americans cut the barbed wire and slipped out to pick up the materials for the bomb. British guards spotted the Americans but failed to catch them. The next day, the British authorities announced harsh measures would be taken until the escapees turned themselves in. Haganah operatives composed a note saying they had tired of being cooped up and had gone into town for some fun. They enclosed some Cypriot currency and signed false names to the note. Nothing further was heard about the incident, and the Hatikvah crewmen began readying their bomb in a section of the camp controlled by the Haganah.

A large part of the job was preparing the gelignite explosive for smuggling onto the British prison ship. First, the gelignite had to be combined with an oily substance and kneaded. Then it had to be concealed for carrying aboard ship. The volunteers tried hiding it inside bars of soap, but this was unsatisfactory. The soap showed the marks of tampering where plugs had been cut from the bar. Shaving-cream tubes provided an answer. The shaving cream could be removed and the gelignite inserted, followed by a final portion of shaving cream to conceal the insertion.

The first stage of the Exodus affair was the occasion that triggered the bomb. On July 18, 1947, the British captured the American refugee vessel Exodus after a battle in which three Jews were killed and scores were injured. Instead of transporting her 4,515 passengers to Cyprus, the British decided to send them back to Europe. This new policy became apparent within a few days, after the prison ships bearing the refugees failed to turn up at Cyprus.

On July 22, with the Exodus passengers on the high seas and heading for Port de Bouc, France, the prison ship Empire Lifeguard was at Cyprus taking on immigrants for Palestine. Among the passengers boarding the prison ship were American sailors from the Hatikvah and a Palestinian leader with their unassembled bomb.

When the order was given to carry out

the bombing, the effort invested in putting a final covering of shaving cream into the gelignite tubes proved its worth. A British soldier squeezed a tube to check its contents. Out came a dab of shaving cream, and the tube passed inspection. But substantial amounts of gelignite had to be carried onto the Empire Lifeguard in larger packages. A nurse escorting an infirm patient carried a package of about five pounds of explosive in her handbag and passed it to one of the American volunteer sailors as he boarded the ship. A British officer wanted to examine the nurse's package, but a superior officer countermanded this decision. A more typical package was a rubber sack, strapped to the small of a man's back and hidden beneath his shirt. A number of such packages were brought aboard.

The interior of the prison ship consisted of large wire cages. The first American member of the bomb crew to board feared that the others would be shunted into separate compartments. He enlisted the help of women in his cage, pointing the Americans out to them. The women called out to the men, pretending that the Americans were their husbands, and the guards permitted them to enter together. When the group had assembled, an American handed a hacksaw to their Palestinian commander, who asked everyone in the cage to start singing.

As the passengers sang loudly, the Palestinian sawed the lock from a hatchcover in the floor of their cage. Opening the cover, he saw a light. He shut the hatch instantly and handed a knife to one of the Americans, instructing him to kill any sailor they found below. But when they descended into the hatch, it was empty. They assembled the bomb, minus its detonator, and returned to their cage for the overnight trip to Palestine.

Two hours before they were due in Haifa, the Palestinian inserted the detonator, which had its own timer to determine the precise moment at which the bomb would explode. All seemed in order. But, as the Empire Lifeguard approached Haifa, the ship's propeller stopped. Then, the anchor was lowered. The passengers trapped in the cage above the soon-to-explode bomb turned to the Palestinian. Wouldn't it be a good idea to remove the detonator? He explained:

"They taught me how to put it on. They didn't tell me how to take it off."

The prisoners thought about notifying the British that a bomb was aboard. But, if they did that, all chance of sinking the ship would be lost. After what seemed an eternity, but was probably only about 10 minutes, the Empire Lifeguard pulled up her anchor and started moving. She entered Haifa harbor.

It was the morning of July 23, only five days after the British had brought the battered Exodus into Haifa. As the Empire Lifeguard was unloading the last of its passengers, a dull boom was heard and the ship shuddered. The passengers continued to file ashore. A British officer, remembering the nurse at Cyprus with the suspicious handbag, shouted, "That girl with the

Hatikvah crew members in Cyprus. From left: Hugh McDonald, Sam Gordon, Harold Katz, Joe Gilden, Murray Greenfield

bag." It was too late to save the prison ship. Slowly, the Empire Lifeguard sank to the bottom of Haifa harbor. The British never caught the bombers.

The bombing was remembered as the most successful attack on a British vessel during Aliyah Bet. It was also costly. After the sinking of the Empire Lifeguard, the British imposed on the Jewish Agency a penalty in money for transporting Aliyah Bet passengers to Cyprus.

* * *

Before being released in Palestine, the Americans who returned from Cyprus were sent to the British transfer camp at Athlit. A delegation of American Jewish leaders visited Athlit to observe conditions for the prisoners at the camp. Judith Epstein, who served two terms as president of Hadassah, a women's Zionist organization, recognized one of the American volunteers and addressed him by name:

"Harold Katz, what are you doing behind barbed wire?"

Paraphrasing Henry David Thoreau's famed comment to Ralph Waldo Emerson when Thoreau went to jail on a matter of principle, the volunteer answered with a question:

"Mrs. Epstein, what are you doing not behind barbed wire?"

When the volunteers were released from Athlit, they made their way to Mossad headquarters in Haifa. Each volunteer was provided with new clothing, purchased at a local store. One of the Hatikvah sailors had prominent tattoos on his forearms and was embarrassed to wear the short-sleeved shirt ordinarily included in the clothing ration. This volunteer was not Jewish, and he was sensitive to the religious tradition that prohibited Jews from wearing tattoos. After discussion of the volunteer's problem, a sympathetic Haganah official stretched the rules and authorized the purchase of a shirt with long sleeves. Months later, higher levels in the Haganah bureaucracy were still raising questions about the extra expenditure for long sleeves.

* * *

After Israel became independent in May 1948, the Haganah reclaimed the Aliyah Bet ships interned by the British in Haifa harbor. The Hatikvah joined the new Israel Navy, but only briefly. Her first sea trials convinced naval officials that the old vessel had a doubtful future as a warship. Next, she was evaluated for use as a passenger carrier. Again, the results were negative, and the Hatikvah went the way of most old vessels: She was sold for scrap.

Edition
JERUSALEM
SUNDAY, JULY 20, 1947

POST

PRICE 20 MILS
VOL. XXII. No. 6161

PROTEST STRIKE AGAINST DEPORTATIONS TODAY

3 REFUGEES DEAD: 4,500 SENT FROM HAIFA

Palestine Post Staff

The Jews of Palestine will down tools at 4 o'clock today in protest against the deportation of the 4,500 refugees who arrived on Friday on board the s.s Exodus 1947 (formerly the "President Warfield") and against the killing of three of the refugees. The funeral of the victims of this fiercest battle so far between the Navy and a Hagana ship will be held in Haifa this afternoon.

DEAD AND WOUNDED

Those who lost their lives in trying to prevent the Exodus 1947 from being boarded by a naval party are:

Hirsch Yacubovitch, 16, from Poland.

Mordecai Baumstein, 23, from a D.P. camp in Germany.

William Bernstein, 23, from San Francisco. He was born in New Jersey, has a mother in Miami and a brother in San Francisco. Was chief mate on the vessel.

The casualties now in Government Hospital:

Arieh Birnbaum, 16, abdominal wound. His wife has been allowed to remain with him.

Moses Engelman, 20, abdominal wounds.

Ernst Weiss 31, burns.

Nathan Berkowich, 23, ill.

William Millman, 31, bullet wound in jaw. Millman comes from Chelsea, Mass., and was helmsman of the boat.

It was officially stated that three sailors of the boarding party were injured in the struggle that occurred in the early hours of Friday morning off the southern coast of Palestine. Several of the destroyers were also damaged when the Exodus 1947 "took evasive action."

EXPECTED IN CYPRUS THIS MORNING

Two members of the United Nations Committee, the Chairman and the Yugoslav Delegate, witnessed the transhipment of the refugees to three deportation ships in Haifa Harbour on Friday. Although the first of these ships sailed on Friday evening before 9 o'clock, it had not arrived in Cyprus last night, more than 24 hours later. The P.B.S. in its noon bulletin yesterday, reported that the deportation ships had sailed for Cyprus, but the Public Information Office announcement yesterday contained no mention of their destination, and inquiries late last night could elicit no information. An official message from Cyprus last night stated that the three deportation ships were expected there at five o'clock this morning.

STOPPAGE OF WORK FOR FUNERAL

Palestine Post Staff

A countrywide stoppage of work will be observed by the entire Jewish community from four o'clock today in memory of the refugees killed on the "Exodus 1947" and as a protest against the deportation of the immigrants. There will be mass protest meetings in towns and villages.

In Tel Aviv and Rehovot there was a general cessation of work on Friday.

The Haifa Jewish community has decided to begin its strike at 2.30 and half-an-hour later Mrs. Goldie Myerson, of the Jewish Agency Executive, will address a public meeting in Herzl Street. Buses will leave the meeting with mourners for the funeral of the three refugees. The cortege will leave from the Government Hospital.

Although places of work generally will close down at four o'clock, urban transport will be resumed at seven o'clock, and restaurants will be open from 7 to 9 p.m. All places of entertainment will remain shut.

During the Tel Aviv stoppage on Friday morning, there was a tense moment when British armoured cars found themselves bottled up in the traffic standstill in Rehov Allenby, but they managed to weave their way out.

2 Dead, 5 Hurt in Two Days

HAIFA, Saturday.—One British constable was shot dead and another constable as well as a Jewish passer-by seriously wounded in Hehalutz Street, Hadar Hacarmel, at 7.00 this evening by three unknown assailants. Two of the three men, described by an eye-witness as "European-looking," escaped on foot in the direction of Wadi Salib.

A Red Shield ambulance took the two wounded men to the Rothschild Hospital, where their condition is reported to be serious. The civilian is Jack Gruendorf, a student of the Technical College here. The two constables were in mufti.

Early on Friday morning, a British soldier was killed and three others seriously injured when a mine was detonated beneath a military car on the Kfar Bilu-Ramle Road, near Kfar Bilu. The vehicle was thrown into a ditch some 50 metres away, and was completely destroyed. A Palestine Electric Corporation transformer in the vicinity was hit by the explosion, causing a break in the electric current and the water supply at Kfar Bilu.

A house-to-house search of part of the village was made and inhabitants screened shortly after the attack.

Jerusalem Attacks — Page 2

British Mediation Fails

WAR THREATENS BETWEEN INDONESIANS AND DUTCH

BATAVIA, Saturday, (Reuter).—Following the crisis in the Dutch-Indonesian negotiations which are understood to have broken down on the question of military and police functions in the newly created United States of Indonesia, the position has become so precarious that M. Gani, the Vice-Premier of the Republic, today made an urgent appeal for the preservation of peace in Indonesia.

"The lights must not go out this week-end," he said. It was unthinkable that the world should allow a nation like the Dutch — who had themselves been oppressed by Hitler—to use force to settle what he called the "remaining minor differences in Indonesia".

Last night, the Indonesian Republican Government, in another "last minute" bid for peace with the Dutch, offered to order the immediate ending of hostilities and all unfriendly action, provided the Dutch took all possible steps to restore confidence in the Republican territory.

All British diplomatic attempts to induce the Indonesians to issue a cease fire order by mid-day today, have failed.

The members of the Second Chamber of the Dutch Parliament have been called for an emergency meeting on Wednesday, to consider the "most serious situation in Indonesia".

Nehru Instructs Sir Abdur

WASHINGTON, Saturday. — Pandit Jawaharlal Nehru, the Vice-President of the Indian Government, cabled Mr. Emanuel Celler, Democratic Congressman, that Sir Abdur Rahman, the Indian representative of UNSCOP, had been instructed to serve with "complete impartiality."

Mr. Celler had cabled Mr. Nehru that Sir Abdur had shown "prejudice and hostility almost to the point of insult to the Jewish point of view," and Pandit Nehru replied: "Our instructions to Sir Abdur emphasized the quasi-judicial character of the inquiry and laid special stress on complete impartiality. I am communicating a copy of your telegram to him."

(Reuter & UP)

UNSCOP To Beirut Today

Palestine Post Staff

After spending five weeks in Palestine, the members of the United Nations Special Committee will leave by road for Beirut today to hear the evidence of the Arab States. Iraq, Egypt, Saudi Arabia, Syria and the Lebanon have all accepted the UNSCOP invitation to give evidence but, despite the intervention of the other Arab States, the Trans-Jordan Government has refused to give evidence unless the Committee goes to Amman.

Should the attempts of the Arab States to alter this situation prove of no avail the Committee, it is understood, will discuss visiting Amman while in session at Beirut.

Yesterday morning the Committee met in private at the Y.M.C.A. and heard—at their request—representatives of the Palestine Government. The Government spokesmen headed by Sir Henry Gurney, the Chief Secretary, are reported to have answered questions on the statements made to the Committee during the public hearings, and to have elaborated on a supplementary memorandum submitted by the Government. The meeting ended about 1 o'clock.

From Jerusalem today the Committee will travel by way of Nablus, Jenin, Acre and Ras el Nakura, and the journey will take about six hours. The party will be met at the Acre crossroads by Mr. R.J.P. Thorne-Thorne, the Galilee District Commissioner, who will escort them to the frontier where they will be greeted by Mr. Khorchid, of the Lebanese Department of Foreign Affairs.

The convoy of cars will leave Kadimah House at 1 o'clock.

Leaving at 1 O'clock

The Committee will start its meetings on Monday at Sofar, in the hills overlooking Beirut.

Syd. Hamid Franjieh, the Lebanese Foreign Minister, held a preparatory meeting yesterday with the Arab States' Ministers to the Lebanon.

The U.N. Headquarters at Lake Success ordered top representatives of UNSCOP to "insist" that the Lebanese Government admit to their territory a correspondent travelling with the Committee.

This action was taken after a sharp note from the Acting Secretary General, Mr. Adrian Pelt, had secured the admission of six representatives of Palestinian newspapers during UNSCOP's interviews with Arab officials at Beirut.

The seventh correspondent, Gerold Frank of the O.N.A. and "New York Post," is still refused entry.

The Assistant Secretary General's cable to Dr. Victor Hoo said, "Please convey to the Government of Lebanon my strong representations to the effect that all correspondents duly accredited with UNSCOP should be given full facilities for following and reporting on the Commission's work."

A spokesman of the U.N. Secretariat at Lake Success said that although the protest from the Palestine Journalists Association against the Lebanese action had not been officially received by the U.N., the position was that all correspondents accredited with U.N. should be allowed to cover the activities of the group wherever it went. He cited the precedent of the Balkan investigation commission. He said it was preferable that the matter should be handled on the spot by the UNSCOP Secretariat.

AMERICAN TELLS STORY OF FIGHT WITH NAVY

Palestine Post Reporter

HAIFA, Saturday — Three lives was the toll paid at the gates of Palestine by the refugees of "Exodus 1947"—but still the refugees did not enter.

Carrying 4,500 souls the largest number to set out together, the vessel was engaged by destroyers in a battle whose echo is still reverberating in the press and wireless of the world.

In addition to the killed, 28 immigrants were taken to hospital with injuries, and three British sailors were injured when the ship was boarded.

For months the arrival of these ships had become almost routine. Then there was a lull of seven weeks, with restrictions tightening up throughout Europe, at Britain's insistent request. On Thursday night the news of the imminent arrival of "Exodus 1947" was broadcast from the ship itself, and yesterday morning there was an official report of its capture near Rafah, and an account of the boarding, which, it was stated, met strong resistance, with the "illegal immigrants using tear smoke, fireworks, smoke bombs, steam jets, oil fuel and various missiles."

"We had no tear gas, no fireworks. We used steam jets, oil fuel, potatoes and kosher corn beef! The British had clubs, tear gas and pistols."

This denial came from Rev. John Stanley Grauer, accredited correspondent of the American paper, the Churchman, and member of the American Christian Palestine Committee, who sailed together with the DP's from Europe, and who told the press here what he had seen.

The ship, built in Baltimore in 1928 for inland water traffic, named the President Warfield, in honour of the president of its shipping line, and displacing 1,814 tons, left for Europe seven months ago, to carry refugees to Palestine. It was driven back by a hurricane had to be refitted, and then sailed again. "We were kicked from pillar to post, knocked about, spied on by the British and Italians." The Warfield finally loaded at Port Bette on the French coast nine days ago. "Everything was done in a legal manner," Mr. Grauer said. "When the ship was loaded the French refused to let us leave, but one night the crew took matters into their own hands and departed from a harbour thought impossible to get out of without tugs.

Died in Childbirth

"The first seven days were comparatively quiet. We had food and water, the people were in high spirits. Then the seas got rough and many were sick. A woman (Polya Abramovitch) died giving birth. She was buried at sea with the crew as guard of honour. The baby, one of two born during the voyage, is well.

"The British authorities have the Hebrew original of what was said at the funeral, but I think I remember it quite well. It was something like this:

"We are burying today, without marker, one more Jew to be added to the list of those millions who have died in these recent years. We are reminded of the First Exodus when countless numbers of Jews were also buried in nameless graves. We go again to our land. If there can be any compensation for the death of this woman it is that we here consecrate ourselves and gain courage for those tasks yet ahead. The way of Aliyah Bet is a hard one. It is, we believe, the only way."

"After days spent in preparation we had planned to beach the ship at seven in the morning (Friday)." At three o'clock, still a number of miles outside the territorial waters the British challenged them, Mr Grauer said, telling them that they were inside the territorial limits. "We turned west and travelled two miles, so that we were then surely out, he added. "Two destroyers came alongside and squeezed the ship between them. British sailors boarded, and at the first assault the bridge was taken.

After a number of the people on board had been injured there was a feeling that further resistance meant death, and the ship gave in. Its navigation, however, was left in the hands of the crew, who brought the Exodus 1947 to Haifa.

Three of the American crew were arrested. The chief mate, William Bernstein (who died last night) was taken to hospital with a fracture of the left temple, caused by a blow with a club. The helmsman, William Millman, was also brought to hospital, with a bullet wound in his jaw. The rest of the crew mingled with the refugees, Rev. Grauer said. He himself was taken into custody, but released, after all his papers and documents were confiscated.

A crowd of young Arabs had gathered outside the window of the Savoy, watching the blond, sunburned, strong-looking young man in the dirty khaki wool shirt, with a soiled American flag worn as a band around his arm, who was so earnestly talking.

Another passenger said today that he judged the Exodus 1947 was boarded 20 miles off the coast and 18 miles outside the territorial waters. The destroyer R 38 struck the ship first, and four men jumped on deck, beginning to fire. Among the refugees there was only one revolver, and that was kept in the hold, but a pistol taken away from a British sailor was

(Continued on Page Two)

Senators Indict British Govt.

WASHINGTON, Saturday (PTA). — Senator Warren Magnuson (Democrat), together with eight other Senators of both parties has introduced a resolution into the Senate directing the Secretary of State to request the British Government to end the emergency regulations in Palestine and restore a civilian administration and civil rights.

This is identical with a resolution introduced in the House of Representatives last week by Mr. Andrew Sommers.

"For too long have the British been permitted to believe that we are not serious in regard to our commitments and rights in Palestine," Senator Wayne Morse of Oregon, one of the co-sponsors of the Senate resolution, declared. "The British have been comforting themselves with the notion that we Americans were merely making sentimental statements, possibly motivated by domestic politics," he added.

Senator James Murray of Montana said the time had come "to quit dilly-dallying on the subject of Palestine and pretending it is a British province and a British problem." It was time for some affirmative and constructive action to be taken by the U.S.

Together with the House resolution, Representative Kenneth B. Keating of New York, a Republican, introduced for insertion in the Congressional Record a brief called "The Legal View of the Palestine Question," as a guide to the resolution which he and 28 other representatives have introduced.

SIX BURMESE OFFICIALS SHOT

LONDON, Saturday (Reuter). — Six leading members of the Burma Government were killed and two wounded in Rangoon today, when a gang burst into the Council Chamber and sprayed the meeting of the Executive Council with bullets.

Details of this "murderous attack" came through to the Burma office in London tonight from the Governor of Burma, Sir Hubert Rance, after Rangoon had been cut off from communication with the rest of the world for some hours.

Sir Hubert stated that while the executive council was in session, a jeep drew up to the main entrance. Five men, armed with sten guns and rifles, went straight to the council chamber.

A guard outside the door was shot and wounded. The three men then entered the council chamber and fired their sten guns. "They then made good their escape in the jeep," Sir Hubert stated.

The following Ministers were killed:— Mr. U. Aung San, Deputy Chairman of the Council; Mr. U. Ba Win, Member for Commerce and Supplies; Mr. Abdul Razak, Member for Education and Planning; Mr. Mahn Ba Kaing, Member for Industry and Labour; Mr. Thakin Mya, Member for Finance; Mr. Ohn Maung, Deputy-Secretary of Transport and Communications.

Clark Supports Stratton Bill

WASHINGTON, Saturday (PTA). — The hearings of testimony on the Stratton Bill for the admission of 400,000 D.P.'s into the U.S. during the next four years, has ended with the Attorney General, Mr. Tom Clark, strongly supporting practically every person who appeared in favour of the Bill.

He spoke on the basis of actual experience and first-hand acquaintance with the subject, while most of the opposition witnesses had based their testimony on a long-standing prejudice against immigration itself. He urged the Committee to bear such prejudices in mind in determining the weight which should be given to their testimony.

CONFERENCE TO FIGHT ANTI-SEMITISM

LONDON, Saturday (Reuter). — In a move to fight the "rising wave of anti-Semitism in the liberated countries," the British Council of Christians and Jews, and the U.S. National Conference of Christians and Jews, have decided to organize an international conference at Seelisberg, on Lake Lucerne, Switzerland, from July 30 to August 5.

Participants in the conference will include government officials and religious leaders from a large number of countries, including university professors from France, Italy, Switzerland, Austria, Czechoslovakia, Germany, Britain and the U.S.

Besides its special subject of anti-Semitism, the conference will set up an International Council of Christians and Jews, and a European Secretariat, which will work from Paris and closely cooperate with UNESCO.

THREE PLAGUE CASES IN AFFULA

AFFULA, Saturday. — Three cases of plague were discovered here today and the men affected taken to the Government Hospital in Haifa.

One of the men had been ill for five days and had been cared for in the local hospital here, while the other two fell ill yesterday. All three of them were employed in the "Emek" Flour Mill here.

A special inoculation tent has been set up in the village by the Senior Medical Officer.

EXODUS 1947 TOP NEWS IN LONDON

By JON KIMCHE

LONDON, Saturday. — The arrival of the "Exodus 1947" in Palestine waters eclipsed all other news here yesterday afternoon. The B.B.C. and the evening papers featured the battle and the arrival as top news.

The "Evening Standard" ran a banner headline across the front page reading "Five destroyers intercept biggest ever shipload of Palestine immigrants. Gas battle in Exodus ship. 4,500 people on board. Casualties both sides. Destroyers damaged."

First Official Reaction

The first official reaction came later in the evening when a Foreign Office spokesman gave detailed information to diplomatic correspondents about the purchase of the President Warfield and her movements since she left the U.S.

This morning the London press and the B.B.C. devote great attention to the arrival and give full and fair accounts of the encounter, but the emphasis is divided.

The "Daily Herald" describes how the ship arrived and how an "amazing dossier" of the ship's history had reached London. It described how the President Warfield "had been bought by a vast smuggling ring to which money is no object," under the heading: "Jew-smuggling code secret out".

But most of the other papers concentrate on the actual events off Palestine.

Banana Code

The "Graphic," "Telegraph," and "Times" similarly feature the battle. The "Worker" and the "Guardian" play up the struggle, but the "Mail" heads the story "Road to Gehenna. Hell-ship captain arrested." The "Express" devotes only two inches, headed "Banana code disclosed," to the statement that Mr. Bevin is expected to ask several European countries once more to tighten security measures against refugees travelling to Palestine. Fresh formal representations are not expected to be made.

The arrival of so large a number of Jews while UNSCOP is still in the country has, however, been received with mixed feeling in Government quarters. While the Foreign Office and the Admiralty have taken full steps to prevent this traffic, some members of the Government are believed to welcome this incident as demonstrating more than any evidence to the U.N. Committee Britain's problem over illegal immigration.

AGENCY CHARGES "CRUELTY"

A statement was issued by a spokesman of the Jewish Agency for Palestine last night as follows:

The freedom-loving peoples of the world must share the shock and revulsion of the Jewish people over the attack launched against the Haganah ship "Exodus 1947" and its cargo of human misery. It is an inglorious exploit which will add no lustre to the annals of the British Navy.

The Mandatory has now extended enforcement of the illegal White Paper to the high seas. To enforce this policy, the Mandatory is driven to utter disregard for human life and freedom.

The ramming of the ship was a heedless and wanton act, fraught with grave peril for the 4,500 refugees aboard, most of whom were women and children. The armed attack was an act of senseless cruelty. It took a toll of three lives and more than forty maimed and wounded.

None but those who witnessed the unloading of the ship and the transfer of its passengers to Cyprus-bound steamers can comprehend the stark tragedy of the last 36 hours. Into those hours were compressed twenty centuries of Jewish homelessness and disaster.

Here were men and women and children who had managed to survive Hitler persecution, who had waited for the democracies to grant them life and liberation, who had travelled the long and painful road to the Promised Land. But they were allowed to remain only long enough to permit soldiers to search their knapsacks.

Today, those who came on Exodus 1947 are once again in exile. But they will not, they must not, long remain so. To bring them and their hundreds of thousands of brothers and sisters to their rightful homeland, the Yishuv will strain every resource, will dedicate its entire strength.

Today, the Yishuv mourns those who fell in a battle to defend their rights as a people. They will be remembered long in Jewish history, they will be remembered by all men who treasure liberty.

DR. WEIZMANN LEAVING TODAY

Dr. and Mrs. Chaim Weizmann are leaving for Switzerland from Haifa this afternoon.

They have been in Palestine for the past five months having arrived here from London on February 8, 1947.

OFFICIAL LOG OF BOARDING, DEATHS

OFFICIAL COMMUNIQUE
No. 191, July 18

In order to remove any doubts which may have been raised by inaccurate broadcasts from the illegal immigrant ship "President Warfield," the following facts are recorded:—

The "President Warfield" arrived in Palestinian waters early on the 18th July, carrying approximately 4,500 Jewish illegal immigrants. In order to avoid being boarded she took violent evasive action which in the ensuing boarding operation resulted in damage to herself as well as to ships of the Royal Navy. Her sides had been planked up and barbed wire had been strung fore and aft. The boarding party met strong resistance backed up by tear smoke, fireworks, smoke bombs, steam jets and various missiles. She also dropped life rafts from a height on to the decks of the naval vessels.

One single shot, and one burst of machine-gun fire were used by one of the naval ships against an immigrant who was threatening to decapitate one of the boarding party with an axe, and another who was about to use a rifle. The shot and the burst both missed, but frightened the men who dropped their weapons. No other fire was used by naval personnel. Some fifty naval personnel in all were used in the boarding party.

The "President Warfield" entered Haifa Port under her own steam on the evening of the 18th. Two illegal immigrants were found to have died from fractured skulls, and a third has since died in hospital from the same cause. Twenty-seven others were admitted to Haifa hospital; some of these persons though not all were suffering from injuries received when the "President Warfield" was boarded. Three naval ratings were injured and admitted to hospital."

INDIAN INDEPENDENCE BECOMES LAW WITH KING'S ASSENT

LONDON, Saturday (Reuter). — The Indian Independence Bill, creating the two Dominions of India and Pakistan, became law yesterday, when the Royal Commission conveyed the King's assent to the Bill in the House of Lords. This ends nearly 200 years of British rule in India.

The ceremony took exactly 15 minutes.

Reports from New Delhi tonight say that the redistribution of the Indian Government portfolios in what amounts to two provisional Governments, one for India and the other for Pakistan, was tonight announced in a communique from the Viceroy's residence.

It said that each Government would deal with its own business and consult the other on matters of common concern. The most important changes in the redistribution of the portfolios are:

India — Pandit Nehru (Congress, Hindu) — External Affairs, Commonwealth Relations and Law.

Mr. Chakravati Rajagopalachari (Congress, Hindu) — Industry, Supply and Finance.

Mr. Jagjivan Ram (Congress, Scheduled Castes) — Labour and Health.

Those retaining their former portfolios in the new India Government include Sardar Vallabhai Patel (Congress, Hindu) Home Affairs, Information and Broadcasting "States Department."

Maulana Abul Kalam Azad (Congress, Moslem) Education and Arts.

Sardar Baldev Singh (Sikh) — Defence.

Pakistan — Liaquat Ali Khan (Moslem League) — Finance, External Affairs, Commonwealth Relations and Defence.

Mr. Chundrigar (Moslem League) — Commerce, Industry and Supply, Works, Mines and Power.

Bevin Sees No Danger to Peace

LONDON, Saturday (Reuter). — Mr. Bevin told a miners' rally today that he saw no danger of another war in this generation. "I sincerely trust that all differences and suspicions may be removed with Soviet Russia and that we, a powerful nation and the central arch of a bridge in international affairs will find a way to unite the U.S. and Russia in the common endeavour for the uplift of humanity as a whole," he told 60,000 miners and their families.

Britain was struggling to plant the seeds of a great peace now and it all depended on the will of the people, he said.

Mr. Bevin declared that he hoped the U.S. would never withdraw from Europe again. He added: "We want to make a crack somewhere in the vicious circle that has the world tied now to get our economies going on the right lines."

Mr. Bevin said that he wanted to see the end of dollar borrowing "because it was unnatural for them and unnatural for us."

U.S. Secretary of War Resigns

WASHINGTON, Saturday (Reuter). — The U.S. Secretary for War, Mr. Robert Patterson, resigned yesterday. He is to be succeeded by Brigadier-General Kenneth Royall, the present Under-Secretary of State for War.

Mr. Patterson gave as the reason for his retirement, which is to take effect on July 30, the imminent merger of the American armed forces, which made him consider his work completed.

"TIGER" ENTERS SIXTH DAY

The "Tiger" area round Nathanya, where two British soldiers were kidnapped last Friday night, today enters upon its sixth day of complete isolation from the rest of the country.

Report on Page 2.

ATTACK ON AGENCY EVIDENCE

By a Political Correspondent

Two new memoranda have been presented to the U.N. Special Committee, one on the political history of Palestine under the British administration, prepared by the British Government, and the other, by the Palestine Government, consisting mainly of notes on some of the evidence given to the Committee by the Jewish Agency.

The first is informative in its presentation, the second largely polemical with phraseology somewhat unusual for a Government publication. The British memorandum, in its 41 pages, surveys political events from the establishment of the administration down to the reference of the issue to the United Nations. While couched in dispassionate terms, it is marred by certain omissions.

Thus, it fails to describe the circumstances which caused the British Cabinet to issue the Balfour Declaration. It makes only cursory reference to the Jewish criticism of Sir John Hope-Simpson's conclusions, and adopts his views that there was practically no room for new Jewish agricultural settlement although three pages later the memorandum itself records the great Jewish agricultural development that occurred after — and in spite of — Hope-Simpson's prophecies. It repeats, without substantiation whatsoever, the myth of Arab landlessness resulting from Jewish settlement.

In a survey which purports to give the political history of Palestine since 1918, it surprisingly omits to mention what conversations were held between the British Government and the Arab States enabling the later to be brought onto the scene.

In the section of the Anglo-American Inquiry Committee, Mr. Bevin's promise to the members to carry out their recommendations, if made unanimously, is left out. So, too, is his recent speech in Parliament in which he gave notice that Britain had no intention of leaving the Middle East. These omissions may be due to the fact that although the statements were made by a Minister of the Crown they were nevertheless not official.

In the parts dealing with settlement it is said that the best land is passing into Jewish hands. But no attempt is made to explain why, if that is correct, the Jews are barred from buying land in the desert of the South.

Historical Summary

The Palestine Government's memorandum in five chapters provides an historical summary of the principal political events since January 1, 1946; notes on statements by Jewish witnesses before the Special Committee; a note on education; a note on the cost of lawlessness in Palestine; and a note on the Jewish Agency's "Political Survey, 1946-47."

The most enlightening chapter is the second. Thus, in reply to Mr. Shertok's statement that "in only 6 per cent of Palestine were the Jews free to buy land," the Palestine Government says that the Jews hold over 15 percent of the cultivable area. "Press censorship is not used to prevent publication of criticism of the Administration," the memorandum claims. Newspaper files tell a different story.

The memorandum's analysis of Government expenditure, with the conclusion that "the Jews receive almost half the benefits of public expenditure," is particularly disingenuous. Included among the Jewish benefits is the expenditure on "police and prisons in excess of what may be regarded as normal." While the memorandum agrees that the benefits to the Arabs preponderate over those to the Jews in agriculture, education, health and social welfare, for example, it points out that the Jews benefit more from, among other Departments, the posts, telegraphs and telephones and broadcasting.

Bearer Bonds

The Government in this memorandum takes credit for the fact that of the recent allocation of £P.1,118,000 of loans out of the Bearer Bond funds, the Jewish local authorities benefited as to 77 per cent. It forgets to mention the fact that the Bonds were taken up by the Jews largely for that express purpose.

In connection with the Jewish Agency's complaint that fuel prices are unnecessarily high in Palestine, the memorandum gives a number of irrelevant figures but does not explain why the price of benzine is not based on the cost here but (as is the case) on the cost at some Atlantic port.

Many more such instances could be given of the Palestine Administration's presentation of information to the United Nations. There is space, however, for only one more which is truly enlightening. In connection of the boycott of Jewish goods by the Arab States the memorandum says:

For these (economic) reasons, and having regard to the political causes which gave rise to the boycott, it has not been considered appropriate to institute any retaliatory measures.

Exodus (President Warfield)

Bill Fry sat at a table at Miller Brothers' Restaurant in Baltimore. He dropped a handful of oysterette crackers into a big bowl of clam chowder and stirred it. He toyed with the soup for a moment but he had no appetite. "Jesus Christ," he thought. "I wonder if I can get that piss-pot across the Atlantic Ocean."

—Leon Uris, Exodus, Book 1, Chapter 27.

"If it stays afloat, I'll get it over there."

—Comment attributed to Captain Vigo Thompson, on seeing the President Warfield for the first time in March, 1947.

The crew who have crossed the Atlantic on this "cockle shell" have shown themselves to possess outstanding courage. Can you imagine it? An angry storm, and the vessel sinks.... You can imagine how great must be their idealism! They risk their lives to help their brothers and sisters! Isn't that an act of true heroism?

—Tuesday, July 15, 1947. Entry in a diary taken from a passenger on the Exodus and translated from the French by the British 317th Airborne Field Security Section, included as confidential Appendix B to the 6th Airborne Division Weekly Intelligence Summary.

Of the 64 vessels that sailed in Aliyah Bet after the defeat of the Nazis, none became more widely known than the Exodus.

But, thanks to a novel by Leon Uris, two ships with the name Exodus exist in people's minds. Israelis who learned in school or from experience about Aliyah Bet know that the Exodus was a heroic little steamer whose 4,515 passengers were forcibly deported to Germany by the British. Others, particularly Americans, know the Exodus as a fictional ship with an entirely different story. Uris' 1957 novel *Exodus* has had untold impact; it has been translated into other languages, including a clandestine Russian translation by a Jew in a Soviet prison. It became a motion picture seen by millions. For countless readers and movie-goers, it has served as an introduction to the story of modern Israel; for many, it is their only knowledge of the subject. The result is that most people who are aware of the Exodus have in mind the fictional vessel. Uris' Exodus succeeded in reaching Palestine with 300 refugee children after a dramatic hunger strike at Cyprus.

The line between fiction and history is further blurred by the fact that Uris included in his book a fictionalized account of the actual Exodus under a different name. Readers of Uris' novel can find this story tucked away in Book I, Chapter 27, where the fictional counterpart of the actual Aliyah Bet vessel Exodus is a Chesapeake Bay excursion boat named the General Stonewall Jackson.

* * *

The story of the real-life Exodus began February 6, 1928, when the Baltimore Steam Packet Company, known as the Old Bay Line, launched a new flagship for its small fleet of excursion liners plying the Chesapeake Bay between Baltimore and Norfolk. Originally to have been called the Florida, the flagship was named the President Warfield in memory of Solomon Davies Warfield, the Old Bay Line's president, who had decided to build the new liner as the utmost in Chesapeake Bay luxury. The specifications for construction of the President Warfield called for 171 first-class staterooms, each with hot and cold running water. She would be licensed to carry 400 passengers and would have a crew of 58. She would have two flagstaffs. One would fly the Stars and Stripes; the other, the British Union Jack.

Warfield died in 1927, a month after the keel was laid. His name survived on the excursion boat, and later in newspaper headlines about the marriage of his niece and ward, the divorcee Bessie Wallis Warfield, to the future King Edward VI of England.

The President Warfield was an anachronism when she was built, and the dying era of bay excursions came to an abrupt end with World War II. The War Shipping Administration requisitioned the President Warfield, and on July 12, 1942, she was transferred to the British Ministry of War Transport for use in the English Channel. After refitting, she crossed the Atlantic in a convoy that lost three ships to attacking German submarines. She spent most of the next year-and-a-half moored on a beach as a barracks ship. On May 20, 1944, she was transferred to the U.S. Navy and became the U.S.S. President Warfield (IX-169). In June, she took part in the Normandy invasion, serving as a control center for logistical operations; every craft entering or leaving port at the Normandy beachhead exchanged blinker signals with her. In February of 1945, she became a troop ferry from Le Havre to staging areas along the Seine River; she made 15 trips in three months, carrying an average of 800 men and as many as 1,028 one time. When the fighting ended in Europe, she returned to the United States, arriving July 25, 1945, at the Chesapeake Bay. She sat, unused, in the James River for a year. The Maritime Commission offered her for sale as scrap in early 1946 but rejected the highest bid of $6,255 as too low. This bid came from the Potomac Shipwrecking Company, of

Washington, D.C., whose partners included George Levin, Louis Levin, and Paul Backer. Later in the year, they offered $8,028, and on October 1, 1946, the Maritime Commission accepted this bid. The buyers had to take delivery within 30 days; before that time, they resold the President Warfield for $40,000 to Samuel Derektor of the Chinese-American Industrial Company. In less than two weeks, Derektor's lawyer asked the Maritime Commission to approve a third sale, to the Weston Trading Company, the Aliyah Bet front; the application, dated November 2, said that Weston wanted to buy the vessel for $50,000 and operate her under Pananamian registry in Western European waters.

On December 3, 1946, the Maritime Commission approved the sale. By that time, tugs hired by the Weston Trading Company had removed the President Warfield from the James River and brought her to Baltimore. The transfer of ownership to the Weston Trading Company took place on December 17, 1946.

Repairs began. The hull and engines were in good shape, but virtually everything else needed rebuilding. A former Merchant Marine officer arriving to join the volunteer crew grabbed a rail on the gangplank and it came off in his hand. He went below to the engineroom and kicked his foot through a rotted steel panel. "This is suicide," he thought. Fourteen electrical fires broke out before the work was completed. The repair bills mounted; Morris Ginsberg of the American Foreign Steamship Corporation guaranteed payment, and the Weston Trading Company made the disbursements from its bank account. Estimates of the total costs, including purchase, ranged as high as $130,000.

As the repairs went forward and the volunteer crew reported to Baltimore, the Aliyah Bet network in the United States worked on the problem of a foreign flag. British intelligence operatives were in touch with the State Department and the government of Panama; their efforts resulted in withdrawal of the Warfield's Panamanian registry. Aware of this effort by the British, Aliyah Bet agents applied for Honduran registry even before the Weston Trading Company bought the President Warfield. But approval did not come quickly. British pressure on Honduras resulted in a requirement that the Weston Trading Company certify that it would not use the President Warfield for running the blockade of Palestine. Weston signed an affidavit to that effect on January 21, 1947, leaving the Honduran consulate in New York no alternative but to issue a certificate of registry. Two days later, on January 23, The Baltimore Sun printed an article headlined "Warfield, Old Bay Line Queen, Exiled to China as Riverboat." The article quoted Captain William C. Ash as saying the President Warfield had applied for Honduran registry in preparation for sailing to China, where she would operate as a riverboat. He identified her owner as the Chinese-American Industrial Corporation. To reach China, he said, she would sail by way of the Mediterranean.

The President Warfield loaded for the voyage. She took aboard canned drinking water, life jackets, army K-rations, and three million cigarettes which could be sold on the black market in Europe to help pay for operations.

On the afternoon of Sunday, February 16, 1947, Baltimore Zionists came aboard for a ceremony. The volunteer crew assembled on the main deck and took the Haganah oath, receiving a Bible and a sweater. Yaakov Dori and Danny Schind of the Haganah mission in New York attended, as did Rudolph G. Sonneborn, the philanthropist leader of the weapons-buying network known as the Sonneborn Institute. I.F. Stone, the journalist whose book about the ships Wedgwood and Haganah had appeared the year before, was also there. Danny Schind presented a Haganah flag to Yitzhak "Ike" Aronowitz, a Palestinian merchant sailor assigned to become the Warfield's captain in Europe. Schind introduced Captain Ash as the man responsible for making the voyage a reality. The gruff-spoken Captain Ash wished the sailors success and said he envied them their role as 20th-century Maccabees.

In the week before departure, a Jewish volunteer crewman married a local Catholic girl in a ceremony aboard ship. Maryland law required that the ceremony be performed by a clergyman. The Reverend John Stanley Grauel, a Methodist minister serving as a volunteer member of the crew, officiated.

On February 25, the President Warfield left Baltimore for the last time. She sailed for the Azores, six days away, but ran into a gale when she was 75 miles from Cape Hatteras. The storm disabled all but six of the 42-man crew, some from seasickness, and others from being battered in the tossing vessel. The craft began filling with water; her inexperienced crew had failed to seal the openings around the mooring cables with cement after she left port. With deep water in the engineroom, the sailors could not open the valves to pump the water out. The water was six feet deep, so a volunteer officer called for a six-foot metal bar. When his request brought no response, he looked around and discovered a crewman trying to saw two inches off the end of a six-foot-two-inch bar. The captain sounded an SOS and planned with an officer to give the order to abandon ship when the last generator failed. The generator gave out, but, as if by a miracle, it returned to operation a few seconds later.

Boarding the Exodus (President Warfield)

The Coast Guard sent help, and Danny Schind summoned an assistant to New York to notify the next-of-kin if rescue efforts failed. The President Warfield struggled back to land under her own power on February 27 and docked at Norfolk for repairs.

The damage from the storm was repaired in three weeks. But the Warfield's cover story, not as solidly built as the little vessel, was damaged beyond repair. News coverage resulting from her near-disaster at sea brought out some interesting facts about the President Warfield. Supposedly bound for China, she carried no charts of Chinese waters. Most of her crew members were Jewish, and some were Palestinian. A reporter for The New York Times put the picture together; his story appeared March 6 under the headline: "Palestine-Bound Mystery Ship."

After fueling at Paulsboro, New Jersey, the President Warfield arrived at Philadelphia on March 22. There, Captain Vigo Thompson, a Norwegian professional sailor, came aboard to take the Warfield to Marseilles. He replaced Captain William Scholastica Schlegel, whom Captain Ash fired during an argument over the need for further repairs. A few of the volunteers decided not to go any further, and new crewmen replaced them.

Early Saturday morning, March 29, the day the President Warfield was scheduled to depart from Philadelphia for Europe, the Honduran Consul General in New York telephoned Captain Ash and said his government had instructed him to go to Philadelphia and remove the President Warfield's Honduran registry and flag. The Honduran official said strong representations from the British embassy in Washington were behind the move.

Captain Ash and the Consul General took the 10:30 a.m. train together to Philadelphia. Before leaving New York, Captain Ash sent a message to the President Warfield's captain to assemble the crew, find a pilot, and leave port as quickly as possible. Captain Ash offered to pay the captain a bonus for every 15 minutes the vessel departed sooner than the scheduled noon sailing.

By the time Captain Ash and the Honduran Consul General arrived at the pier, after lunching at the bar of the Bellevue-Stratford Hotel in Philadelphia, the President Warfield was headed for the open sea. She left the dock at 11:10 a.m.

* * *

The President Warfield stopped for fuel at Ponta Delgada in the Azores on April 5, 1947. Her local fuel agent, a Jew who operated under a British franchise, was denied permission to supply her. The Warfield's crew bribed guards at the dock and filled the tanks themselves.

A few days later the President Warfield arrived at Gibraltar and entered the straits at night. A signal light flashed to ask her identity. The President Warfield replied, "Go to Hell" and continued to Marseilles.

Intense British activity persuaded Aliyah Bet officials that the President Warfield should not stay long at Marseilles. British intelligence agents kept the vessel under constant surveillance. Photographers taking pictures of the vessel for the British sold extra copies of their work to crew members of the President Warfield. On April 27 the British Embassy in Washington complained to the State Department that the American vessel intended to carry illegal immigrants to Palestine. British diplomacy won an agreement from Honduras not to object to the interception of a ship whose registry had been withdrawn; a proposal to seize the President Warfield on the high seas was forwarded to the British Prime Minister on April 30.

Hurrying out of Marseilles, the President Warfield rammed and damaged a French vessel. The American vessel left behind unpaid fines of 30 million francs for infractions of sanitary and port regulations.

The President Warfield headed for the west coast of Italy, anchoring in Portovenere at the beginning of May. British agents in Italy picked up the chase; within a few days of her arrival, an Italian gunboat dropped anchor between the President Warfield and the exit from the harbor. The President Warfield remained at Portovenere for seven weeks.

The young Haganah agents selected to command the voyage to Palestine came aboard during this time. They and the Americans eyed one another skeptically. The Americans wondered about entrusting their lives to these youngsters, while the Palestinians looked on the free-wheeling behavior of the volunteers as dangerous to security. A crisis flared when a number of Americans refused to stay aboard ship while the Palestinians enjoyed shore privileges. The Americans who went ashore in defiance of orders were taken to Milan for the Haganah equivalent of a court-martial and threatened with being sent home. A sullen, angry day followed; the tension broke after an American found a soccer ball and started a game that blossomed into vigorous competition between the Americans and the Palestinians. They returned to Portovenere and kept up the new-found spirit with campfires and singing on the beach.

The Exodus (President Warfield) at Sete

When the time came to leave Portovenere, Haganah officials presented the Italian port captain with an official-looking letter ordering the withdrawal of the gunboat that blocked the President Warfield from leaving the harbor. The President Warfield steamed off at top speed, before it could be discovered that the document was bogus. Later, the gunboat gave chase, but the President Warfield vanished in the darkness and by the next morning was off Toulon in French waters.

The President Warfield stopped next at Port de Bouc, near Marseilles, and began preparing for her passengers. Bunks for 5,000 people had to be built. In the evenings, Americans caught the train to Marseilles; one night a volunteer quarreled in a cafe with a British officer and knocked him cold. A British agent bought drinks for a group of volunteers but became drunk himself and told the Americans his government was prepared to fight the Jews to ensure access to Arab oil. On July 4, some of the volunteers asked for a day off. The Palestinians could not understand why the Americans wanted time off when so much work remained. The Americans explained that they felt about Independence Day the way the Socialist Palestinians must feel about May Day. A Palestinian in authority weighed this explanation and offered the Americans a half-day. The Americans barricaded themselves in the galley and got drunk.

On July 9, 1947, the President Warfield slipped out of Port de Bouc to pick up her passengers. She headed west along the French coast to the small port town of Sete across the Bay of Lyon. On shore, some 70 trucks filled with refugees carrying visas for Colombia moved toward the harbor. Half of the refugees boarded before dawn on July 10. Passports had been prepared for only 2,000, so the documents were collected aboard ship and sent back to shore

After the battle

for the next group of passengers; French officials raised no objection. By noon, more than 4,500 passengers were aboard, and the President Warfield was getting up steam.

Before the President Warfield could sail, Haganah leaders received word that the French government was about to order the vessel detained. Moments later, the order came through.

On that morning of July 10, British Foreign Secretary Ernest Bevin was meeting in Paris with his French counterpart, Georges Bidault, when a clerk interrupted to whisper a message to Bevin and his aides. British intelligence had noted the President Warfield's arrival at Sete the night before and relayed the word to higher authority. Bevin announced that the President Warfield was loading in Sete and angrily confronted Bidault with a demand that France redress this affront. Bidault gave orders to detain the President Warfield. One of the secretaries in the room was a Haganah agent; before the order could be transmitted, the secretary slipped out and telephoned the news to Haganah headquarters in Paris.

The President Warfield sat at the dock in Sete through the day as Haganah officials tried without success to arrange for her release. The local Haganah commander, Shmarya Tzameret, an American-born member of Kibbutz Bet Hashita, offered $10,000 to a French pilot to come aboard at 2 a.m. and guide the President Warfield to sea. The pilot accepted, and the President Warfield prepared again to sail. When the pilot failed to show up, an American volunteer officer swam ashore and cast off the lines; the President Warfield executed a difficult turn in the small harbor and made for the sea. Almost immediately, she went aground. Her young Palestinian captain improvised a series of maneuvers that freed her from the mud, and she was on her way.

There was no need to hide the refugees below deck, for the British already knew where the President Warfield was. As soon as the refugee vessel reached international waters, a British warship appeared and began following her.

For a week after her escape from France, the President Warfield steamed through the Mediterranean with her British escort.

Organization of the refugees aboard the President Warfield was strict. A food detail carried dried rations and buckets of barley soup around the vessel for distribution to the passengers. Youth-group members served as traffic police to regulate the passage of people and prevent any movement that could threaten the vessel's stability. Everyone except infants and expectant mothers had jobs to do.

The public address system played the chorale from Beethoven's Ninth Symphony and carried news broadcasts in English, Hebrew, Yiddish, and Hungarian. Hebrew lessons were given, and a handwritten ship's newspaper was produced. At night, there was singing on deck, and the crew entertained the passengers with stories and skits. Rough seas brought an outbreak of seasickness, and the sanitation crew could not keep the toilet troughs from overflowing; an epidemic of diarrhea ensued. On July 16, Polya Abramovich, a passenger, died giving birth to a son. The vessel halted at sunset for her funeral; the crew served as a guard of honor, and the Haganah commander delivered a eulogy likening the refugees' voyage to the Biblical exodus from Egypt.

The day of the burial at sea the President Warfield received orders to beach herself at Tel Aviv between 6 p.m. and 7 p.m. on July 17, staying outside territorial waters until the last possible moment, and then making a dash for the beach. The Warfield's design as a bay ferry might allow her to reach shallow waters where the bigger British ships would not dare go. The Haganah prepared to assemble thousands of people at the beachhead to meet the refugees in the surf. Beyond that, the Haganah was ready to mobilize additional thousands by word of mouth in less than half an hour to create diversionary incidents all over Palestine.

More ships joined the British escort, which grew into a task force composed of the cruiser Ajax, four destroyers, a frigate, and two minesweepers. On July 17, a group of Americans and Palestinians lined up on the bridge of the President Warfield and in mock-ceremony saluted the British warships while the refugee vessel's public address system played Elgar's "Pomp and Circumstance" march. This show of irreverence toward the Royal Navy did not take away from the seriousness of the Warfield's battle preparations. That day, leaders on the refugee craft opened their sealed orders for hiding the Haganah agents on board if the British captured the vessel. They discussed the likelihood of someone's being killed; the conversation tailed off after Bill Bernstein, an American volunteer, said he would probably be the one to die.

To resist British boarders, the Warfield crew rigged wire mesh around the promenade deck and across openings. They ran pipes to spread the deck with slippery oil at the moment of boarding, and to spray live steam at the boarders. They hammered planks across open areas and piled sandbags around the wheelhouse.

The Exodus after her capture

Both sides knew the confrontation was only a matter of time. But their schedules did not agree. The British commander on July 17 maneuvered his ships into position to entrap the refugee vessel before she could complete her expected run for the beach. The British expected the Warfield to make the attempt near the Sinai-Palestine border, at dawn on Friday, June 18. The Haganah, changing the Warfield's orders, chose a later time: 11 p.m. on Friday.

At 2 a.m. on Friday, June 18, the refugee vessel was 23 miles off the coast. In another 90 minutes she was due to change course and proceed northward, skirting territorial waters as she headed for the landing site. Before this could happen, the British attacked.

Shortly after 2:30 a.m. on July 18, the British warships turned on their searchlights and illuminated the refugee vessel from end to end. She was no longer the President Warfield; in the night, she had changed her name. Blue-and-white Jewish flags flew from her staffs fore and aft, and signs in English proclaimed her name as "Haganah Ship—Exodus 1947." The alarm sounded on the Exodus, and the crew rushed to their stations. A British destroyer announced that the Exodus had entered territorial waters and called on her to stop and be towed to Haifa. The captain of the Exodus cursed the British as liars. By radio, the Exodus accused the British of piracy.

The Exodus began to turn. British destroyers approached from both sides and rammed her, snapping the pipes that had been readied to squirt oil and steam. Sailors and marines in battle dress raced across boarding bridges that neatly fit the Exodus' deck. The boarders captured the wheelhouse quickly, clubbing Bill Bernstein unconscious and shooting another American point-blank in the jaw. After the initial surprise, the defenders fought back. The Palestinian captain and an American volunteer regained control of the vessel by disconnecting the steering apparatus from the controls in the wheelhouse. From below, using auxiliary controls, they steered the Exodus on a radical course, veering into the British ships that tried to pull alongside. One after another, the British destroyers retired from their boarding attempts, too damaged to continue. In two hours, the British succeeded in putting aboard only 40 men, a number of whom were captured by the unarmed Jews. Near daybreak, the British used small arms fire on deck and mortally wounded two Jews, one of them an orphan of 15 who was shot in the head. At 5:15 a.m., the battle was over. With no further hope of beaching the Exodus, the Jews agreed to surrender. Bill Bernstein, who had been knocked out by a blow to the head early in the battle, lay dying in the captain's cabin; shipmates wept at his side but could do nothing to help him. In all, 146 Jews had been injured; 28 of them were hospitalized.

An American volunteer took over as captain, and Palestinians and Americans went to their hiding places or disappeared among the refugees. At 4 p.m., as Haifa grew quiet in preparation for the Jewish Sabbath, the Exodus was towed into port. Three American crew leaders were led off under arrest. They were temporarily released from jail two days later to serve as pallbearers at the funeral of Bill Bernstein. Later, they were deported. A Jewish work crew came aboard to clean the stinking vessel and, as usual, walked off with the Haganah members who had hidden from the British.

* * *

The refugees were placed aboard three prison ships used by the British to transport Aliyah Bet immigrants to Cyprus. After the convoy sailed from Haifa, the British commander opened his sealed orders and was astonished at what he read. Instead of Cyprus, the destination was Port de Bouc, France.

When the convoy failed to turn up at Cyprus a day after leaving Haifa, anxiety arose in Palestine that the British had begun a new policy. Determined to make an example of the Exodus, and angry about her escape from the harbor at Sete, British Foreign Secretary Bevin wanted the passengers returned to France.

On July 28, the prison ships reached Port de Bouc and anchored outside territorial waters. About 60 infirm and elderly passengers agreed to go ashore. The others refused, and the French government announced that it would not force them.

The ships remained off Port de Bouc for more than three weeks. On August 21, the British Colonial Office notified the Jewish Agency that if the refugees did not go ashore, they would be deported the next day at 6 p.m. to the British Zone of occupied Germany. The refugees ignored the ultimatum; 20 minutes after its expiration, the prison ships sailed for Germany.

On September 8, the ships arrived at Hamburg, where 2,500 British troops stood ready at the harbor with tear gas and clubs. Some of the refugees on the first ship to unload staged a sitdown strike, and soldiers dragged them ashore. The refugees on the second ship got off quickly, and the British found a bomb powerful enough to sink the vessel; Haganah agents had smuggled it aboard in Port de Bouc, but it failed to go off at Hamburg as planned. When the British detonated the bomb on shore, it blew out 100 windows of a nearby barracks. On the third ship, the Jews refused to leave and battled for two hours

British soldiers place Exodus passengers aboard trucks in Germany

against 300 paratroopers and military police who forced their way aboard.

The expulsion to Germany had at least one silver lining. An American volunteer accompanied his refugee sweetheart on a prison ship to Germany. There, behind barbed wire in an internment camp, they found her mother, who had been presumed dead at the hands of the Nazis.

Almost a year after the expulsion to Hamburg, the last of the Exodus passengers reached the newly independent State of Israel. On September 4, 1948, another American-manned volunteer vessel, the Calanit, arrived at Haifa with 320 refugees from the Exodus among her passengers. Formerly known as the Mala, and before that as the Mayflower, this craft had served in the administrations of Presidents Theodore Roosevelt through Herbert Hoover as the United States Presidential Yacht. Because she reached Israel after the establishment of the State, the Calanit was not considered an Aliyah Bet vessel. But she carried passengers of the Exodus to the completion of their Aliyah Bet journey. And she brought the flag of the Exodus home to Israel.

* * *

More than any other event of Aliyah Bet, the story of the Exodus captured the attention of the outside world. This was due not only to the plight of the Jews, but to the way the British mishandled the situation from the standpoint of public relations. The development of the story in the press can be seen in these headlines. All are from The New York Times except where indicated.

British Bring Ex-Bay Liner into Haifa after Long Fight, Baltimore Sun, July 19.

Refugees Being Returned to France, July 21.

British Fight Terrorists in Jerusalem: Holy Land Disorders Follow Deportation of Warfield's Passengers, Baltimore Sun, July 21.

Terrorist Tension Reaches New High as Refugees Sent to France, July 22.

French Foreign Office Spokesman Said Jews Victims of Fraud, July 25.

French Bar Using Force on Refugees, July 31.

France to Renew Invitations to Jews: Will Try Again to Induce 4500 Deported Immigrants to Go Ashore En Masse, August 1.

Exodus Refugees Get an Ultimatum, August 22.

British Assailed on Refugee Threat, August 22.

Exodus Refugees Begin Forced Trip to German Camps, August 23.

Jews Sent Back to German Port: 4400 from Exodus Refused to Land in France, Baltimore Sun, August 23.

British Bid for Aid in the Exodus Case, August 24.

Exodus Refugees Reach Gibraltar, August 27.

Utmost Tact to be Used by British in Persuading Jews to Disembark, September 6.

* * *

The British suffered more than negative press coverage from the Exodus case.

In the United States, Members of Congress denounced the British, and President Harry S. Truman expressed his concern. Some 20,000 persons attended a memorial program July 25 at New York's Madison Square Park for Bill Bernstein.

French-British relations were strained. In Britain, the opposition headed by former Prime Minister Winston Churchill attacked the Labor government for bungling the Exodus affair. In Palestine, insurrection and violence reached new heights. And in the United Nations, the Special Commission on Palestine recommended that the British leave and allow the establishment of Jewish and Arab states.

* * *

After Israel became independent in 1948, the Exodus remained moored in Haifa harbor, too old and damaged for further use. In 1951, Haifa Mayor Abba Khoushi proposed that the battered little vessel be preserved as a musuem of Aliyah Bet. Before this plan could be put into action, the Exodus caught fire August 26, 1952, and burned to the waterline. Her hulk was towed out of the way of the harbor traffic and abandoned at nearby Shemen Beach. Twelve years after the fire, an Italian firm cut the hull into two sections in an effort to salvage it for scrap; an attempt to raise the sections failed August 23, 1964. Shortly after that, the Hayama ship repair cooperative, under contract to the Israel Port Authority, raised the hulk, towed it to the Kishon River, and scrapped it.

* * *

In Washington, D.C., the Smithsonian Institution displayed a model of the Exodus. Some viewers complained that the museum's plaque explaining the model was obscure to an extreme; the plaque said only:

> Built for the Old Bay Line as the President Warfield, this steamer later was involved in the Jewish immigration strife on the Palestine coast.

Later, the Smithsonian allowed a second plaque to be placed alongside the model of the Exodus. This second plaque told more of the story:

> In early 1947, the President Warfield joined the "illegal immigration fleet" transporting refugees from Europe to Palestine, and was renamed Exodus.
>
> On her final voyage in July 1947 with 4550 refugees aboard, Exodus was stopped by British naval units. In the ensuing struggle her American Chief Mate William Bernstein was killed.
>
> Exodus was one of ten vessels in the "illegal immigration fleet" manned by volunteers from the United States, Canada, and Latin America. The fleet pursued its mission against a British blockade of the Palestine Coast during 1946-48.

The inscription concluded with the names of the 10 vessels and an explanation that the plaque was presented to the museum "by the American volunteers in tribute to the spirit of their mission and the courage of their passengers."

In 1987, 40 years after the voyage, veterans of the American volunteer operation brought to Israel a replica of the plaque for presentation to the Clandestine Immigration and Naval Museum in Haifa.

Edition

JERUSALEM FRIDAY, OCTOBER 3, 1947

POST

PRICE 15 MILS VOL. XXII, No. 6...

JEWS READY TO TAKE OVER IF BRITAIN QUITS

At the Jewish Elected Assembly on Mount Scopus in Jerusalem and before the United Nations at Lake Success yesterday the leaders of the Jewish Agency proclaimed the readiness of the Jewish people to take over the temporary administration of Palestine under the supervision of the United Nations as soon as a decision to set up a Jewish State is taken. The speaker in Jerusalem was the Chairman of the Jewish Agency, Mr. David Ben Gurion, while in New York it was Dr. Abba Hillel Silver, who declared that the Jewish Agency was prepared most reluctantly to accept the Partition of Palestine in the interests of achieving a solution.

Column One

By David Courtney

ORDINARY people have a lot to be afraid of. In spite of Governments separately and together, which are said to be legislating for the peace of men's bodies and souls, there are very few portents of the time when ordinary people will not have a lot to be afraid of: bankruptcy, prison, the loss of a job, the policeman's knock at the door, cholera, the baying of a siren, riot and war. It is not much use seeking the deeper cause in Moscow or even in Washington; and not in the exercise of the veto or the nationalisation of steel. But if we don't find the cause soon, there will be something new for ordinary people to be afraid of. Hunger bears in its shrivelled womb more than death from starvation. The fungi of perpetual crisis include more than a wave of suicides. Multi-headed fear grins with an inventive cruelty. The dispute over Security Council membership may help. The playing of Italy and Finland against Balkan aspirants to U.N. may be for the world's good. It doesn't look like it. It is hard to believe that it will save a single life in India or Egypt, or fill a stomach in Bessarabia, or stop the throwing of stones, if that should be today's intention, along the road from Jerusalem to Jaffa.

■

THE cholera in Egypt is getting worse. All that can be done about it now is being done. Plenty of vaccine is there and presumably plenty of means to vaccinate. It is a bit late but better than never; and apparently something is also being done about cleaning up Egyptian filth. The point seems to be that millions of people in Egypt and India and a dozen other countries still work their guts out for nothing better than conditions of life in which a cholera epidemic is as simple as life and death and not surprising to anyone. Democracy and a so-called world responsibility have been in existence long enough to have done better than that. Countries like Egypt, India and China have been under rich and powerful imperialisms long enough to have got at least the benefit of a w.c. and a wash-basin out of it.

■

THE sordid spectacle of half the world is no credit to the other half. Veto or no veto, Sir Alexander Cadogan or Jamal effendi Husseini, League of Nations or U.N., it makes an odd and depressing background for the Security Council to wrangle against in its peculiar discussion of what constitutes a nation fit to be a member of U.N. The Soviet exercise of the veto against the membership of Italy and Finland may come under the heading of dog-in-the-manger tactics; but it was logical and characteristic of the Council as a whole. A State may leave its peasantry and slum-dweller to grovel in dirt; no matter: that, presumably, is no concern of Democracy and no disqualification for U.N. The attributes peculiar to the Yemen are missing in the States of Bulgaria, Hungary and Rumania; and those three States must therefore remain outside U.N.

■

DEMOCRACY needs a better definition than anyone has lately given it, or one day, in its own confusion, it will disappear. Until it gets out of its muddle, ordinary people will go on having lots to be afraid of. When it gets out of its muddle, perhaps even the hooligans who throw stones along the Jerusalem-Jaffa highway will not throw them any more. Today's strike is fair enough. Its prospects seem to have frightened some people; but it is fair enough. No one can say that the Arabs have nothing to complain about; and a strike is a fair instrument of protest. To conjecture on the day of the event is unwise; to fear that the event will degenerate into the throwing of stones and the tossing of knives is even sillier. Fear gives half the stimulus it wants. There is so much that ordinary people have to be afraid of that it is foolish to be afraid too soon or to provoke in fear the thing that is feared.

Jerusalem, October 3.

After Midnight

The Brooklyn Dodgers won the third game in baseball's World Series yesterday, when they beat the New York Yankees, 9-8. The Yankees had won the first two games.

WE CAN PROVIDE SECURITY -- *Silver*

LAKE SUCCESS, Thursday. — Rabbi Abba Hillel Silver, member of the Zionist Executive, presenting the Jewish Agency's case before the U.N. Ad Hoc Committee on Palestine today, warned that the world had now reached "one of the important crossroads of history."

The United Nations' course was fraught with destiny for the Jews, the Arabs and the U.N., he said.

Referring to Mr. Creech Jones' statement last Friday, Dr. Silver declared: "When Britain brought the Palestine case to the U.N., surely one could presuppose that she would loyally cooperate in any U.N. solution.

"Otherwise the British Government might just as well have announced six months ago what it declared the other day. Why were six critical months lost, during which time the situation in Palestine was permitted to deteriorate most gravely?"

Mr. Creech Jones' statement seemed to imply that Britain not only did not wish to assume sole responsibility for implementing the Palestine report, but reserved to itself the right of refusing any cooperation in implementing the U.N. decision. The question was whether in taking such a position Britain was helping to solve this difficult problem, and whether its course would enhance the authority and prestige of the U.N.

In view of Britain's declared reluctance to impose her policy by force, he said, one might be pardoned for inquiring why Britain had not hesitated to use 100,000 to impose a policy on Palestine of which no international body approved.

Nothing Offered

Reviewing the British attitude towards Partition proposals in the past, Dr. Silver said that it seemed that the UNSCOP Report was no more acceptable than the two earlier reports. "Britain has indicated no support of this latest report and offers instead -- nothing.

"The failure of Britain to give the U.N. a measure of guidance and support, and her announced intention of an early withdrawal from Palestine -- which we welcome -- made it more imperative than ever that the General Assembly proceed as speedily as possible," he declared.

Referring to the minority recommendation for a bi-national state, he said: "We find it wholly unacceptable, even as a basis for discussion." Such federalisation would force the Jews to be a permanent minority in an Arab state, and the Jews would have no control over immigration, he added.

Partition, as proposed in the majority report, was never contemplated by the Balfour Declaration. However, if Partition were decided, the Jews would point out their objection to the elimination of Western Galilee from the Jewish State. To exclude Jerusalem "would also be a particularly severe blow," he said.

Although the Jews had maintained reservation about Partition, Rabbi Silver said they were prepared to accept it. They were also prepared to accept the proposal for economic union, but "the Jewish State must have in its own hands those instruments of financial and economic control necessary to carry out large-scale Jewish immigration and related economic development."

The Jewish State must have independent access to those world sources of capital and supplies which were indispensable for the accomplishment of these purposes, he stressed.

The majority economic plan would in effect mean that the Jewish State would provide a large subsidy to the Arab State, but the Jews were prepared to assume this burden in order to find a way out of the present intolerable impasse. "Sincerely and without reservations, we bring an offer of peace and friendship to the Arabs.

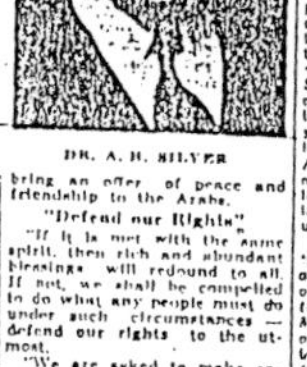

DR. A. H. SILVER

"Defend our Rights"

"If it is met with the same spirit, then rich and abundant blessings will redound to all. If not, we shall be compelled to do what any people must do under such circumstances — defend our rights to the utmost.

"We are asked to make enormous 'sacrifices' to attain what we should have attained long ago." Dr. Silver added. "In sadness we are prepared to make this sacrifice. Beyond it we cannot and will not go."

The Jews favoured an international authority to supervise the U.N. decisions during the transitional period, he said. Full use should also be made of the "trained manpower available in Palestine," which was prepared to help the U.N. maintain law and order.

The Jewish people were not impressed by idle threats. If the British forces were withdrawn from Palestine, then the Palestine Jews were prepared to provide without delay the forces needed for security, Rabbi Silver declared.

Referring to Jamal eff. Husseini's address, he recalled with satisfaction that similar threats at the Special Session in April did not influence either the Assembly or UNSCOP.

"Why does the Arab Executive now come to ask 'justice and equity' from the U.N. whose authority it has flouted and whose competence to decide the future of Palestine the Arab spokesman has categorically denied?"

Denying the Arab allegations about the origin of the Jews, he said that history should not be "a story out of the Arabian nights."

Certain facts could not yield to wishful thinking and "one would assume that the Arabs of Palestine would be among the last people on earth to wish to engage in genealogical research."

D.P. Problem

Taking issue with the sixth recommendation of UNSCOP's 11 unanimous proposals, suggesting that the U.N. Assembly initiate an international arrangement for dealing with the D.P. question, Dr. Silver recalled that the Anglo-U.S. Committee had reported that Palestine offered the only hope for the D.P.'s.

The Jewish Agency strongly hoped the world's nations would welcome those D.P.'s who wished to emigrate elsewhere, but "it would be most unjust, most unkind and bitterly resented" if refugees were to be compelled against their will to emigrate to other lands.

The Jewish Agency assumed, he said, that the transfer of powers and the functions of the administration for the two peoples would be inaugurated immediately and consummated as rapidly as possible instead of after the transition period.

It was also hoped that after the definition of the boundaries, the establishment of the States by the U.N., their territorial integrity and sovereign rights should be respected similar to those of other nations under the Charter.

It was the realization that an Arab-Jewish agreement was impossible that had prompted Mr. Bevin to turn the issue over to the U.N. "It must be clear to everyone that no settlement of the Palestine problem was possible without some enforcement," he said, adding:—

The Jewish Agency hopes the transition from the present status of the country to a new status of two independent states will be attended by a minimum of friction and conflict.

VACUUM MUST BE FILLED -- *Ben Gurion*

Palestine Post Staff

The Elected Assembly of the Jewish Community of Palestine yesterday proposed to the United Nations that a provisional Jewish government should be set up immediately after their decision to establish a Jewish State, to take over from the Mandatory Power and rule under the supervision and with the assistance of U.N.

The resolution was adopted after Mr. David Ben Gurion, Chairman of the Jewish Agency Executive, had told delegates from all over the country that they must consider three major points — security, the establishment of the Jewish State, and the achievement of Jewish-Arab agreement.

Speaking for 90 minutes at an open session presided over by Dr. A.H. Fraenkel at the Rosenbloom Hall of the Hebrew University on Mt. Scopus, Mr. Ben Gurion said that on security depended not only the fate and peace of the country today, but also the fate and peace of the future Jewish State. The anti-Zionist policy of the British Administration in the past 10 years, the destruction of Jewish resources in Europe, the creation of the Arab League, and the existence of Arab armies in neighbouring states and in Palestine all increased the problem of security, he stressed.

We can face all the difficulties, within Palestine or from abroad, only by the mobilization of the entire Yishuv and of all the Jewish people in the world. Men, resources, funds, science, organizing ability and economic strength must be mustered for the establishment of a "security regime." Every section of the country — youth, labour, industry, employers and employees, villagers and townsfolk, — must be mobilized.

SIR ALAN SEES BEN GURION, KHALIDI

The High Commissioner, Sir Alan Cunningham, yesterday saw Mr. David Ben Gurion, the Chairman of the Jewish Agency Executive, and Dr. H. F. Khalidi, Secretary of the Arab Higher Executive, at separate interviews.

Nobody knew whether a final decision would be taken at the present U.N. session, he continued, but the termination of the Mandate was certain. Referring to Mr. Creech Jones's statement at the U.N. that the British Government would not be able to implement a policy which was not acceptable to Jews and Arabs, Mr. Ben Gurion said that if Jewish-Arab accord were possible, no help would be needed.

While Mr. Creech Jones has declared that the British are not prepared to undertake by themselves the task of imposing a policy in Palestine by force of arms, and that they are not prepared to carry out any U.N. decision, they continue to use force with all the means at their disposal against Jewish immigration — a policy rejected by several international bodies.

Even after the Colonial

(Continued on Page 3.)

U.S. INITIATIVE WILL DECIDE

By GERSHON AGRONSKY

LAKE SUCCESS, Thursday. — In a democracy the highest executive is unashamedly susceptible to public opinion, whatever its permanent officials may feel about a wave of resentment at any given moment, which they would prefer to dismiss contemptuously as stemming from pressure groups. Thus, the White House now seems to have awakened to the realization that the American public will not easily swallow a deal with Britain over Palestine which would leave London as the arbiter in defiance of the purposes for which she was originally granted a Mandate.

Within the past 24 hours there have been hints from Washington that as far as the White House is concerned Palestine's future is to be decided on the highest political level, not by administrative pundits. This reinforces the hope that the American delegation at the U.N. Assembly will be instructed to support the UNSCOP majority report.

French Support

Other straws in the wind point to similar support from other quarters. France does not consider that she is in a position to carry the torch for the Jewish people. But if the Assembly is faced with a proposal that the report be accepted, the French will not bar the way. Holland, too, will back up the report, to which her delegate on UNSCOP subscribed.

Most surprising of all, perhaps, is the rumour that M. Simic, who was a member of the UNSCOP and who is the Yugoslav delegate at the Assembly, is prepared to countersign the majority report against his own minority report which recommended a federal plan for Palestine.

Hints have been heard that the Latin Americans are wobbling and that as many as ten of the South American countries might abstain on the final count. This speculation need not be taken tragically; for in the end it is United States' initiative that will decide.

Back to Washington

Thus, whichever way you turn, you are back full circle to Washington. In this connection the greatest danger is future British stalling. When the likelihood of the necessary two-thirds majority for the Sandstrom recommendations becomes inescapable, Britain is likely to propose, either herself or through a friendly stooge, some new delaying device. The present United Nations Assembly will become, however, a grotesque caricature if it allows any such device to destroy the UNSCOP report as the Woodhead Commission stultified the Peel Report.

Nevertheless, the opportunities for stalling appear unlimited, for the present Assembly is due to wind up on November 20 without having completed its agenda and it has been suggested that another special Assembly for Palestine should be called for February.

(Earlier Cable — Page 3)

STOP PRESS
PROSPECTS BETTER

By J.Z. LURIE, Palestine Post Correspondent

NEW YORK, Friday. — Anglo-American negotiations over the acceptance of the Majority UNSCOP Report are proceeding apace, with prospects of both accepting the Report and of its getting a two-thirds majority looking good today, though they may change again by tomorrow.

The crux of the present negotiations is the implementation of the Report — who would provide the forces necessary. The latest suggestion is that the small powers of UNSCOP be called upon, thus providing for the contingency that the Big Powers, including the U.S. and Russia, are to be kept out of the picture.

ARAB THREATS "BASELESS"

NEW YORK, Thursday (Palcor). — Mr. Frank Buxton, who was a member of the Anglo-American Committee of Inquiry on Palestine, wrote in a letter to the "New York Herald Tribune" today that he considered Arab threats of a boycott of the Western Powers, should the United Nations decide on Partition, to be baseless. American economic interests would in no way be impaired, he said.

SIDE-TRACKED

LAKE SUCCESS, Thursday (Palcor). — The Arab States' resolution that the U.N. Assembly should include on its agenda the question of international cooperation to prevent immigration "likely to disturb friendly relations between nations" has been side-tracked to the Social, Humanitarian and Cultural Committee instead of being put before the Political Committee for action, as its sponsors desired.

Palestine was not mentioned in the discussion, but there is no question about the real purpose of the resolution, although Faris Bey el Khoury (Syria) replied, when asked by the Soviet delegate what kind of immigration he meant, that he was referring to the resettlement of war refugees.

3,000 on 2 Seized Ships

Palestine Post Bureau

HAIFA, Thursday. — One of the two long-expected refugee ships which were intercepted about six miles south of here this evening and boarded by a Naval party was brought into port just before 11 o'clock, with approximately 2,000 passengers and was manoeuvred against the quayside by a tug.

She is the Paducah, about 800 tons, re-named the Geulah (Redemption). The second ship, the Northlands, re-named the Medinat Hayehudim (Jewish State), is expected here about 8 o'clock tomorrow morning with about 1,000 refugees.

It was officially stated that they had been boarded by the Navy within territorial waters. The statement added that no resistance occurred in the capturing of the Geulah about 4 p.m., but some opposition was met when the Navy boarded the Medinath Hayehudim 44 minutes later.

The deportation vessels, Empire Comfort and Empire Shelter are also in the harbour tonight. The two ships can only take a few hundred passengers.

It was learned here that the refugees will be taken to Cyprus, at least for the present.

The trim, black-and-white Geulah is a former excursion boat. She bore no signs of damage. On the upper structure were the words "Haganah Ship Geulah" and the Zionist colours fluttered aloft.

Across the jetty from the vessel were moored the two deportation ships, Empire Shelter and Empire Comfort, ready for the transhipment.

The port area was filled, as usual on such occasions, with troops of the Sixth Airborne Division and Palestine police. Searchlights mounted on lorries floodlighted the sea. Some of the soldiers carried walkie-talkie radio equipment.

A gangway was placed against the ship and steel-helmeted soldiers boarded her to relieve the naval party. A Naval officer called down "Everything O.K." and there were obvious signs of relief among the soldiers.

Told in Hebrew by an interpreter that they would be taken to Cyprus and that their baggage would be searched and returned later, the refugees came quietly off the vessel. The first off were a middle-aged couple carrying a child. As the rest came down, children could be seen curiously peeping out of the portholes. Another announcement invited the refugees out, and after a sick man had been helped down by two soldiers, there followed a procession of elderly people, some of them limping and others obviously ill.

The refugees entered the D.D.T. tent, and then handed over their scanty baggage for inspection. The search was extremely thorough, and resulted in a slow transhipment to the Empire Comfort. Tinned foods, water-bottles, loaves of bread — everything the refugees carried — was minutely inspected.

A number of expectant mothers and some sick people were taken to the Government Hospital here.

One woman who fainted was treated by an Army doctor, but neither he nor three newspapermen nearby could understand what language she spoke. One of the correspondents, all of whom were kept behind barbed wire away from the refugees, remarked that most of the refugees looked as if they had seen better times, and that 10 years ago they would probably have been able to pay their own passage to Palestine.

SPIRITS HIGH

A radio broadcast was heard in Palestine early yesterday morning from one of the two refugee ships. The announcer said that spirits of the refugees were high.

At the end of the broadcast the refugees could be heard singing Palestinian songs.

CAIRO MAY BE ISOLATED

By VICTOR AZAM, Palestine Post Correspondent

CAIRO, Thursday. — The health authorities are now debating whether to declare Cairo an infected area, following five deaths reported yesterday and the appearance of twenty high cases today. There were 49 more deaths in the whole of Egypt today.

Measures to prevent a cholera epidemic in Palestine were discussed this week by Dr. A. Katznelson, head of the Vaad Leumi's Health Department, and Dr. T. Krikorian, Acting Director of Medical Services.

Government laboratories were preparing sufficient vaccine to inoculate the entire population, Dr. Krikorian said, although for the present only people living south of the Beersheba-Gaza road and staff and workers at airfields, airports and railway junctions were being vaccinated.

FOURTH ARAB NOTE

LONDON, Thursday (Reuter). — A fourth Arab State — Saudi Arabia — has sent a note to Britain on the Palestine problem, a Foreign Office spokesman said today.

In the past week, notes have been received from Iraq, Syria and the Lebanon, following the conference at Aley recently of the Arab League Political Committee.

RUBOVITZ'S DEATH NOT PROVED
FARRAN FOUND "NOT GUILTY" OF MURDER

By M.W. JACOBS

Captain Roy Alexander Farran, a 26-year-old Regular Army Officer and former Deputy Superintendent of the Palestine Police, was acquitted yesterday by a General Court Martial in Jerusalem of the charge of murdering Alexander Rubovits on the night of May 6-7, near the Jerusalem-Jericho road.

A cry of "Good show" and loud clapping from the rest of the Court, which was filled with police, soldiers and some civilians, greeted the announcement of the finding by the President, Brig. R.H. Maxwell, Commander, South Palestine District, shortly after 3 o'clock in the afternoon. The trial, which occupied just over eight hours in all, began on Wednesday morning.

Continuing its considerations of the admissibility of an Army notebook which the Prosecutor, Mr. Maxwell Turner, alleged had been given to Farran while he was held in Allenby Barracks, the Court opened yesterday morning with evidence by Lt. Col. P. H. Labouchere, who had been Farran's Commanding Officer when he was in the 3rd Hussars.

He considered Farran an officer of "outstandingly high reputation," Lt.-Col. Labouchere said. When he went to Syria to bring Farran back, he told him that he would be tried by General Court Martial. They returned to Allenby Barracks on June 17 and, in the presence of Superintendent K. P. Hadingham, he told Farran that he was to regard him, the witness, as his legal adviser.

Examined by Mr. R. A. Fearnley Whittingstall, the Defence Counsel, Lt.-Col. Labouchere said that he had given Farran a letter of resignation from the Police and that Farran had signed it in his presence.

"I told him to write down all matters to do with the case he could think of," the witness continued.

Mr. Turner: *Have you any legal qualifications?*

(Continued on Page 3.)

CONSERVATIVES BUSY WITH HOME AFFAIRS

By GEORGE LICHTHEIM, Palestine Post Correspondent

BRIGHTON, Thursday. — Home affairs occupy almost the entire attention of the Conservatives meeting here for their 40th annual conference.

Little room has been allotted on the agenda to imperial matters, including a brief reference to Lord Beaverbrook's and Mr. Bevin's projected Empire Customs Union, which has already been turned down by all the Dominions. What discussion there will be on the Colonies will again relate to customs matters, and here the main argument will be over the possibility of fostering Empire free trade in the face of America's objections.

Closer union between Britain and the Colonies will be urged and an attempt made to distinguish Conservative Colonial policy from that of the Labour Government.

Palestine Not on Agenda

By tacit consent of all concerned, controversial issues like India, Burma, Egypt and Palestine do not appear on the agenda, there being no disposition to challenge the Government's policy on these matters. The Marshall Plan receives very brief mention.

Somewhat faint applause greeted the only speaker at this morning's session who praised Mr. Churchill's Pan-European campaign. Compared with the Labour Conference at Margate last May, this quiet and rather pedestrian meeting with no organized opposition except on industrial questions, where something like a fight is promised between the Party leadership and certain stalwarts wedded to complete laissez-faire.

Churchill on Saturday

The most applauded speaker today was a Conservative Trade Unionist, whom the Assembly regarded with a certain nostalgia, many no doubt wishing themselves able to speak in authentic proletarian accents.

But although overwhelmingly middle-class and somewhat self-consciously genteel, the Assembly contains a fair proportion of youthful elements, including many ex-servicemen, and there is plenty of applause for any speaker who attacks the Left-Wing Ministers.

So far, nobody has said an unkind word about Mr. Bevin.

Massacre In India

NEW DELHI, Thursday. — Two thousand Hindu and Sikh refugees were slaughtered by a Moslem gang which attacked their convoy at Tandlianwala, 25 miles west of Lyallpur in Pakistan, a report from Amritsar said last night.

The attack, said to have been the largest mass killing since India was partitioned into two independent states, was reported to have taken place on September 28.

More than 30,000 lbs. of cooked food was flown in two R.A.F. Dakotas from Delhi this evening to supply 100,000 Hindu and Sikh refugees marooned at Mangowallah in Pakistan's West Punjab, and another convoy of 23,000 Hindus and Sikhs are also marooned in a camp near Rawalpindi.

Announcing this at a press conference, a military spokesman said that the movement of refugees by rail had not been started yet because of the floods both in East and West Punjab. The movement by foot and road transport in both directions was being started in some areas, he added.

(U.P. and Reuter)

GANDHI IS 78

NEW DELHI, Thursday (AP). — Sorrow over the communal strife which cast its blight on the free India he had such an important part in creating, today overshadowed Mahatma Gandhi's 78th birthday. Stricken with influenza, he spent the day fasting and squatting crosslegged before a charka (cotton spinner), praying and meditating, while a stream of well wishers, rich and poor, from all walks of life, called on him. Though declared a public holiday by the Indian Government in honour of the occasion, there was little festivity.

During the day, Mr. Gandhi found time to prepare a birthday message to the people which he planned to deliver personally at a prayer service tonight.

BOYCOTT BOMB AND FALSE ALARM

The sirens in Jerusalem were sounded twice within an hour yesterday afternoon — once when an Arab boycott bomb exploded about 3 o'clock and again, an hour later, when construction blasting resulted in a false alarm.

About LP.100 damage was caused by the boycott bomb when it exploded in the doorway of a grocery shop owned by Mr. Nicolas J. Zaphiriadis, a Greek, in Mamillah Road. Mirrors and interior fittings were damaged but no one was hurt.

11 INJURED AS CAR EXPLODES

Palestine Post Reporter

HADERA, Thursday. — An officer and 10 soldiers were slightly hurt when an Army vehicle was blown up on the outskirts of Hadera at 6 o'clock tonight. The explosion was heard all over the town, and windows were smashed in nearby houses.

Soldiers in other vehicles in the convoy later broke into the houses and attacked the occupants, but a mounted Police detachment which appeared prevented further violence.

A man who is believed to have been one of the attackers is reported to have been captured. It is not known whether he is a Jew or an Arab.

Geula (Paducah) and The Jewish State (Northland)

The whole journey, from the despatch centres, through the collecting centres and staging points, to the port of embarkation, was in Russian-occupied territory and was extremely well-organized.

—*British intelligence report on the arrival of The Jewish State at Haifa.*

And then it strikes me, it is I who have changed. Before, as the captain, I felt sorry, deeply feeling the misery of these people, wishing to help, but now I am one of them. Their problems are my problems.... What happens to them happens to me.

—*Rudolph Patzert, captain of the Geula, describing the capture of his ship and passengers.*

As the passengers from the Exodus sweltered on British prison ships outside Port de Bouc in July and August of 1947, the Mossad for Aliyah Bet prepared a response to Britain's new deportation policy. If the British intended to send refugees back to their countries of origin, the Mossad would arrange things so that the British would have a new problem: the Russians. That summer, the Mossad reached an agreement with Soviet authorities to allow Jewish refugees to embark for Palestine from Soviet-controlled Eastern Europe. The agreement included an understanding that the Russians would reject British attempts to return the refugees.

By the time this agreement came into being, the ships that would transport the immigrants from Eastern Europe were already being refitted in the French Atlantic port of Bayonne. They were two former Coast Guard vessels purchased for Aliyah Bet by the Weston Trading Company.

The older of the two was the Paducah, a former icebreaker. Commissioned on September 2, 1905, she had been used as a training ship on the Chesapeake Bay and had a top speed of about 10 knots. The Paducah was partially refitted in Miami, Florida, after the Weston Trading Company bought her early in 1947 for $77,500 from Mary Eurich Angelo. She sailed from Miami to Europe with an American volunteer crew. The Paducah's companion ship, the Northland, sailed from Baltimore, where she had undergone repairs at Pier 4 on Pratt Street. The Baltimore Sun on January 23 quoted Captain Ash of the Weston

Trading Company as saying the war-surplus Northland had been bought for $50,000 for resale to the Danish government. Built in 1927 as an icebreaker, the Northland saw combat duty in World War II, sinking at least two enemy ships.

* * *

Some of the volunteers had been to sea before, and others received their first training while crossing the Atlantic. Before the departure from Baltimore, a volunteer with Merchant Marine experience cleaned out most of his shipmates in a crap game. He stocked up on beer, cigarettes, chocolate, and other supplies to share during the voyage and kept aside a few hundred dollars for his own use in case of emergency. At sea, the volunteers' lack of experience showed up in activities other than dice games. Aboard the Northland, a volunteer who had been an infantryman during the war became seasick every time he took his two-hour turn at the wheel, but the landlubber insisted on learning the job; he cleaned up after himself each time and refused to be replaced. A former Royal Canadian Air Force pilot who knew how to navigate by the stars noticed one night that the Northland was sailing off course toward Africa. After some confusion, someone discovered that the ship's novice 18-year-old helmsman was wearing a heavy steel wrench under his belt, and the metal had been deflecting the needle of the ship's magnetic compass.

Security precautions were impressed upon the American volunteers. But, as in previous sailings from America, others were already in on the secret. As the Northland sailed from Baltimore on May 1, flying the Panamanian flag, a sailor on one of her tugboat escorts was heard to comment: "There goes the Jewish navy." Before the two ships went to Bayonne for refitting, they entered the Mediterranean and stopped at Marseilles and Port du Bouc, two French ports that were frequently used by Aliyah Bet ships to deliver cargo, refuel, and make other arrangements. Before the Northland sailed on June 2 for Bayonne, a group of volunteers dropped into a bar in Marseilles; when the accordionist saw the strangers enter, he interrupted the tune he was playing and broke into "Hatikvah."

A disagreement arose over the participation in the voyage of a Black sailor. Haganah officials in France were unreceptive to his desire to remain part of the crew. They had sent two other Black seamen back to the United States, but the third was persistent and told the Palestinians: "You can't keep a man down without going down yourself." He had volunteered for Aliyah Bet in New York with a Jewish shipmate from the Merchant Marine, and he wanted to go to Palestine. Another Jewish volunteer who had been a Merchant Marine officer reminded the Haganah officials that there were Black Jews, such as the Falashas of Ethiopia. He argued also that a Black member might be a helpful addition to the crew if the British deported them to Kenya. A confrontation flared, and the Palestinians backed down; the Black sailor stayed with the crew and wound up in a British internment camp in Cyprus.

In Bayonne, the crews of the two ships became friendly. They spent almost two months there while hired workmen built sleeping racks for passengers, and the volunteers chipped and painted. At first, the Americans were restricted in their movements for reasons of security, and visits to Paris were forbidden. One volunteer with relatives in Paris decided to sneak off to the capital for a weekend. He arranged for a buddy to take his duties aboard ship; the arrangement seemed to be working smoothly until the two shipmates bumped into each other in the Paris subway on Sunday morning. Both were disciplined when they returned to ship.

After a few weeks in Bayonne, what may have seemed like small lapses in security exploded into something much bigger when a British newspaper printed a sensational article on Aliyah Bet and the volunteers. The article went into details of the clandestine operation, noting that Palestine was code-named "Oklahoma" and refugees were referred to as "bananas." It described the American volunteers as cynical adventurers and riff-raff of the New York underworld. A group of seamen discovered the power of publicity when they visited a Bayonne cafe the night after the article appeared; the owner, instead of giving his usual curt nod of greeting, rose and welcomed them with a respectful handshake.

Exposure in the press brought an end to attempts at secrecy in Bayonne. After their

The Geula (Paducah)

cover was blown, the Palestinian shu-shu boys spoke Hebrew in the street and sang Hebrew songs on deck. In free time, the sailors went to the nearby resort town of Biarritz, which was empty of tourists in the summer of 1947; one volunteer got the impression that a carton of American cigarettes could buy the whole town. At one point, the volunteers decided they needed more pocket money. Although they worked without salary, the volunteers received a small allowance for spending in port. They delegated a tough-talking shipmate who had been a cab driver in Montreal to negotiate for them. After three-quarters of an hour closeted with the Palestinian in charge of the pocket money, the ex-cabbie emerged with a stunned look and informed his shipmates that he had allowed himself to be talked into accepting a reduction of 10 per cent. "That guy is the biggest con-man I ever met," the Canadian volunteer said of the Palestinian.

During the refitting in Bayonne, orders came through from Aliyah Bet headquarters in Paris to prepare for a larger number of refugees. The deal with the Russians had been made. The ships being refitted in Bayonne would deliver from Eastern Europe a complement of refugees approximately equal in number to the Exodus passengers. Instead of rebuilding the Northland to accommodate 1,700 persons, the new order required space for 3,000.

On August 4, the Paducah sailed for the Black Sea. Her route took her around Portugal and Spain to Gibraltar. The Paducah had orders to pass through the Straits of Gibraltar at night, but the cover of darkness was not enough to prevent her being spotted by the British. Thirty miles from Gibraltar, a British aircraft flew over the Paducah. British warships soon arrived and began following the Paducah. She stopped briefly at Bone, Algeria, to make engine repairs which the commanders said had been necessitated by the inexperience of the crew. The Paducah proceeded across the Mediterranean to the Aegean Sea, through the Dardanelles and the Bosphorus, and up the Bulgarian coast to Constanza, Rumania. British warships followed the Paducah until the entrance to

The Jewish State (Northland)

the Dardanelles; there, the Paducah left her British escorts behind and took on a local pilot to guide her through the passages to the Black Sea. Needing to refuel, the Paducah received instructions to proceed to the Bulgarian port of Varna. There, she waited for two weeks without receiving fuel. Then she backtracked more than 50 miles to Burgas, another Bulgarian Black Sea port, to pick up fuel and passengers.

Meanwhile, in Bayonne the Northland fought a bureaucratic battle with French authorities in early August. The Exodus, in her hurried departure from France in July, had incurred certain charges which remained unpaid. Now, as the Paducah steamed eastward to pick up passengers for Palestine, the Northland was being held at Bayonne to pay a fine of 30 million francs on behalf of the Exodus. British agents had pointed out that the Northland and the delinquent Exodus were owned by the Weston Trading Company. To free the Northland to sail, Aliyah Bet officials in Paris sought the aid of Leon Blum, the former three-time Prime Minister of France. Blum was the first Jew to head a French government. In retirement since 1946, he played an instrumental role in preventing British pressure from halting the flow of immigration through France. Through Blum, the Mossad appealed to French officials to rescind the fine in view of the refugees' plight.

When the Northland was finally free on August 28 to leave Bayonne, she followed the Paducah eastward, also encountering British destroyers as she passed Gibraltar. The destroyers trailed the Northland to the Dardanelles, where they reported her passage on September 12, and then waited for her to return from the Black Sea.

When the Northland caught up with the Paducah in Burgas on September 21, Bulgarian authorities would not permit the American volunteers to go ashore from the Northland. The Bulgarians told the Palestinian commander of the Northland that this was because Americans were imperialists. The commander replied that he would not go ashore if his men were confined to ship, and the Bulgarian officials relented. Later, members of the Northland crew heard that their restriction was due not to ideology but to the Bulgarians' unhappy experience with the volunteers from the Paducah, who had gotten drunk and started to fight with Russian troops.

When the time for departure came, events in Burgas marched forward with a stern regularity. Bulgarian authorities closed the port, and the passengers arrived at dockside on sealed trains. They boarded the ships at night.

Unlike previous Aliyah Bet passengers, who received their ship assignments from the clandestine Jewish refugee network in Europe, the refugees departing from Bulgaria had to be approved by Communist authorities. Virtually all came from Rumania. It was speculated later that considerable amounts of money changed hands to make their exit possible; according to one source, Aliyah Bet paid the Rumanians and Bulgarians a flat sum for each refugee permitted to leave.

The Northland boarded her passengers first. At the last moment, 80 additional children turned up on the dock. No place had been allotted for them on the ship; they were taken aboard anyway.

Fuel for the Paducah arrived September 24, on Yom Kippur, the Jewish Day of Atonement. Almost 1,400 passengers came by train the next day. The Paducah left Burgas at 5 a.m. on September 26. By that time, the Northland had already pulled away with almost 2,700 aboard and was waiting in the Bay of Burgas with a Bulgarian pilot. On deck, religiously observant Jews prayed. Aboard the Paducah in the Black Sea, American crewmen and refugee children stood at the rail and watched a glorious sunset. A child with a clear, high voice sang the opening Hebrew words of Hatikvah, the Jewish national hymn, and the others on deck joined in. Two Yiddish songs followed, one a children's tune with new words about Palestine, the other a march asserting the determination of the Jews who fought the Nazis in the ghettoes of Europe.

The two ships headed for the Bosphorus, where the Haganah expected trouble from British-instigated local officials. The Northland tried to avoid anchoring at Istanbul, but a Turkish health officer came aboard. The commanders feared he would detain the refugee ships on grounds of inadequate sanitation.

As was the custom in ports almost everywhere, officers of the Northland offered the Turkish official and his companions American cigarettes and bottles of American blended whisky. The Northland officers also prepared a valise containing part of the cash carried by Aliyah Bet ships for use in emergencies. With $25,000 aboard in various currencies, they had decided to try offering a bribe of $6,000; they had concluded it would be worth paying up to $10,000 to avoid being detained in Istanbul for two or three days. As they presented the papers of the Paducah and Northland, they opened the valise. The Turkish official certified the documents, picked up the valise, and left without counting the money.

The two refugee ships resumed their voyage toward Palestine, crossing the Bosphorus the night of September 27 and arriving at the Dardanelles on September 28. As they emerged from the Dardanelles into the Aegean Sea, the Paducah and Northland found their Royal Navy shadowers waiting for them. At this stage, the British were cordial. They warned of minefields in the Aegean and advised the Northland to change course. The shortest path was through the minefields, and the Northland's American captain chose this more direct route; through the night he shouted commands at his young helmsman as they steered through the mined waters. On this occasion, as on others, the captain fortified himself with alcohol. At another point in the voyage, the captain announced that Jews did not know how to drink; this resulted in a drinking contest in which a Jewish former Merchant Mariner drank the captain under the table. Crewmen carried the captain to his bunk.

When the ships re-entered the Mediterranean, the plan was for the Paducah to transfer her passengers to the Northland and return to Europe for more refugees. At the last moment, this proved impossible. The Northland was overcrowded with almost 2,700 people and would have been unable to carry 4,000 for any length of time. On the Paducah's deck, 150 passengers had no place to lie down; on the Northland, hundreds more had no sleeping space. The weather was good, and this mitigated the passengers' discomforts.

The time came for the ships to take their Hebrew names for the run to Palestine. The Paducah became the Geula, a Hebrew word meaning "redemption;" the Northland became Medinat HaYehudim, "The Jewish State."

Near Crete, with two British destroyers continuing to follow them, the Aliyah Bet ships received new orders: they were to split up, with the Geula proceeding to Haifa and The Jewish State heading for Tel Aviv. The maneuver diluted the strength of the British pursuing force, but only briefly. The Jewish State steamed off with only one British destroyer in pursuit, but within three hours three more had joined the procession.

Aboard the Geula, crew and passengers readied cans of conserves for use as missiles, and they prepared water hoses to spray at boarders. In the radio room, crew members destroyed the Geula's powerful transmitter to prevent its falling into British hands. Radiomen went below with a small American army radio and hand generator, and continued to transmit messages to the Haganah in Palestine. The transmissions were still going through after the British boarded the Geula. But the order to resist capture never came through, and, when the boarding party arrived, the British captured the Geula without difficulty and prepared to tow her to Haifa.

The Jewish State continued on her course toward Tel Aviv. When she was about 90 miles from shore, the British destroyers began to approach. Until then, they had maintained a distance of a mile or more. Now, maintaining their gentlemanly tone, the British addressed the passengers of The Jewish State in four languages: German, Yiddish, Rumanian, and Bulgarian. The British asked the passengers why they should suffer and urged them not to listen to the Haganah leaders. The British said they would take the passengers to Cyprus. The Jewish State declined the invitation and prepared for the confrontation. Knowing that the British would inevitably win a head-on fight, the Haganah commander of The Jewish State asked the American captain to do everything possible to run the ship aground at Tel Aviv, where at least some of the passengers would have a chance of escaping along the beachfront.

"Leave that to me," said the captain. An American volunteer in charge of the duty shift carried out the maneuvers that followed. The Jewish State made a 90-degree turn as two British destroyers approached. Operating on the principle that no captain is prepared to lose his ship, the refugee ship succeeded in forcing the British vessels to veer aside rather than risk colliding at sea with The Jewish State. The British returned, spraying water hoses on deck and shooting tear gas as they came alongside The Jewish State. Another left turn by The Jewish State, and the British ships spread out again. These maneuvers were repeated from about two p.m. until early evening, each round taking about an hour as the ships jockeyed for position. Each time, The Jewish State resumed course and continued to position herself for a final run to the Tel Aviv beach under cover of darkness.

In the fading daylight, with the lights of Tel Aviv in sight, the British ships received orders to engage the refugee vessel. This time, when The Jewish State turned left once again, she collided with a British destroyer. The impact of the collision put a dent in The Jewish State, but it collapsed the bow of the British vessel, which was no match for the heavily plated former icebreaker. The British ship was so seriously disabled that she spent the next half year undergoing repairs.

The battle became a race to the beach. A British destroyer moved in from the other side and sent commando troops onto the bridge of The Jewish State. The defenders of The Jewish State disconnected the controls and abandoned the bridge. They had organized the defense so that, even if the British took the bridge and the deck, the Jews would continue to control the ship. The outside handles of doors leading below deck had been cut off in preparation for this battle, and the below-deck area became a redoubt protected by 300 unarmed Jewish fighters.

Controlled from below deck, and guided from above by sailors in two forward portholes with telephones, The Jewish State continued due east, toward Tel Aviv. A British destroyer steamed alongside. Finally, the British boarders captured the engine-room. The diesel fuel line was cut, disabling The Jewish State's propulsion and electrical systems. The ship ceased to function. A second destroyer pulled alongside. The ventilation system no longer operated, and the Jews below deck were forced to open the doors to allow passengers to breathe.

The Jewish State was towed to Haifa. An American volunteer whose scalp had been creased by a British bullet went to the sick bay. As he lay on a bunk next to a refrigerator in which medicine was stored, the body of a baby accidentally suffocated by its mother during the British tear gas attack was placed in the refrigerator.

Late on the night of October 2, the captured Geula was towed into Haifa harbor as news correspondents waited on the pier. The Jewish State arrived the next day. British agents, trying to pick out the Americans, searched for single men in clothing that appeared non-European. By prearrangement, the sailors had attached themselves to refugee families, and young women passengers claimed that the volunteers were their refugee husbands from Eastern Europe. Passengers from the Geula told an agreed-upon story: they traveled from Europe at night and did not know from which port they departed. A few imaginative ones claimed that they had sailed from Poland. When this drew laugh-

British troops board the captured Geula

ter, a youth retorted that with the Haganah, all things were possible. For several days, the passengers remained at Haifa, and rumors circulated that the new British deportation policy would result in their being sent to South Africa. In the end, after detailed searches and interrogation, the passengers were put aboard transports for Cyprus.

As in previous Aliyah Bet voyages, some crew members escaped in Haifa by hiding in the water tanks of both ships until cleaning workers came aboard and took the sailors ashore past the British guards. Aboard the Geula, an American volunteer prone to claustrophobia had second thoughts about spending a day or several days confined in the darkness of the water tank; he climbed out and went to Cyprus. Haganah representatives in Cyprus gave him an identity document in the name of another person, as they did for the other Americans interned there; he kept his certificate throughout the next four decades without ever meeting the man whose name he borrowed. Aboard the Jewish State, an American volunteer who escaped by the water-tank route disregarded orders to lay low and went to a movie his first night in Haifa. During the movie, he noticed that some of the British soldiers who had boarded his ship were sitting in the next row; at the intermission, he made a discreet exit.

Most of the Americans passed themselves off as refugees and went to Cyprus. Among them was the hired captain of the Jewish State. Many years later, veterans of the American volunteer crew would speak with admiration of the non-Jewish captain's accompanying his passengers to internment camp. Aboard the Geula, the non-Jewish captain also joined his passengers for the trip to internment camp in Cyprus. He took the fictitious name Mendel Levy, and a woman passenger pretended to be his refugee wife. Much later, the captain wrote about his reactions as the British were rounding up his passengers for internment: "The faces ... subtly seem to have changed. And then it strikes me, it is I who have changed. Before, as the captain, I felt sorry, deeply feeling the misery of these people, wishing to help, but now I am one of them. Their problems are my problems.... What happens to them happens to me."

In Cyprus, one of the volunteers mused aloud that he would prefer to be at Coney Island with an American woman, and a refugee told him that an American woman was coming to their camp that day to speak. The visitor was Golda Meir, a Jewish Agency official who had emigrated to Palestine from Milwaukee in 1921 as Golda Meyerson. She explained to the refugees that the British wanted to make a deal to send the Jews from the Exodus to Palestine in place of Cyprus internees who were waiting their turns to enter Palestine. The occupants of the Cyprus camps made it clear they did not like the British proposal to delay their entry to Palestine; after her speech, the future Prime Minister of Israel sat with crew members of the two ships, and they talked animatedly for an hour about the past and future of the Jewish people. After a few weeks in Cyprus, the Americans were transferred back to Haifa as part of the monthly quota of Jews permitted by the British to enter Palestine. Some of the Americans did not wait for their formal release in Palestine; they escaped from a bus transporting them from Haifa to a British transfer camp, and they went underground in Palestine, some to take up residence there and become soldiers in the War of Independence, others to return to the United States. One former Merchant Marine officer, fed up with what he viewed as the Palestinians' improper and unprofessional treatment of the Jewish volunteers, signed on for another Aliyah Bet voyage but insisted on receiving the higher status and pay of the non-Jewish crew members.

* * *

When the British left Palestine in 1948, the ships parted ways. The Geula was sold for scrap. The Jewish State became the A-18, the principal warship of the Israeli Navy.

Prime Minister Ben-Gurion decided that she would be named the Elath, for the harbor where Israel would create a new Red Sea port. This was the site of Israel's southern port in the time of King Solomon; in time, it would be an important seaport again.

Many years after Aliyah Bet, one of the American volunteers who had settled in Israel moved to an apartment in Jerusalem with his family. One day, talking with the family that occupied the apartment across the hall from his, the former sailor learned that his neighbors had escaped from Europe as passengers on his voyage. He was struck by the change in their appearance; on the Aliyah Bet ship, the refugees had a pitiful, wretched aspect; in Jerusalem, in the 1960s, they were a pleasant-looking Israeli family sharing in the modest comforts available in the new country. They told him that, aboard ship, the refugees had looked up to the Americans. "To us, you were like gods," they said. "You came to rescue us."

LATE Edition

THE PALESTINE POST

JERUSALEM
FRIDAY, JANUARY 2, 1948

8 PAGES

PRICE: 30 MILS
VOL. XXIII. No. [illegible]

Column One

By David Courtney

BELATEDLY, "The Times" has deduced what for some weeks has been manifest: the Mandate, *de facto*, has been given up. The lag between the surrender in fact and the surrender in law has created the promised vacuum and is producing the chaos and bloodshed foretold by British spokesmen. The Palestine administration is "fundamentally in a false position," says "The Times." It is indeed. It has been put into that fundamentally false position by a policy which claims sole responsibility for law and order whilst disclaiming its performance. The administration "cannot adopt means whereby the responsibility can be discharged": that is the explanation given by "The Times" for the pitiful failure of the British Government to exercise its Mandatory functions in this last and humiliating phase.

SUCH is the result, if not the immediate purpose, of Bevin's policy, which is ultimately the policy of the whole Government. The Colonial Office is not unaware of the disastrous consequences. Through a London spokesman it has said, in commenting on the breakdown of the Mandate, that the sooner the British troops get out of this mess the better. It is a statement characteristic of a Government incapable of modifying a bad policy except under the compulsion of panic. There are London reports of a desire on the part of the Foreign Office and General Staff to prolong the Mandate beyond May 15. If true, no such proposals would stand a ghost of a chance before the U.N. An earlier message attributed to Bevin the intention of proposing immediate abrogation of the Mandate. It would not be a surprising move, however much in contradiction with the Foreign Minister's emphatic attitude before the Cabinet a month ago.

MR. Bevin, who has gone to much pains to build up a reputation for sticking robustly to his guns, has surrendered them one after the other. If his surrenders had been acts of grace or good sense, he would have done less violence to his country's name and his Party's principles. Instead, they were acts of bad faith and political misjudgment. Misjudgment if not bad faith has produced in Palestine the dilemma to which "The Times" referred to on Wednesday; for it is evident that Mr. Bevin and his advisers were under the impression that the successor authority in Palestine would bring chaos and bloodshed with it, not that the departing Mandatory would leave behind it chaos and bloodshed as its only contribution to the U.N. plan. Happily, "The Times" has not attempted to excuse the Government's impotence at this stage by recalling the decision not to take part in the implementing of Partition. There could hardly be a sillier excuse. The implementation of the responsibilities of the Mandate is what is missing. The keeping of law and order is only part of the U.N. plan in the sense that it is part of all civilized government, mandatory or otherwise. It may also be part of U.N.'s calculations [illegible] gree that U.N. has a right to expect a retiring trustee to hand over its trust in fair order and condition.

IF the British Government, today, is in a fuss and a pother at the way its plans have miscarried, it has only itself — not the Arabs, or the Jews, or U.N. — to blame. The insistence upon exclusive responsibility for law and order, whilst lacking the will and withholding the means to enforce law and order, is a state of affairs produced neither by accident nor exigency. It is difficult to brush aside the suggestion that the gap between the Palestine Administration's responsibilities and its means of discharging them, to which "The Times" refers, is itself a factor of deliberate policy. The withholding of the means is nothing less than a refusal to employ them. The prim assertion of sole responsibility may be part and parcel of the policy which refuses to exercise it. There is evidence enough to show that the false position into which the Palestine Administration has been put is exactly where Mr. Bevin intended it to be put.

Jerusalem, Jan. 2.

FOREIGN AND COLONIAL OFFICES DISAGREE
CONFLICTING VIEWS ON PALESTINE

By GEORGE LICHTHEIM, Palestine Post Correspondent

LONDON, Thursday. — The latest events in Palestine are understood to have accentuated the chronic differences between the Colonial and Foreign Offices, and the Cabinet is now faced with conflicting advice on the question of evacuation. A Cabinet meeting to discuss Palestine is scheduled for next week, by which time it is expected that both departments will have prepared their briefs.

High Foreign Office officials are reported to be maintaining an illogical position, coupling strict neutrality with postponement of the evacuation, and even a reconsideration of the terms of the Mandate's abrogation.

Contrary to the impression prevailing yesterday, it is now believed that the Colonial Office may support the demand for an earlier termination of the Mandate, provided that order is energetically maintained in the meanwhile, and that the U.N. Commission is given a chance to take over responsibility.

Since the Colonial Office inclines to the carrying out of the U.N. plan, it is perhaps not surprising that it advocates giving up the Mandate earlier than was originally intended, and letting the Jews aid the Commission in maintaining order. It is believed that Jewish circles, though aware of the risks of this course, would prefer it to the Foreign Office's counter-proposals envisaging the reopening of the whole question of the establishment of independence this year.

The Cabinet will presumably be asked by Mr. Bevin to consider the wider danger inherent in large-scale fighting in Palestine, coupled with the worsening situation in Greece. Observers commenting on this line of reasoning, which is at the moment fashionable in Foreign Office quarters, point out that this danger has been brought about by Mr. Bevin's own refusal to assist the implementation of the U.N. plan.

Retain Mandate

Naturally, the conclusion drawn by the Foreign Office is not that Britain should actively assist the U.N., but rather to postpone the evacuation and retain the Mandate for some further period and try to gain Arab and Jewish support for some fresh political settlement. It is believed that one object of Mr. Eden's current visit to Baghdad is to discover how far this line is likely to obtain Iraq's support.

Partition on The Agenda

LONDON, Thursday. — Palestine will "naturally" be discussed when Mr. Bevin holds talks next week with the Iraqi Premier and Foreign Minister, a Foreign Office spokesman stated today.

Salyh Jabr Pasha, Iraq's Premier, will leave Baghdad for London on January 7. The main topic of the talks is understood to be the Anglo-Iraqi Alliance which Iraq wants to revise immediately. One of her major demands is the immediate withdrawal of all British forces from Iraqi territory.

Mr. Anthony Eden, former British Foreign Secretary, left Baghdad for Teheran today. (U.P., A.P. and A.N.A.)

Arabs Lobbying Against Partition

LONDON, Thursday (JTA). — A five-point diplomatic plan for defeating the Partition scheme is being pushed with the utmost determination by Arab diplomats in London, according to highly reliable British sources.

This plan, which Middle East quarters claim "has already secured the support of very influential circles," amounts in practice to the undoing of UN's decision to divide Palestine into two independent States. Assuming that the situation in Palestine deteriorates irreparably, the scheme strives for the following solution — (1) calling the U.N. "Little Assembly" which would then postpone the date of implementing Partition, and (2) establishing a kind of temporary rule for, say, 18 months.

The British would then be invited not to evacuate Palestine in the meantime, they suggest.

Britain Ignores Arabs' War Declaration -- Ben Gurion

Palestine Post Bureau

TEL AVIV, Thursday. — Mr. David Ben Gurion, chairman of the Jewish Agency Executive, charged in a statement to the press today that the British Colonial Secretary and his representatives in Palestine did not distinguish between attackers and attacked, despite the open declaration of war by the Arabs.

Mr. Ben Gurion criticised the Government's "righteous neutrality," by which it tried to disarm the Jews of their defence weapons while not seriously interfering with the aggressors when they brazenly looted Government arms and stores, and murdered and stole before the very eyes of Police, sometimes without interference. He added that the stubbornness with which the British retained the Trans-Jordan Arab Legion in Palestine and sought to fetter the Haganah appeared suspicious.

After stating that the Jews would not be deterred by the Government's betrayal of its last obligation, Mr. Ben Gurion said that the defence scheme this time differed from that in previous disturbances. The Jews had to defend the Jewish community of Palestine, the borders of the Jewish State, the recommendations of the U.N. General Assembly and all peace-loving inhabitants of the Jewish State — Jews, British, Arabs or others.

But, he said, the Jews did not this time stand alone. The war declared by Hitler's Middle East disciples was against the entire U.N. organization.

Mr. Ben Gurion lashed out against "sensation mongers" who sought to associate the Zionist movement with the "Eastern" or "Western" powers. They ignored the fact that both sides had been united in the General Assembly in support of the Jewish State, he said, and the Zionist State relied on this unity.

In demanding moral and material aid from the United Nations, Mr. Ben Gurion warned the Jews that they must rely primarily upon their own effective, enterprising and imaginative defence.

"We have not and shall not wage war against the Arab people, just as our resistance to the treacherous White Paper was not a war against the British people," he said. He stressed the Jewish determination to live in peace with the Arabs, but also to resist any attack.

He described the present sacrifices as "the birth pangs of the Jewish State," and said that the people would accept them with love, faith and devotion.

480 KILLED, 1,000 HURT

Official figures place the total casualties in Palestine from November 30 to the end of 1947 at 480 dead and 1,000 injured, 401 of them seriously, it was announced in Jerusalem yesterday.

The dead were 204 Jews, 208 Arabs, six other civilians, 12 British soldiers, five British Police, 11 J.S.P.'s, one Jewish S.P.C., two T.J.F.F., and one Arab S.P.C.

The injured were 379 Jews, 512 Arabs, four other civilians, 34 British soldiers, five Jewish prisoners, 17 J.S.P.'s, one Jewish S.P.C., nine Jewish Police, 26 British Police, four Arab T.A.P.'s, five Arab S.P.C.'s and four T.J.F.F.

Village Cafe Shot Up

JAFFA, Thursday. — Two Arabs were killed and nine were injured when steel-helmeted I.Z.L. raiders in battle dress dashed into town in a jeep early this afternoon and sprayed the side-walk tables of a cafe with automatic fire.

The party entered Jaffa through Manshieh Quarter and drove through King George Blvd. As the jeep swerved into Falameh road, the raiders shot the persons sitting at the tables. They then sped down the street, crashed through the Arab road block near the border, and disappeared into Tel Aviv.

An official statement said that the party in Army uniform wearing the badges of the Royal Irish Fusiliers, was led by an officer of the unit. After an investigation, it was stated that no jeep of the Royal Irish Fusiliers was in the area at the time of the shooting, and that no personnel were missing.

TAKEN FROM BED

HAIFA, Thursday. — Before the eyes of his parents, Moshe Bodek, 19, was taken out of his bed early this morning and kidnapped by a large group of armed, masked men.

He was carried out through the window of his house at 7 [illegible] Street.

The Purloined Letters

The two consignments of mail stolen from a train on December 27 consisted of letters and parcels from the United States, Switzerland, Egypt, Haifa, Jaffa, Tel Aviv and Tulkarm, it was officially announced in Jerusalem yesterday.

The stolen mail from Switzerland included letters and parcels for the Jerusalem and Tel Aviv areas; letters from the United States and Egypt for the Jerusalem area; and local letters and parcels for the Jerusalem district.

POST OFFICE CLOSED AGAIN

Palestine Post Staff

The General Post Office in Jerusalem was closed again yesterday when the Arab workers, who had reported for duty on Wednesday, stayed away. They demand that the Jews return to work and that a 50 per cent Arab and 50 per cent Jewish guard be posted on the building.

It was learned last night that the Post Office hoped to find a solution to the problem shortly.

The offices of the Department of Education in Jerusalem have been split into Arab and Jewish sections. The Arab staff is now accommodated in the Department's stores offices in St. Louis Way (Telephone 4611), while the Jewish branch is off Princess Mary Avenue above Mr. Lewin-Epstein's surgery (Telephone 4613).

The examination centre is in the Jewish office, but an Arab examination officer is available at the Arab office.

A number of Jewish employees in Consulates in the Security Zones are reported to have been warned by Arabs not to come to work. It is understood that the matter is to be discussed by the Consulates concerned, some of which are considering opening branches in Jewish quarters if their Jewish staff are not afforded protection.

KILLED IN AMBUSH

TIBERIAS, Thursday. — Ambushed this afternoon while patrolling fields in Genosar settlement near here, David Baer, 20, one of the settlers, was killed, and Yaacov Weinreich, also of Genosar, and Gideon Salomon of Yakuk settlement were wounded.

Haganah reinforcements fought the Arabs for about four hours. The gang reportedly came from Kuseiriya village north of Yakuk, and consisted of men from Safad and Syria.

WATER RESERVOIR UNDER FIRE

GAZA, Thursday. — Strong fire was directed at a water reservoir on the Negev pipeline between Dorot and Ruhama settlements at 8.30 last night. The fire was returned by the defenders. There were no casualties.

BROADCAST TO ARABS

TEL AVIV, Thursday. — In an Arabic broadcast last night, the Jewish Defence Forces said that any village offering shelter to Arab gangs would be regarded and treated as accomplices.

The Defence Forces would, as hitherto, refrain from harming innocent people, but would mercilessly attack organized bands. The broadcast appealed to peace-loving Arabs to expel gangsters from their villages.

Reprisal Raid On C.R.L. Murderers

Palestine Post Bureau

HAIFA, Thursday. — Seventeen dead and 31 wounded are the figures given by the Government Hospital here of casualties sustained in an attack on Balad-esh-Sheikh village near here last night. Jewish sources reported that the attacks were carried out by the Haganah.

Most of the villagers at Balad esh-Sheikh are employed at the C.R.L., where 39 Jews were killed on Tuesday.

The attacking force, which used Brens, Stens, rifles and grenades, lost three men killed. They are Haim Ben-Dor, a son of Mr. Yitzhak Ben-Dor, the Jerusalem correspondent of the Hebrew daily "Davar," Hanan Belinger and Amos Gal[illegible], 21.

Another Haganah party which attacked Hawassa village found the perimeter houses deserted, and only women and children in other houses. No action was taken against them.

Buildings Blasted

Palestine Post Bureau

TEL AVIV, Thursday. — A spokesman of the Jewish defence forces said today that three buildings were demolished in Salameh village during the night in a raid to disperse gang concentrations in the village, which had been the base for attacks upon Hatikva Quarter.

The Haganah force occupied the village for about two hours, during which the men were screened. A quantity of illegal arms was seized.

A heavy barrage of automatic fire, punctuated with loud explosions, kept the people in the neighbourhood awake through the early hours of the morning.

No casualties were reported by either side.

A Haganah patrol detected an Arab sniper opposite the Shapira Quarter this afternoon. The sniper fired twice at a Jewish truck, but missed. A Haganah man shot and silenced the Arab.

This evening, three Jews were brought to the Hadassah Hospital from the Hatikva Quarter, wounded by Arab snipers. They were Bluma Yanovitz, 20, Abraham Ben Ami, 18, and Shlomo Haskelevitz, 18.

HAGANAH KILLS TWO NAZIS

Palestine Post Staff

Two Germans, one of them known to be a member of the Nazi Party, were killed by the Haganah in Jerusalem yesterday, Jewish sources said last night. One of them was said to have been in touch with Arab terror bands and to have been an informer.

According to the same sources, booby traps placed by the Haganah in the doors of Jewish shops temporarily evacuated were discovered by troops, who brought mine-detectors at the request of Arabs.

Yesterday afternoon, one Arab was killed in the Sanhedria Quarter of Jerusalem in a Haganah action. Another Arab was wounded.

The same sources reported that the attempts of the Arab villages of Jabaliya and Tel er-Rish to form peace pacts with their Jewish neighbours at Holon had been stopped by the Arab Higher Executive, which had also ordered the removal of posters in Arabic in Tulkarm condemning the attacks [illegible].

APPEAL FOR PEACE

Another Appeal in leaflet form has been distributed by the Haganah in Arab villages and towns, Jewish sources reported in Jerusalem yesterday.

Summarising the effect of a month of rioting on Arab workers, fellaheen and merchants, the leaflet pointed out that many workers had been thrown out of employment as a result of economic dislocation and the inability to sell to the Jews.

In the border areas of Jaffa and Tel Aviv and in Jerusalem, Arab merchants had been forced to leave, and their economic life had been stifled.

"The Food situation in the Arab camp has worsened, and the price of pittah (Arab bread) has increased — in some cases it has doubled — while a black market has set in for food and for goods stolen from trains."

The leaflet added that the dislocation and economic hardships would get worse, and the Arabs had only themselves to blame for it all.

"We shall have peace in this country if you turn the war-mongers and inciters away from your towns and villages. Peace unto those who desire peace, the message ended.

HAGANAH FIGHTER SENTENCED

Palestine Post Staff

The first trial of a Haganah man arrested in the disturbances ended in the Military Court in Jerusalem yesterday when David Michael Kagan, a 21-year-old ex-soldier, was sentenced to five and three years' imprisonment — to run concurrently — when he was found guilty on charges of discharging and carrying a firearm. Kagan was accorded special treatment.

After Mr. A. N. Elkayam, one of the mukhtars of the Ezra and Hatikva Quarters of Tel Aviv, had told of an attack from the direction of Salameh village on the morning of December 8, two Red Shield men told of seeing Kagan bringing in the body of a man. They both testified that Kagan was unarmed, and a J.S.P. also said that he saw the accused without arms.

Closing the case for the defence, Mr. E. D. Goitein referred to the "extremely hurling language" used by the Military Prosecutor in the opening stages of the case. He said: "The remarks were of a purely political character and were not relevant" as to whether Kagan held or fired on that day. He used the charming word "thug" for people in a field defending themselves against an Arab attack. Soldiers in the field may win a Military Cross — all these boys can look forward to is a Military Court. They do what other soldiers do — in fighting for their country — they obey orders and run the risk of being killed night and day.

"These boys are fighting for their country against attackers who show no mercy or pity, and if they are caught they are liable to long sentences or to be hanged. They ask for nothing more than to be allowed to do a simple duty — to defend themselves, but they have to act as conspirators to carry out that duty. That is the thanks they get for doing some of the work which should be done by the Police and Army. If that is a 'thug,' then it is an honourable term."

Stating that if ever there was justification for a defence force in Palestine "this case has shown it," Counsel stressed that someone had to do the job of defending the Jews.

Referring to Police evidence as a "made-up story," Mr. Goi[illegible]

(Continued on Page 2)

BOARDING PARTY WITHOUT ARMS
LANDING TO TAKE THREE DAYS

NICOSIA, Thursday. — The Pan York and the Pan Crescent, renamed the Independence and Ingathering of Refugees, both flying the Zionist flag and carrying between them 15,300 visaless Jewish refugees, entered Famagusta harbour at dawn today. Their disembarkation began in the afternoon.

The ships did not put up any resistance when intercepted last night outside territorial waters. Both captains immediately agreed to being escorted into Famagusta by five destroyers and two cruisers — the heaviest escort ever employed for illegal immigrant vessels.

According to figures so far available, the passengers include 1,300 children, more than 1,000 of them under five years of age; 1,000 unaccompanied youths under 17; and six babies born on the voyage (four more are expected at any moment).

Troops Without Arms

The Pan York was the first ship to be boarded by British troops when they dropped anchor one mile off shore shortly before eight o'clock this morning. Among the boarding party were a number of troops of the Sixth Airborne Division, who arrived in Cyprus from Palestine only yesterday. They did not carry arms.

The disembarkation is proceeding slowly, as the authorities are anxious not to separate families. It is expected that the whole operation will take more than three days. The refugees are being taken to the Caraolos and Xylotymbou camps.

For the first time, immigrants were permitted to carry off their luggage without search on board.

By six o'clock tonight, more than 1,500 refugees from the Pan York, including expectant mothers and two sick children, had been accommodated in a camp with the 1,500 who came off the Pan Crescent.

The British authorities commended the "excellent organisation" among the immigrants, whose leaders stood on gangways to relay instructions passed from the bridge.

The organization aboard the vessels was excellent, the military stated, and medical arrangements made it possible to leave the sick on board while awaiting a break in the weather. Fifty-five doctors were among the passengers.

The professional crews, according to an authoritative statement, must be prepared to be sent back home, but the immigrant crews will be accepted either into Cyprus or Palestine camps.

All newcomers will be treated in the same way as the 11,000 refugees now in Cyprus camps, a Foreign Office spokesman stated in London today, and can expect to reach Palestine before May 15, by which date the Cyprus camps will have been cleared. (Reuter, AP, UP)

CYPRUS CAMPS TO BE ENLARGED

By [illegible], Palestine Post Correspondent

NICOSIA, Thursday. — The military authorities have just been given approval by the Cyprus Government to extend the detention camps' accommodation to take 41,000 "illegal immigrants," I have been privately informed.

Extensions are to be made in the existing camps, while the Jewish Immigrants' compound at the Nicosia Military Hospital will also be enlarged. These extensions which were being planned by the Army since early October, have now been hastened, due to the arrival of the Pan York and Pan Crescent.

Squeezed In

The existing accommodation in existing camps is — Xylotymbou 21,000 in seven camps and Caraolos 9,000 in five camps. The new batch which has just arrived will be squeezed into the present camps with considerable congestion in several of them, and by converting all tents and Nissen Huts now used as kitchens etc. into living quarters.

Pay Corps soldiers disembarked here from Palestine yesterday, as their HQ has now been transferred to Cyprus. Some 30 tons of military cargo arrived with them, nine tons of which is understood to be Pay Corps stationery.

More Than Enough

LONDON, Thursday (UP). — An Admiralty spokesman confirmed today that there was "more than enough accommodation" on Cyprus for the Pan York and Pan Crescent refugees.

He indicated that the Cyprus Government could even offer further accommodation for more immigrants.

700 More Arrive at Nahariya

Palestine Post Bureau

HAIFA, Thursday. — The s.s. United Nations, a two-masted schooner with about 700 refugees, beached herself at Nahariya at 1 o'clock this afternoon, and the immigrants went ashore.

The United Nations was at sea for nine days. There were 90 children and infants and many women on board.

A 24-hour curfew was later imposed on the town, and a cordon of troops of the Sixth Airborne Division was thrown around it.

It was officially reported that 100 persons were arrested on the beach, of whom 42 were detained. The others were Palestinian citizens.

GOVT., REBELS CLAIM GAINS

ATHENS, Thursday. — Conflicting reports continue to come in concerning the front around Konitza, just south of the Albanian frontier, with the Greek War Ministry claiming that the guerrillas had been routed and a guerrilla communique asserting that the ring surrounding the town had not been broken.

According to the official Greek communique, Government forces entered Konitza last night, after dislodging the guerrillas and inflicting heavy losses on them. There was no mention of the direction in which the guerrillas retreated, but their primary escape route appeared to have been to the north-east, towards the Grammos Mountain stronghold.

"The battle-weary Konitza garrison of less than 1,000," the communique says, "which has withstood savage frontal attacks for seven days by 6,000 Communist guerrillas, is now being evacuated and relief forces are taking over."

There are no reports of foreigners fighting with the guerrillas in the Konitza operation, although military sources said that a substantial number of them had been trained in Albania and Yugoslavia and that all arms and ammunition had come from there.

Meanwhile, UNSCOB, in a report sent to Lake Success from Salonika last night, said that events might impel it to recommend the convocation of a special session of the General Assembly. (AP & Reuter)

JEW KILLED, 3 HURT IN JERUSALEM

Palestine Post Reporter

Arab attacks in Jerusalem yesterday resulted in the deaths of one Jew and injuries to three others. Buses and an ambulance again came under Arab fire, while following a violent explosion shortly before 7 p.m. it was officially reported that three Arab houses had been blown up near Malha village.

Shmuel Mizrahi, a 50-year-old street cleaner who worked in Talpiot, was found stabbed to death in Deir Abu Tor early in the afternoon. He leaves a wife and nine children.

The dead man, who lived in the Old City, had not been home since the beginning of the disturbances. He was in working clothes when passers-by found his body in the street. He was last seen alive about 11 a.m., travelling in a truck in the direction of Deir Abu Tor. There was a girl in the vehicle with the driver.

Three persons were injured when heavy fire was directed at a No. 11 bus near Givat Shaul at 4.45 p.m. The crews of two Police armoured cars which were at the scene drove their vehicles forward to shield the bus from the firing and helped the passengers to take cover in ditches. They then engaged the attackers and laid down a heavy barrage in the Lifta area.

One of the armoured cars raced into town and escorted a Red Shield ambulance to pick up the wounded. The ambulance was fired on and one tyre was punctured. The first-aid men had to crawl towards their vehicle with the three injured persons and an expectant mother suffering from shock. The injured are Shimon Halevi, 14, seriously hurt, Tikva Molart 17, and Shlomo Freiman, 44.

There were no casualties when a grenade was thrown and shots were fired at an armoured bus in the Sheikh Jarah Quarter at 1.30 p.m. The bus was on the way to Mt. Scopus.

Just before 11 p.m., a violent explosion shook the city. The explosion was preceded by small-arms fire directed at a pill-box in the Sheikh Jarah Quarter. A few minutes later, the rear of a house across from St. George's Cathedral was blown up and extensive damage was caused. A Bren-gun was found near the spot.

Jewish sources reported that the earlier explosion, in which three houses were blown up near Malha village, had been caused by a Stern Gang attack.

A young Arab in European clothes who appeared to be acting suspiciously was questioned by a J.S.P. patrol in the New Montefiore Quarter yesterday afternoon and handed over to an Army patrol.

HELPED 60,000

NEW YORK, Thursday (UP). — The year end report of the United Jewish Appeal in the U.S. announced today that in the past year it had helped approximately 60,000 European Jews, the majority of them [illegible] new homes in Palestine and elsewhere. This year its plans provide for the resettlement of 125,000 Jews on the continent.

The Aid Committees are seeking to provide reconstruction help and defence of the Jewish State in Palestine as well as assistance to Jewish refugees attempting to reach the U.S. Of the 60,000 Jews assisted by the agency, approximately one half had settled in Palestine, 25,000 in the U.S. and the remaining 5,000 in other countries, at a cost of 134 million dollars.

The report stressed that in addition to the U.N. decision to allow 15,000 Jews to enter the Jewish State within 1948, and 25,000 to come to the U.S., the U.J.A. hoped that the American Congress would permit enlarged refugee immigration to the U.S. The report maintained that this would have a "salutary effect on the immigration policies of other nations."

NO CONTACT WITH OLD CITY

For the third day in succession, no Jewish vehicles entered the Old City of Jerusalem from outside the walls, and Jewish inhabitants were again unable to return to their homes.

The escorted bus which was ready to go off daily was once more delayed because of the road blocks placed at Jaffa Gate and in Mamillah Road by Arabs.

All day Arabs checked every person entering the Old City, and it was reported that Police and troops were also required to produce identity cards.

The failure of the bus to get through has caused hardship to hundreds of families. One woman reported that she had not been able to get to the Jewish Quarter to see her seven-year-old son since Tuesday.

A Jewish Agency spokesman said in Jerusalem yesterday that the Government had to arrange to get the convoys through and the Agency would give all help possible.

Referring to the fact that 25 bodies were awaiting burial, the spokesman said that it might be necessary for the security forces to shoot their way through to the cemetery; something must be done. He believed that the Haganah would be willing to cooperate provided their arms were not taken away — they had assisted in repelling attacks at the cemetery on Tuesday and their arms had not been seized.

Some of the bodies are those of persons killed last Saturday. Two attempts to bury them on Monday and Tuesday were both stopped. The funeral which came to the cemetery on Tuesday came under heavy fire. A British Constable and a volunteer burial society worker were killed in a two-hour battle, and the funeral returned to town.

Atzmaut and Kibbutz Galuyot (Pan Crescent and Pan York)

I said that I could not believe that the Jews would any longer proceed with illegal immigration, since it must be a dead loss to them and would be of no pressure value.

Bevin questioned this.

—United States Secretary of State George C. Marshall, in a memorandum of a meeting December 5, 1947, with British Foreign Secretary Bevin.

British rule in Palestine had been broken, not by the terrorist, but by the almost despised illegal immigrant. He—and the men and the women who brought him—had undermined the moral claim of the British to rule in Palestine, and this was at the root of all else that followed. It was the homeless wanderer returning to Zion with neither visa nor passport, other than those indelibly stamped upon him by history. It is to the unquestionable credit of the British that after this last demonstrative show of strength they had, in the end, neither the heart nor the will to carry on a fight for which all moral sanction was so patently lacking. The Pan ships had provided the conclusive evidence. They were a bigger triumph for the Mossad than its directors had realized at the time, for they had demonstrated to the British the purposelessness of further struggle and bloodshed.

—Jon and David Kimche, The Secret Roads.

The last major American involvement in Aliyah Bet was set in motion on Saint Patrick's Day, 1947, with the purchase of the freighters Pan York and Pan Crescent.

More than nine months elapsed before the two ships were able to sail from Bulgaria with the largest number of refugees ever carried in Aliyah Bet. During this time, political events outside the hands of the men operating Aliyah Bet dominated the scene. British diplomats intervened with one government after another to prevent the ships' sailing, pressing the case with the U.S. Department of State until almost the last moment. As political circumstances changed, Zionist leaders in Palestine disagreed over whether the operation should go forward. The British turned the Palestine question over to the United Nations, which appointed a Special Commission to study the issue and make recommendations. Some Zionist leaders feared that a refugee voyage of this magnitude would appear provocative and alienate governments voting in the United Nations. Others argued that it was necessary to keep up the pressure on the British and maintain the momentum toward an independent Jewish state. The United Nations General Assembly voted on November 29 to recommend the partition of Palestine into Jewish and Arab states, and the Arab League announced its determination to prevent the Jewish state from coming into being. The plans for the refugee voyage went forward. By the time the Pan York and Pan Crescent left Europe with more than 15,000 refugees in the last week of December, the rapid succession of events during 1947 had outrun the earlier aims of Aliyah Bet. But the British had not yet departed from Palestine, and the Jews had not yet won the right of free entry to their future country.

* * *

The sister ships had been banana carriers in the service of the United Fruit Company. As such, the Pan York and Pan Crescent would be better suited than other types of vessels for Aliyah Bet. Compared to freighters with deep holds, banana carriers with their extensive, shallower decks were less difficult to convert for transporting large numbers of passengers.

Paul Shulman, a young former U.S. Navy officer who was a volunteer adviser on the purchase and refitting of ships for Aliyah Bet, went to New Jersey with two $125,000 checks in his pocket on March 17, 1947, to buy the Pan York and Pan Crescent in the name of the FB Shipping Company. The company was an Aliyah Bet front, and its name was derived from the initial letters of the motto "F--- Britain." At the contract signing, when asked what the company initials stood for, Shulman replied, "Far Better."

The purchase of the Pan York and Pan Crescent put the American branch of Aliyah Bet into the cargo business. To defray expenses, and to put British intelligence off the track, the refugee-smuggling organization looked for legitimate cargo to carry.

* * *

The Pan Crescent was the first to sail for Europe, going to Venice for refitting. The Italian city was occupied at the time by the British Army, and Royal Navy warships used the harbor. It was not long before the Aliyah Bet men in Venice became aware that the British were inquiring about them.

Paul Shulman, who had arrrived in Venice to help supervise the preparation of the Pan Crescent, was called in for questioning by the local police. The Italian officer who questioned Shulman made no secret of his anti-British feelings. Instead of arresting the American volunteer, the official filled Shulman in about British intelligence activities and gave him a permit to carry a gun.

On the night of April 30, 1947, as the Pan Crescent sat in the harbor at Venice, a limpet mine exploded and blew a hole in her side. She began to tilt dangerously, and the chief engineer directed emergency efforts to sink her straight down into the water and prevent her from toppling over. Shulman, notified by telephone of the explosion, tried without success to find a motor launch to take him to the scene. He hired a gondola and observed that the two gondoliers paddled faster when he drew his gun. The damage could be patched; within a few days, the hole created by the explosion was sealed with timber and concrete, and the ship was pumped dry. The work to prepare the Pan Crescent for her refugee voyage started again, and the Haganah ordered extra precautions against further sabotage.

The Haganah worried about how to overcome British efforts to keep the Pan Crescent from leaving Venice. The bomb damage could render the Pan Crescent no longer eligible for a certificate of seaworthiness, and this alone could be grounds for the Italian authorities to refuse permission to leave the harbor. As the work went forward during the summer, Ada Sereni, in charge of Haganah activities in Italy, struck a deal with the Mayor of Venice. According to Shulman, the deal took shape as follows.

Haganah representatives had been keeping their eyes on a British warship moored at Venice. Their purpose was to contrive defenses for the Pan Crescent against hostile boarding parties. After the seizure of the Exodus at sea in mid-July, they wanted to equip the Pan Crescent better, with live steampipes on her gunwales, and with trailing wires that could foul the propellers of attacking warships. Not having the blueprints of the British ship, the Haganah men went to the dock to make visual estimates of the height of her deck and other factors they needed for their planning. They were observed visiting the warship at dockside, and the British made representations to the local Italian authorities.

When Ada Sereni went to see the Mayor of Venice to ask his help in releasing the Pan Crescent to sail, he was sympathetic, but he dropped a figurative bombshell. He told her that Haganah men had been seen snooping around the British vessel, and he confronted her with the accusation that the Haganah intended to place a bomb on the British ship in retaliation for the explosion on the Pan Crescent. In Shulman's words:

"Ada was a wonderful actress besides being a wonderful woman. She said: 'Yes, it is so; but how did you find out?'

"He said: 'You cannot do this. It cannot be done, and you must stop it.'

"She said we would stop it (which we had never intended to do in the first place) provided he did two things which we wanted. First was to make sure the drydock was available to us. And the second was to have a cocktail party for all the officers of this ship on the night of sailing."

To escape, the Pan Crescent needed time to get clear of the Venice lagoon and enter international waters. Because the lagoon was shallow and had an extremely narrow channel, it would have been relatively easy for a British ship to force the Pan Crescent aground in the lagoon. As the Mayor promised, a cocktail party for the British officers took place the night of sailing, and the Pan Crescent was able to disappear from Venice before the British realized what was happening.

The escape of the Pan Crescent from Venice had a further element of deception, occasioned by the visit of two ships of a United States destroyer squadron in which Shulman had served in World War II. Most of the officers knew Shulman, who had been second-in-command of a destroyer in the war, and he carefully avoided contact with them in Venice. As the Pan Crescent was preparing to sail, Shulman noticed in his hotel one of the American officers, a captain with whom he had once had a run-in. While on shore patrol in a Chilean port, Shulman had ejected this captain from a brothel. Now, to avoid being spotted by him, Shulman hired a prostitute and instructed her to go to the American captain and say she was a present from an old friend. When the American captain walked off with the prostitute, Shulman and a group of Haganah men left without being seen.

The Pan Crescent sailed for Constanza, Rumania. Aboard her were a number of American volunteers who had arrived only that day from France, where they had left her sister ship, the Pan York.

* * *

The Pan York took a different route. After arriving at Marseilles, she augmented her crew during the summer with some experienced American volunteers who had reached France as prisoners of the British. These Americans had been aboard the Exodus when the British captured the refugee ship July 18. The British put the Exodus passengers and crew aboard prison ships and tried to return them to France, but the refugees refused to get off at Port de Bouc. The British prison ships sat outside Port de Bouc for almost a month, drawing the attention of the world press to the determination of the refugees not to give in to the British. Except for a few elderly or infirm passengers who went ashore, the refugees rejected offers of sanctuary in France and stood firm in their demand to be allowed into Palestine. As the refugees' protest went forward, the Haganah sent word to about 10 of the American volunteers to go ashore and report for new assignments. One task that awaited them was helping smuggle explosives to their comrades aboard the prison ship Empire Rival outside Port de Bouc. Using small boats, the Americans ferried the makings of a bomb to the Empire Rival inmates under the noses of the British.

Then the Americans went to nearby Marseilles for further orders. One volunteer who had lost about 20 pounds from eating poorly aboard the Empire Rival asked the Haganah to let him go to the Riviera for a rest. With a buddy, he went to Monte Carlo for a few days and won at roulette. Then they went to Nice for a week, lost their winnings, and had to ask the Haganah for money to return to Marseilles. There, some of the Americans were assigned to the Pan York for a fully legal voyage carrying cargo.

With the Americans aboard, the Pan York sailed to the Atlantic coast of Morocco to pick up a cargo of phosphate from Safi, south of Casablanca. The Americans had a week of leisure on the Moroccan coast, enjoying the beach and blue skies. One smoked hashish for the first time in his life and concluded that it was not worth the trouble. From Safi, the Pan York sailed north to deliver her cargo to two French ports, Brest and Rouen, and then headed back into the Mediterranean. Although one purpose of the Pan York's cargo run had been to provide her with the cover of an ordinary merchant vessel, British intelligence was on the lookout for her, and a Royal Navy destroyer was on her trail when she passed Gibraltar on September 29 en route to the Mediterranean coast of France. When the Pan York reached Port de Bouc, American volunteers noticed that the three prison ships filled with passengers from the Exodus were no longer there. They had left for Hamburg, Germany, and two of the Americans asked the Haganah to send them ahead to Hamburg to rejoin their friends. Instead, the Americans received orders to join the Pan Crescent in Venice. About a half dozen Americans without passports and a handful of Palestinians with refugee papers accomplished this by boarding a small boat near Monte Carlo, sneaking ashore in Italy at Ventimiglia, taking a train to Milan where they stayed for several days, and then catching another train to Venice. Cajoling their way out of encounters with police at several points on the journey, they boarded the Pan Crescent at Venice and she sailed the same night for Constanza, Rumania.

* * *

Trailed by British destroyers all the way to the entrance to the Dardanelles, the Pan York left France and followed her sister ship to Constanza, arriving on October 10, a few days after the Pan Crescent.

Moored side by side at Constanza, the two ships underwent their final preparations through most of October, November, and December. On free evenings, the Americans went to the restaurant of the Hotel Carlton, where a violinist played. Russian officers also ate there, and the Americans and Russians came to recognize one another. The Americans struck up friendships with young Jews in the Rumanian port. They went to movies together, and some of the Americans were invited into the home of a well-to-do Jewish widow who had attractive daughters and served good food. One American took advantage of his presence in Rumania to obtain permission from the Haganah to visit his native town of Satmar, where he had lived until the age of six months. He found the house he had lived in, met a number of his relatives, and persuaded some to sign up to travel on his ship.

Workmen at Constanza installed bunks equipping each ship to carry more than 7,000 refugees. The bunks were typical Aliyah Bet accommodations; they were wooden benches slightly less than six feet long and two feet deep. Originally they were to be almost 20 inches wide, but their width was reduced by four inches to increase the number of spaces by 20 per cent. The biggest passenger liners in the world were 10 times greater in tonnage but carried only one-third as many people. Drawing on the experiences of earlier voyages, and seeking to take no chances with the lives of the passengers, the Haganah made provisions for health and security. Plans for each ship called for a surgical operating room, 24 doctors, and 40 nurses. Plans were made to organize the passsengers into groups of 50, with a refugee leader for each group. On each ship, some four dozen handpicked refugees would serve as security guards.

* * *

American volunteers who had served on earlier Aliyah Bet vessels filled key jobs on the Pan York and Pan Crescent. One volunteer, for instance, was put in charge of 3,800 refugees on the Pan York. But the role of the Americans was different this time. On this voyage, they were neither the majority of the crew nor the men in charge. On the one hand, they were outnumbered by hired sailors, Spaniards on the Pan York and Italians on the Pan Crescent. Ze'ev Venia Hadari, an Aliyah Bet official, later explained where the Americans fit in: "Since the Pans could not be entrusted to a foreign crew, efforts were made to find professionals for key positions who would provide a solid core with higher motivation and dedication."

On the other hand, although the Americans were handpicked veterans of earlier Aliyah Bet voyages, they were excluded from the top jobs, which went instead to young Palestinians. In Hadari's view, the Americans had the better qualifications to run the operation; he commented:

"Since they were qualified seamen as well as Zionists, volunteers and with experience in immigration operations, they were fitting candidates for positions at the top of the command structure on the ships. Meeting their Israeli counterparts highlighted their greater experience and skills. Nevertheless, the Mossad preferred the small coterie of young Israelis, all from the same age group, who had gone through youth movement, Kibbutz and Palmach together."

* * *

Anna Pauker, the Rumanian Foreign Minister was both a Jew and an anti-Zionist. The British tried to intercede with her, but they failed to destroy a deal the Haganah had made with the Communist authorities to allow Jews to leave for Palestine. Preparations went forward in Rumania for the selection of the immigrants to travel aboard the Pan York and Pan Crescent.

A hitch developed when the Soviet Union objected to the use of Constanza as the port of embarkation. It was virtually a Soviet naval base, and the Russians did not want the embarrassment that would result from their allowing the refugees to board there. The Russians suggested Bulgaria as an alternative, and the Haganah negotiated for the use of the Bulgarian port of Burgas.

The Atzmaut (Pan Crescent)

In both Rumania and Bulgaria, the Haganah's deals involved money. The amounts that changed hands have never been made public. Estimates have ranged from five dollars per immigrant to fifty dollars.

The British, apparently unable or unwilling to believe that money alone could purchase Communist cooperation, suspected that political cooperation was the price.

* * *

Stung by the loss they suffered in world opinion in the Exodus incident, the British sought to take the propaganda initiative away from Zionists. To prepare public opinion, British spokesmen launched a campaign against Communist influence in the Middle East. The opening shot in this campaign was fired a few days after the Pans reached Rumania. On October 15, the British Foreign Office announced that the Pan York and Pan Crescent had arrived in Constanza and were preparing to take illegal immigrants to Palestine. Unofficially, the Foreign Office called journalists' attention to the appearance of a connection with the Soviet Union; the Russians had announced in the United Nations their support for the partition of Palestine, and now thousands of Jews from Communist Rumania were planning to sail for Palestine. Along with this, the British pressed their case against immigration of any large numbers of Jews, Communist or non-Communist, as an irritant that could invite violent Arab reactions. This view was reflected the same day, October 15, in a editorial in The Times; the London newspaper said His Majesty's government could hardly "allow the position of the Arabs to be prejudiced by admitting illegal immigrants to Palestine so long as she retains the Mandatory responsibility for safeguarding their interests."

At the diplomatic level, the British continued their efforts to prevent the voyage. On October 30, a memo from British Foreign Secretary Ernest Bevin sought the help of the United States in bottling up the two ships at Constanza, plus a third ship then berthed at Norfolk, Virginia. A memorandum from the British Embassy in Washington to the Department of State the next day, October 31, asked the United States to block further movement of Jews from the American zone of Austria to join the 28,000 Jews already in Italy; the memo noted: "It appears probable that as many as 17,000 illegal Jewish immigrants may reach Palestine waters from the Black Sea in the near future, thus threatening to fill the Cyprus camps to capacity."

Secretary of State George C. Marshall had sent a secret reply November 7 to Bevin emphasizing "the concern with which the Government of the United States shares with the Goverment of the United Kingdom over the activities of vessels engaged in the clandestine emigrant traffic to Palestine." Marshall told Bevin that "the Secretary of State has in person called in Jewish leaders and informed them with the greatest possible emphasis that unless immediate and effective steps were taken to stop this clandestine activity he would have no other recourse but to treat the matter publicly."

Marshall reported that "armed cutters of the United States Coast Guard have the Colonel Frederick C. Johnson under 24-hour surveillance at Norfolk and all possible steps are being taken to prevent the sailing of this vessel." As to the Pans, Marshall wrote that the Jewish Agency said it "would do everything within its power to prevent further incidents but indicated that the Agency did not have complete control of the Jewish Underground." Marshall informed Bevin that the Jewish Agency had said it knew of no sailings scheduled from Europe or the Black Sea in the next five or six weeks. As matters developed, the Jewish Agency's statement had the appearance of being true, if only in a technical sense.

The Jewish Agency told the truth in saying it could not control the underground. At the last moment, the Jewish Agency tried to prevent the voyage. The American delegation to the United Nations, acting on instructions from President Truman, informed the Jewish Agency that the British had evidence the ships were bringing Communists to Palestine. American support might halt if the ships were allowed to sail, the Jewish Agency was told. Hurried discussions took place in Palestine, and the Jewish Agency voted to halt the sailing. On December 21, Ben-Gurion ordered the Pan York and Pan Crescent not to sail. But Mossad Chief Shaul Avigur, giving priority to the immigrants' hopes of escaping from Europe to Palestine, refused Ben-Gurion's order. On December 22, the Pans sailed from Constanza to the Bulgarian port of Burgas on the Black Sea. On the same day, eight railroad trains carrying more than 15,000 Jews left Rumania to meet the refugee vessels at Burgas. It was six weeks and one day after the date of Marshall's memo.

* * *

At Burgas, the operation was a larger version of the sailing of the Paducah and Northland three months earlier. The ships pulled into the harbor, and railroad trains bearing the refugees arrived. The loading took more than two days. Well-organized, it went off without snags, and the Pan York and Pan Crescent sailed.

The next worry on the part of the Haganah was whether the vessels could pass through the Bosphorus without being detained by Turkish authorities, who were also feeling British pressure. The Turkish government declined to take responsibility for stopping the voyage, and the refugee vessels passed the Bosphorus without incident.

Once the Pans entered the Mediterranean, the dilemma of the British became a practical problem with only one solution: Cyprus. The Haganah's deal with Soviet-controlled Rumania ruled out any possibility of the refugees' being returned to their country of origin. The ships would not return to Bulgaria, nor could the British force them to; the British warships were barred by an international agreement from entering the Dardanelles. After the disastrous international reactions to the Exodus affair, sending the passengers to Germany was out of the question. And the British would not let the refugees enter Palestine. No other country would take the Jews, nor would they accept deportation to another British colony without violence.

On shore, the Jewish Agency and the British worked out a compromise. The two sides agreed that the refugees would sail directly to Cyprus and not resist internment. It remained for the commanders at sea to work out the arrangements; they accomplished this after the Pans had passed Cyprus and were heading for Haifa. The British destroyer Mauritius came alongside the Pan York and hailed her Haganah commander. They negotiated. The Haganah commander was not prepared to surrender the ships on the high seas nor to sign away the claim of the passengers to enter Palestine. He told the British that the Jews would not resist being taken to Cyprus by force. Under the agreement the commanders worked out, the British sent unarmed boarding parties onto the ships, and the Haganah continued to operate the radio room and manage the internal affairs of the floating refugee camps.

On January 1, 1948, the convoy entered

Famagusta harbor at Cyprus. The unloading took four days. Crew members mingled with the passengers and avoided speaking English. One American tried to fool the British by speaking Hungarian, but his poor command of the language was evident to a Hungarian-speaking British soldier at the port, and the volunteer soon found himself under interrogation. Taken to a building for questioning, the American saw a British interrogator hitting another prisoner, an Aliyah Bet commander who had served in the Royal Air Force. Also being questioned was a non-Jew who had sailed as a volunteer on several Aliyah Bet ships. At 40, he was one of the old men of the crews, and he responded crustily when accused of being an American deserter; the veteran sailor said he had been taking cargoes to England when his questioner was a baby soiling his diapers. The questions the British were asking seemed to have nothing to do with the Haganah. They wanted to know about Communists, Russians, conditions in Rumania, and the like.

The apparent British obsession with Communists was not confined to the questioning of the crew. A special contingent of investigators was sent to Cyprus to conduct a massive search for Communist agents among the passengers. The investigation began as soon as the Pan York and Pan Crescent reached Cyprus. Security agents interrogated passengers, went through their belongings, and searched the ship from top to bottom. The hunt was fruitless. It continued for almost a week, producing 10 crates of documents but no proof.

The only Soviet agents discovered aboard the Pan York and Pan Crescent existed in the minds of the British, and of gullible diplomats and journalists. The British Foreign Office succeeded in obtaining American press coverage of its claims that the ships were loaded with Communists and other subversive agents, but the story appeared before the shipboard investigation actually took place. Afterwards, it was a different story. The charges of Communist infiltration faded as the British turned to other problems. Their time in Palestine was running out.

* * *

In contrast with the other Aliyah Bet ships, which became known by their new Hebrew names, the Pan York and Pan Crescent were generally remembered as the Pans. One reason for this is that, unlike the other Aliyah Bet ships, they did not reach Palestine with their Hebrew names displayed on banners. Instead, they sailed directly to Cyprus as the Pan York and Pan Crescent. Their new Hebrew names appeared almost as a postcript for the record, after the capture by the British had already been negotiated. During the voyage, the vessels had used Hebrew code-names; the Pan York was the "Ahot" (sister, in Hebrew) and the Pan Crescent was the "Haver" (friend, in Hebrew.) The night of the surrender to the British, the question of their names did not come up until late in the negotiations, after almost every other detail had been covered. Requests for instructions were radioed to the Haganah in Palestine, but hours went by with no decision. Finally, the order to rename the ships came through at midnight. The names were said to have been chosen by Ben-Gurion himself. The Pan Crescent became the Atzmaut (Independence) and the Pan York became the Kibbutz Galuyot (Ingathering of the Exiles.) The commander of the Pan Crescent was the first to receive the radiogram with the new names. He chose Atzmaut for his ship and then notified the Pan York that it would become the Kibbutz Galuyot.

* * *

On the way to Cyprus, the captain of the Pan York, a Palestinian Jew who had sailed in the United States Merchant Marine, asked permission to stay aboard his ship in the harbor with a skeleton crew. This was a departure from previous Aliyah Bet practice; in the past, when the British captured a ship, the Haganah had to resign itself to the loss of the vessel. The captain of the Pan York was reluctant to give up his ship so easily; he wanted to maintain her so that she would be ready to sail again after Israel became independent. He received written permission from the British to stay aboard, but at first none of his shipmates would agree to accompany him. The ice broke when a non-Jewish ship's officer from the Basque country volunteered; others followed, and the skeleton crew was assembled. Each week, the British delivered fuel to the Pan York so that she could operate her engines, and the crew judiciously saved some of each shipment. When Israeli independence came on May 15, 1948, the ship hoisted its own flag; on her side appeared the name "Pan York — Haifa." The significance of the captain's insistence on staying with his ship quickly became evident. The Pan York was ready to sail and began almost immediately to transport refugees to Palestine from Cyprus. Joined by her sister ship, the Pan Crescent, she became the mainstay of Israel's new merchant fleet. Each ship took about 4,500 passengers per voyage, and in a short time they transported some 60,000 immigrants to Palestine. The official history of the Zim line, Israel's state-controlled shipping company, says that the country's merchant fleet started with the Kedmah, a vessel that carried 300 passengers. But, in practical terms, the real beginning of the Israeli merchant fleet was achieved by the Pan York and Pan Crescent. At the time, the Zim line received $100 for each immigrant it transported. The little Kedmah could earn $30,000 on a voyage; one of the Pans could bring in 15 times as much in a single trip. Just as Aliyah Bet vessels from the United States became the first warships of Israel's navy, so did the American-purchased Pan York and Pan Crescent provide the nucleus of the new country's merchant fleet.

* * *

Some of the American volunteers stayed in Cyprus as skeleton crew members. Others returned to Palestine in refugee shipments, or escaped. One volunteer escaped by boat to Kibbutz Sdot Yam near Caesarea and became a crew member on another Aliyah

Bet vessel that was captured by the British in late April. When he returned to Cyprus as a prisoner, two British soldiers recognized him. He was beaten and taken to Larnaca, where he was put on trial and sentenced to two months in jail for violating Cypriot law in escaping from the island. Later, he went to Israel to live.

* * *

Israel became independent, but the British did not depart from Haifa until June 15, a month after independence. As the Pan York sailed toward Haifa from Cyprus after independence had been declared, a British destroyer signaled to her off Acre that a berth had been arranged for her in port. Unable to establish radio contact with Israel to obtain instructions, the Pan York sailed on. A British health official sought permission to come aboard but was refused by the Pan York's captain, who felt he must do everything possible to prevent his ship from falling into British hands. Soon, a Royal Navy tugboat arrived. The captain of the Pan York rejected papers presented to him for his signature. Two British sailors grabbed him and took him to jail to await trial. After being convicted on a charge of disobeying His Majesty's orders, the Pan York captain was released June 10, 1948. He was the last Jew arrested by the British in Palestine.

What the British Knew (and Didn't Know)

It is hoped that the red herring of "refugees" drawn by the Jews over their colonization and expansion programs in Palestine has been to some degree exposed.

—*Conclusion of British "Report on Jewish Propaganda concerning Immigration into Palestine," 317th Airborne Field Security Section, Haifa, March 20, 1947.*

In some ways, the British were highly successful in their intelligence efforts. When they were playing their familiar role as an imperial power, the British knew what to do. At the diplomatic level, they intervened with many governments including that of the United States to restrict Aliyah Bet activities. From North America, they noted the purchase and Atlantic crossings of ships. Across Europe, British agents traced the flow of refugees from country to country and anticipated their embarkation at various ports. At European seaports, they observed the comings and goings of ships of many nations and took note of suspicious traffic. At Gibraltar they identified American ships bound for Eastern Europe and tracked them all the way to the Dardanelles. In the Mediterranean, British aircraft pinpointed the positions of Aliyah Bet ships as they neared Palestine; within hours, warships of the Royal Navy arrived to intercept the refugee vessels. Except for the Haim Arlosoroff, no American vessel reached shore before being captured.

In Palestine, where their role was that of an occupying force pitted against a determined and organized local population, the British were less successful. As soon as a ship entered Haifa port, the Jewish underground stood ready to put the British at a disadvantage. On ship after ship, Palestinian and American members of the crew eluded capture by becoming stowaways aboard their own vessel. They hid in a water tank for a day or more until a work crew came aboard to clean the ship. When the cleaning crew walked off the ship, the stowaways went with them dressed as workmen. The ploy succeeded time after time, evidently because the British failed to penetrate the Jewish work force in the harbor. On one of the first American-manned ships, crew members disguised as refugees were sneaked ashore by Palestinian Jews who came aboard the captured vessel in medical teams.

In other respects, the British let their

own preconceptions color their view of reality. This was particularly so with regard to questions involving Zionism, which did not rank as a respectable political belief in British official thinking, and with regard to Jews themselves, who were sometimes stereotyped in British documents as conspiratorial, untrustworthy people. Had the British not allowed their prejudices to blur their interpretation of what was happening, they might have understood better that Jewish nationalism was a real force, supported by people prepared to fight and endure hardship, and that the Zionists meant what they said. But the British were trapped in their own narrow view and did not understand, until it was too late, that the Jews who had committed themselves to Aliyah Bet had a very simple goal; they wanted nothing more, and nothing less, than a free Jewish nation in Palestine.

Interception by the Royal Navy

In March of 1947, for instance, Captain J. Linklater, the Commanding Officer of the 317th Airborne Field Security Section, reported that the passengers on Aliyah Bet ships were not really refugees. Aliyah Bet, the British officer concluded in a secret report based on interrogation of passengers on the American-manned Haim Arlosoroff and Ben Hecht, was essentially "a deliberate campaign of Jewish propaganda to ... gain world-wide sympathy for the Zionist cause on entirely bogus humanitarian grounds." The British report went on to characterize Aliyah Bet as "a well organised and potentially lucrative plan for encouraging carefully selected Jews to enter Palestine for the purpose of developing the country. It does not appear, in any way whatsoever, to resemble a plan for saving the starving, ill, and crippled masses of Jews in Europe today, and of offering them sanctuary in the Holy Land."

The report depicted the refugees as brainwashed by Zionist teachings:

> Discussion with recent immigrants has shown that they have undergone intensive indoctrination and are only too eager to produce parrot-fashion phrases describing the "agricultural potential of Palestine, benefit to the world, assistance to the Arabs, Jewish nation etc" which suggests that a vast propaganda machine is at work, at least in Europe itself, for the express purpose of persuading Jews to leave their homes and set up better ones in Palestine.

The report described, matter-of-factly, how Aliyah Bet ships looked when they reached Palestine:

> The Jewish settlers on board are mostly in a disgusting state of filth and squalor,

> poorly dressed with few clothes, wild eyed, with hang-dog looks on their faces, hair dishevelled, and unshaven. Many are hysterical. The ships themselves are, if possible, in an even worse condition, with garbage and litter lying deep on the deck and stinking in a foul manner.

The British report did not accept this at face value. To support its conclusion that the miserable appearance of the passengers and ship was only a Zionist propaganda ploy, the report adopted a conspiracy theory; it quoted an unnamed "reliable Jewish source" as informing the British "that discipline during any illegal voyage is good, and that orders are given about a day before reaching land to convert the ship into a veritable pigsty ... for the purpose of selling the 'refugee' story."

To bolster this interpretation, the field security officer cited photographs taken aboard one ship departing from Europe:

> Anything less like the ship which finally arrived in Haifa is hard to imagine. The photos show smiling, plump, and confident faces of settlers and pioneers bound for the shores of a promised land. Their hair is tidy and well brushed, their boots polished, and their clothes sound, smart and sufficient. The untidiest person shown is a member of the American crew....

Whatever their inner feelings toward Jews, some British officers evidently felt no great constraint to avoid snide comments when discussing the refugees. A British report on the capture of the Biryah noted that the legs of about 100 people were dangling over the

A view from the Exodus

side of the crowded refugee boat. The report writer volunteered the observation that the thought of using the passengers' legs as fenders was tempting. He wrote that this thought "was filed for future reference." The author of this report held the rank of lieutenant commander in the Royal Navy, and he addressed his comments to the British naval officer in charge at Haifa. Such departures from professionalism indicate that an officer who went on record with a sophomoric comment toward the refugee had no overwhelming fear that his superiors would object.

Lack of familiarity with Jews and their culture colored the understanding of the British, and, consequently, their behavior. In August 1947, it became known that the Bible was among books confiscated from passengers of the Exodus and burned. The Commanding Officer of the Empire Rival transporting the Exodus passengers back to Europe explained that he regretted this but no one in his command knew Hebrew, and so he imposed a blanket ban on all books in Hebrew and Yiddish, and all books dealing with Jews and Palestine.

The Hebrew language was not the only area of ignorance on the part of the British. A report on the arrival of The Jewish State on October 2, 1947, professed mystification at the inclusion of England in a shipboard banner alluding to historic oppressors of the Jews: "Another banner in English bore the rather cryptic message 'Greece, Rome, Spain, Germany, — England?' "

This report, like others, was an amalgam of analysis and supercilious comment on Jews. It veered off into music criticism:

> Groups of Jews in various parts of the ship began to sing Hatikvah lustily and in many different keys. This noise was interrupted at frequent intervals by slogans such as "The land of Israel to the people of Israel" and "We want a national home," shouted in chorus, with energy but badly out of time.

The report noted that the well-organized land transport of the refugees was conducted in Russian-occupied territory. It concluded that the voyage "may be the beginning of another phase in the Russian anti-British campaign in the Middle East."

* * *

The suspicion of Soviet influence was later expanded upon by Captain Linklater, the same British officer whose report in March had concluded that the refugees were not refugees. As other British officials at various levels sought reasons to avoid complying with the November 29 United Nations vote partitioning Palestine into Jewish and Arab states, Captain Linklater now labored mightily, but unsuccessfully, to prove that Jewish immigrants from Eastern Europe were Russian spies.

This was reminiscent of an earlier British inclination to depict Jewish refugees as German agents in World War II. In 1940, the British interned as "enemy aliens" a group of Jews who had reached England from Germany the year before on the refugee ship St. Louis. Later, the British postulated German espionage as a reason for refusing the Jews of another refugee vessel entry to Palestine. This vessel was the tiny refugee boat Struma. In the winter of 1941-42, she sat helpless in the harbor at Istanbul. The Jewish Agency asked Britain to admit the Struma's passengers to Palestine as part of the annual quota of immigrants. The British refused, citing among their reasons a possibility there could be German spies among the more than 760 Jews shivering aboard the Struma. The preposterousness of this objection, put forward in all seriousness at about the same time as the Nazis were adopting their "Final Solution" plan for exterminating the Jews of Europe, was pointed out in the House of Lords by Sir Josiah Wedgwood. He told the Peers on March 10, 1942: "That allegation regarding the Jews is a bare-faced excuse which supplies fresh evidence of anti-Semitism." By that time, there was no opportunity to investigate; the Struma had gone to the bottom of the Black Sea two weeks earlier with all but one of her passengers.

Captain Linklater, however, had ample opportunity to investigate. If evidence existed that Soviet agents lurked among the Jewish immigrants seeking entry to Palestine, it could be found by investigating the more than 15,000 Jews who had received permission to leave Soviet-controlled areas of Eastern Europe for the Middle East aboard the refugee ships Atzmaut and Kibbutz Galuyot. As the two Aliyah Bet vessels arrived at Cyprus on January 1, 1948, Captain Linklater and five assistants trained in various languages embarked on a round-the-clock research project that occupied six days. They interrogated refugees and examined whatever documents they could find. Not surprisingly, the investigators found that some of these survivors of World War II had served in the Red Army. One passenger's belongings included pictures of Joseph Stalin, the Soviet dictator. The investigation produced 10 crates of paper. But the investigators found not a single Russian spy among more than 15,000 passengers.

* * *

The theme of Russian influence was transmitted by the British through diplomatic channels to the United States, where agents of the Federal Bureau of Investigation questioned returning Aliyah Bet sailors about contacts with Russians, Communists, and others suspected of Soviet influence. The American investigation took on a life of its own and continued into the years of the Cold War. One Aliyah Bet volunteer, interrogated by FBI agents twice in the 1950s about contacts with an American Jewish Communist, heard no more from the investigators and assumed that the matter was closed; many years later, he obtained his FBI file through the Freedom of Information Act and learned that he himself had been suspected of being a Communist.

Aboard the captured Exodus

The Story Continues

After the American volunteers completed their Aliyah Bet service, their lives took many directions.

Some returned immediately to the United States. To pass through the British-controlled exits from Palestine, they used false names and false identity documents provided by the Haganah. When they reached France, they reported to United States consular officials and said they had lost their passports. To account for the passage of time since their departure from the United States, they invented stories of travel and romantic adventures in Europe. The consular officials, not necessarily believing these stories, provided them with travel documents valid for a one-way journey to the United States. The volunteers paid for their transportation. Officials escorted some volunteers directly to the airport at Paris and placed them aboard home-bound aircraft. When they arrived in the United States, volunteers underwent questioning by agents of the Federal Bureau of Investigation. Some of their families and next-of-kin also were questioned and investigated. The FBI men wanted to know particularly about contacts with Communists and Russians. Serving as a volunteer in Aliyah Bet violated no American law, and no volunteer is known to have been charged with any crime as a result of the FBI investigations.

A substantial number of volunteers stayed in Israel to fight in the War of Independence. Paul Shulman became the first Commanding Officer of Israel's new navy. Other volunteers put their World War II military specialties to use in Israeli ground and air units. Four former Aliyah Bet sailors died in battle as members of Israeli combat units, and two others were killed by enemy sniper fire while serving on kibbutz settlements. Another, seriously wounded while heroically taking part in fighting in Jerusalem, refused to accept a medical discharge. He went to the United States for brain surgery and returned to Israel to take up an army career.

Some of the men who fought in Israel's War of Independence returned to the United States after the fighting stopped in 1949. Others stayed on to make their lives in the new Jewish State. Those who stayed in Israel included most of the Zionist youth-group members who had joined Aliyah Bet with the intention of settling in Palestine. Most became members of kibbutz communities. Others went into business or professional life. One became an actor. Another became a tour guide. In all, about one in four of the American volunteers continue to live in Israel four decades later.

* * *

As the years went on, the story of Aliyah Bet became an important element in the history of modern Israel. Many books and articles reflected an appreciation of the impact the refugee voyages had in weakening the British hold on Palestine. Yet the role of Americans in this historic undertaking remained a well-kept secret.

Anyone curious about the American role in Aliyah Bet would not learn much from going to a library. Even in books that noted the volunteers' involvement, facts were mangled. A simple example involves the most widely publicized of the American vessels, the S.S. President Warfield, which became the Exodus 1947. The American origin of this vessel became, in print, a near-unfathomable mystery. Jon and David Kimche, whose book *The Secret Roads* is a history of Aliyah Bet, misplaced the Exodus by almost 1,000 miles in writing that the former Chesapeake Bay ferry had plied the Mississippi River. Meyer W. Weisgal went further adrift, recalling in his 1971 autobiography *So Far* that the Delaware-built vessel came from Latin America. Ze'ev Venia Hadari, a former member of the Aliyah Bet leadership, turned the excursion boat into a corvette in his book, *Voyage to Freedom.*

Inattention to the American role went much deeper than these trivial examples. The Exodus was, after all, famous; she therefore could not be ignored by those who wrote books. Of other American vessels, less was known, and no serious attempt was made to tell their stories. Of the remarkable American operation that resulted in buying and equipping the ships and hiring their crews, neither Israeli nor American history had much to report.

The Encyclopedia Judaica, in its article on "Illegal Immigration," (Vol. 8, 1248-54) virtually ignores the American role. Aside from two passing references to the presence of American sailors in Aliyah Bet, the only clue to American involvement is a sentence devoted to the activities of the pro-Revisionist Hebrew Committee of National Liberation.

An article on "Illegal Immigration" in the *Encyclopedia of Zionism and Israel,* produced with the help of the Jewish Agency, is less informative. This article (Vol. 1, pp. 531-33) by Yehuda Bauer of the Hebrew University makes no mention of American sailors. Except for one sentence devoted to the Ben Hecht, it gives no hint of American ship-purchasing efforts.

These lapses involved simple facts. They did not entail evaluation or interpretation, elements which were also notably absent from discussion of the American role in histories of Aliyah Bet.

* * *

Not that the American volunteers tried to keep their activity secret for so long. On the contrary, after they had returned to the United States or taken up their new lives in Israel, many were proud to talk about what they did for Aliyah Bet. There was no longer any reason to prevent the story from becoming known. Once Israel had become independent and the need for secrecy had passed, the story belonged to the public. Some of the volunteers interviewed for this book said they felt slighted by the way the American contribution was ignored in history books.

One reason for the historians' failure is evident. Information was not easy to obtain. The operations of Aliyah Bet had been conducted in secrecy, and many events went undocumented. Where records had been kept, they were not always available. Many documents are believed to have been lost in a fire that destroyed files of the Zim shipping lines. Another rich source of information about the American role was lost when Danny Schind died in 1953 at 44. Probably more than any other person, Schind knew the story of the American contribution. He was both the supervising manager who saw the overall picture of the American operation, and the busy worker who carried in his head the details. A second untimely death further depleted the sources of first-hand information; Davidka Nameiry, Schind's successor in New York, died in 1966 at 58. As years passed and memories faded, the difficulty of obtaining accurate recollections from participants increased. In time, the blank chapter in the Aliyah Bet history took on a force of its own. Research which ignored the American contribution became a basis for further work that reinforced the omission. The story of Aliyah Bet became set in a mold that excluded attention to the American role.

But, although information was not readily at hand, it could be found. There were photographs and newspaper clippings that hinted at the story to be compiled. There was material in archives. There were participants who could be interviewed. There were American volunteers from each of the American-purchased vessels. There were Americans who had sailed on other Aliyah Bet vessels. There were Palestinian commanders who remembered the Americans and what they had done. And, although the American role was largely ignored in histories and autobiographies, parts of the story had been preserved in books by journalists who covered Aliyah Bet.

The same type of research that led to the compilation of this book could have been done long before now, by others with greater resources. A small industry has grown up around research into Aliyah Bet, with substantial sums of money for staff and materials. At Tel Aviv University, an entire research project is devoted to Aliyah Bet. But at this research facility, the term "American contribution" evidently has a meaning other than the role of the volunteer sailors in Aliyah Bet. In the midst of our research for this book, Professor Anita Shapira, the director of the Tel Aviv University project, asked us to donate $15,000 to the project if we wished to continue using its files. We declined to pay for information which should be in the public domain. We gathered information from this and many other sources in compiling this book.

Despite the lack of academic interest so far, this subject is worth pursuing. In addition to its place in the history of Aliyah Bet, the story of the American volunteer operation can shed light on other topics of interest. For one thing, it holds insights into the much-discussed relationship between American Jews and the State of Israel. Aliyah Bet was one of the few instances in which American Jews have become directly active in Israel's struggle. Further inquiry could shed light not only on American Jewish life but on Israelis' attitudes toward Americans. Some of the sailors interviewed for this book perceived the issue as follows: When Americans give money, Israelis know how to deal with it. But Israelis have difficulty understanding Americans who choose to live in Israel, and still greater difficulty understanding the Aliyah Bet volunteers' embracing a mission that held no glory but involved hard work and perhaps danger.

The Aliyah Bet volunteers who made their lives in Israel are also of interest. Only a tiny proportion of the American Jewish population has chosen to live in Israel. And many of those who have immigrated to the Jewish state have later returned to America. The reasons for this are many and complex, and the experience of the Aliyah Bet volunteers stands out in stark contrast. A substantial proportion of the volunteers decided to immigrate to Israel. An overwhelming majority of these immigrants remained.

* * *

Why the historians of Aliyah Bet virtually ignored the American role remains an unanswered question.

At least part of the failure was that many of those who wrote about Aliyah Bet did not know the facts about the Americans.

Many sources at the time the history took shape lacked at least part of the truth.

Many memories, almost four decades later, lacked at least part of the truth.

But, all along, the truth was there. It only needed telling.

Appendix A

Refugee vessels from America

Ten American-purchased and American-manned vessels sailed in Aliyah Bet from 1946 through January 1, 1948. They carried more than 32,000 people, or more than 46 per cent of the 69,563 immigrants who sailed from Europe from August 1945 until Israel's independence in May 1948.

The American vessels did not begin operating from Europe until more than a year after the surrender of the Nazis. During their actual period of operation, the American vessels accounted for more than half of the immigrants sailing for Palestine. In percentage terms, the American vessels carried:

—More than 50 per cent of the 63,515 immigrants who sailed between the first American voyage in June 1946 and Israel's independence in May 1948.

—More than 56 per cent of the immigrants who sailed between the first American voyage in June 1946 and January 1, 1948, when the last American voyage ended.

An 11th American-manned vessel, the Calanit, formerly the Mala, reached Israel in July 1948 with about 1,200 immigrants. Because she sailed after the State of Israel was proclaimed, she was not considered part of Aliyah Bet for historical purposes. Her American crew members were among the founders of Kibbutz Sasa. This vessel was once the Mayflower, the yacht of United States Presidents from Theodore Roosevelt through Herbert Hoover.

* * *

The following summary includes, for each vessel, its Aliyah Bet name, former name in parentheses, former use, embarkation points, date and place of capture, and number of immigrants. The passenger totals and dates are from the Israel Defense Ministry.

1) Josiah Wedgwood (Beauharnois)

Canadian corvette.

Embarked passengers near Savonna, Italy.

Captured and taken to Haifa on June 27, 1946.

1,257 immigrants interned at Athlit.

Next use: Israel Navy corvette K-20, Hashomer.

2) Haganah (Norsyd)

Canadian corvette.

Embarked refugees at Sete, France. Transferred passengers at sea to the Biryah (Akbel II), which was captured and towed to Haifa on July 1, 1946, with 999 immigrants who were interned in Palestine.

Sailed to Baka, Yugoslavia, and embarked passengers there.

Captured, taken to Haifa on July 29, 1946.

2,678 immigrants interned in Palestine.

Next use: Israel Navy corvette K-18, Haganah.

3) Haim Arlosoroff (Ulua)

Coast Guard; revenue cutter during Prohibition era.

Embarked passengers at Trelleborg, Sweden, and Metaponte, Italy.

Beached February 28, 1947, at Bat Galim, Haifa, after battle with British.

1,348 immigrants interned in Cyprus.

Next use: Sold for scrap.

4) Ben Hecht (Abril)

Private yacht; smuggling vessel; Coast Guard vessel PY-31.

Embarked passengers at Port de Bouc, France.

Captured and taken to Haifa March 8, 1947.

600 immigrants interned in Cyprus.

Next use: Israel Navy commando vessel K-24, the Maoz.

5) Hatikva (Tradewinds)

Coast Guard cutter.

Embarked passengers on two successive nights at beaches in Italy.

Captured and taken to Haifa on May 17, 1947.

1,414 immigrants; interned in Cyprus.

Next use: Sold for scrap.

6) Exodus 1947 (President Warfield)

Chesapeake Bay excursion ferry.

Embarked passengers at Sete, France.

Captured off Haifa July 18, 1947, after battle with British.

4,515 immigrants. Passengers were returned to France, where all but a few refused to go ashore, and then taken to Hamburg, Germany, where they were forced ashore and interned.

Next use: abandoned near Haifa harbor. Plans to convert her into a museum of Aliyah Bet were dropped after she caught fire in 1952. She was later scrapped.

7) Geula (Paducah)

Coast Guard training vessel.

Embarked passengers at Burgas, Bulgaria.

Captured and taken to Haifa October 2, 1947.

1,388 immigrants. Interned in Cyprus.

Next use: Sold for scrap.

8) The Jewish State (Northland)

Coast Guard icebreaker.

Embarked passengers at Burgas, Bulgaria.

Captured and taken to Haifa October 2, 1947.

2,664 immigrants. Interned in Cyprus.

Next use: Israel navy warship A-16, the Elath.

9) Kibbutz Galuyot (Pan York)

Banana carrier.

Embarked passengers at Burgas, Bulgaria.

Sailed directly to Cyprus by agreement with British, arriving January 1, 1948.

7,623 immigrants.

Next use: Zim passenger carrier.

10) Atzmaut (Pan Crescent)

Banana carrier.

Embarked passengers at Burgas, Bulgaria.

7,616 immigrants.

Sailed directly to Cyprus by agreement with British, arriving January 1, 1948.

Next use: Zim passenger carrier.

11) Calanit (Mala)

Presidential yacht (from Theodore Roosevelt through Herbert Hoover) known as the Mayflower.

Embarked passengers in France.

About 1,200 immigrants, including a contingent of refugees deported to Germany from the Aliyah Bet vessel Exodus 1947.

Arrived at Haifa July 11, 1948.

Appendix B

Men of the Secret Fleet

From North America

(Names compiled from crew lists, interviews, and correspondence received through May 25, 1987.)

Eddie Abadi, *The Jewish State, Calanit*
Harold R. (Hess) Abells, *The Jewish State*
Sydney A. Abrams, *Geula*
Eugene Alexander, *Haim Arlosoroff*
George (Shmuel) Appley (Applebaum), *Haganah*
Murray Aranoff, *Exodus*
Ajzyk Asatanowicz, *Wedgwood*
Ash, Captain William C.
Lester Avrahamson, *Haim Arlosoroff*
Marvin Bacaner, *Wedgwood*
Pierre Baird, *Geula*
Louis (Arye) Ball, *Geula*
Mordechai Barkan, *Wedgwood*
Yisrael Barnea, *Haganah*
Kurt Baruch, *Exodus*
David Baum, *Haganah*
Mordechai Baum, *Haganah*
Ralph Baum (Banai), *Haganah*
Shmuel Beeri, *Exodus*
Gidon Belkin, Nahshon, *Atzmaut*
Shimshon Belman, *Wedgwood*
Yakov Ben-Yisrael (Woodrow), *Hatikvah*
Bertram Berg, *The Jewish State*
Elihu Bergman, *Geula*
Jeno Berkovits, *Ben Hecht*
Jack Bernstain, *Ben Hecht*
Arthur Bernstein, *Haim Arlosoroff*
Jack Bernstein, *Haim Arlosoroff*
William Bernstein, *Exodus*
Louis Binder, *Ben Hecht*
David Blake, *Geula*
Mordechai Blockman, *Wedgwood*
Philip Bock, *Geula*
Joe Buxenbaum
Lou Braisley, *The Jewish State*
Hy Braverman, *Hatikvah*
Shabtai Breen, *LaNegev*
Louis Brettschneider, *Ben Hecht, Geula*
Albert Brownstein, *Geula*
Miguel Buiza, *Geula*
Yitzhak Calic, *Calanit*
Paul Christie, *Geula*
Eli Cohen, *Wedgwood*
Nat Cohen
Walter Rexie Cushenberry, *Ben Hecht*
Johanan Dreyfus, *Calanit*
Howard (Eddie) Edmondson, *The Jewish State*
Duke Efros, *Haim Arlosoroff*

David Eisen, *Mishmar HaEmek*
Dave Endin (Bender), *The Jewish State*
Ira Feinberg
David Fendel, *Haganah*
Heine Franz Fleigler, *Wedgwood*
Ben Foreman, *Exodus*
Yakov Frank, *Haganah*
Eli Freundlich, *Ben Hecht*
Irving Galil, *Mala*
Hal Galili (Fineberg), *Hatikvah*
Jared (Gerry) Gibraltar, *The Jewish State*
Peter Gilbert, *Geula*
Joe Gilden, *Hatikvah*
George Goldman, *Geula*
David Goldstein, *Mala*
Myron Goldstein, *Exodus*
Martin H. Gooen, *Geula*
Sam Gordon, *Hatikvah*
David Gotlib, *Wedgwood*
William A. Gottlieb, *Wedgwood*
John Grauel, *Exodus*
Walter Greaves, *Ben Hecht, Geula*
Murray S. Greenfield, *Hatikvah*
David Greer, *Geula*
David Leo Gutman, *Ben Hecht, Geula*
Avraham Halevi, *Haganah*
Hillel HaRamati, *Latrun*
James Heggie, *Ben Hecht*
Harry Herschkowitz, *Ben Hecht*
Gad Hilb, *Haim Arlosoroff, Kibbutz Galuyot*
Albert Hirschkoff, *Ben Hecht*
Stanley Jacks, *The Jewish State*
Laz Kahan (Kahansky), *The Jewish State*
Moshe Kallner, *Geula*
Eli Kalm (Kalmanowitz), *Exodus*
David Kaplan, *Ben Hecht*
Eddy Kaplansky, *The Jewish State*
Harold Katz, *Hatikvah*
Moshe Katz, *Wedgwood*
Elliot Kaufman, *Wedgwood*
Paul Kaye (Kaminetzky), *Hatikvah*
Benjamin Kazicki, *Ben Hecht*
David Kellner, *Geula*
Uri Kirstein, *Wedgwood*
Arnold Kite, *Geula*
David Kochavi (Starek), *Exodus*
Louis (Label) Koenigsberg, *The Jewish State*
Bernard Kogan, *Wedgwood*
Lawrence Kohlberg, *Geula*
Arye Kolomeitzev, *Wedgwood, Exodus, The Jewish State*
Joseph Kramer, *Haim Arlosoroff*
Benny Kulbersh, *Geula*
Siegfried (the Rabbi) Kusnitski, *The Jewish State*
Augustine L. (Duke) Labaczewski, *Hatikvah*
Arye Lashner, *Haganah*
Frank Lavine, *Exodus*
Aaron Lebow, *The Jewish State*
Harold Leidner, *Exodus*
Alvin Lerner, *Wedgwood*
Sol Lester, *Exodus*
Aaron Levine, *Calanit*
Phil Levine, *Calanit*
Hyman Robert Levitan, *Ben Hecht*
Bernie Levy, *Hatikvah*
Josh Lewis, *Hatikvah*
Morris Lewis (Nezinsky), *The Jewish State*
Joe Liberson, *Calanit*
Jacob Lichtman, *Wedgwood*
Marvin Liebman, *Ben Hecht*
Haakom Liliby, *Ben Hecht*

Baruch (Bernard) Linsky, *Haim Arlosoroff*
David Lipshutz, *Geula*
Wallace Litwin, *Ben Hecht*
David Livingston, *Haim Arlosoroff*
Avi Livni (Lifshitz), *Exodus, Kibbutz Galuyot, Atzmaut*
Daniel Lombard, *Geula*
David Lowenthal, *Exodus, Kibbutz Galuyot*
Norman Edward Luce, *Ben Hecht*
Abbot Lutz, *Exodus*
Richard MacGarva, *Geula*
Arye Malkin, *Wedgwood*
Danny Malovsky, *Exodus*
Dani Maltese, *The Jewish State, Calanit*
Henry Mandel, *Ben Hecht*
Sam Marcus, *Haim Arlosoroff*
Reuven Margolis, *Exodus*
Louis Markowitz, *Ben Hecht*
Bernie Marks, *Haganah, Exodus*
Hugh McDonald, *Hatikvah*
Irving Meltzer, *The Jewish State*
Mendy Mendelson, *Wedgwood*
Kalman Michaeli, *Haim Arlosoroff*
Hans Miller, *Haganah*
Milton Miller, *Wedgwood*
Dave Millman, *Exodus*
William Millman, *Exodus*
Dov Mills, *Exodus*
Philip Mittelman, *Wedgwood*
Zvi (Ranger) Monash, *Haganah*
Captain Morgan, *The Jewish State*
Haim Myers, *Tel Hai*
Nat Nadler, *Exodus*
Al Naftal, *Exodus*
Yakov Nahalieli, *Yucatan*
Bailey Nieder, *Geula*
Al Nemoff, *Hatikvah*
Benny Newman, *Calanit*
Rachmiel Newman, *Haim Arlosoroff*
Robert Nicolai, *Ben Hecht*
Ben Ocopnick, *Haim Arlosoroff*
Rudolph Patzert, *Geula*
M. Pekofsky, *Haim Arlosoroff*
Mike Perlstein, *Hatikvah*
Menahem Peretz, *Haganah*
Adrian Phillips, *Hatikvah*
Yakov Pleet, *Wedgwood*
Haim Pomerantz, *Wedgwood*
Al Potashnick, *Haim Arlosoroff*
Lenny Prager, *Calanit*
Isidore Rabinovitch, *The Jewish State*
Charles Rattner, *Wedgwood*
Zeev Rauff, *Wedgwood*
Zvi Rav, *Haim Arlosoroff*
Philip Reich, *Wedgwood*
Arnie Reuben, *Hatikvah*
Shepard Rifkin, *Ben Hecht*
Stanley Ritzer, *Exodus*
Roger Rofe, *Exodus*
Francisco Romero, *Geula*
Marvin (Abby) Rosenberg, *Hatikvah, Mala*
John Rosenfeld, *Geula*
Buddy Robbins, *Wedgwood*
Willie Rostoker, *Haim Arlosoroff, Kibbutz Galuyot*
Leonard Rotter, *Geula*
Gerald Rubenstein, *Hatikvah*
P. Rubin, *Hatikvah*
Hyman Rubin, *Wedgwood*
Paul Rubin, *Catriel Yafe*
John Sandin, *Geula*
Harry Nathan Schatz, *Ben Hecht*
Manfred (Shel) Schelasnitzki, *The*

Jewish State
Shmuel Schiller, *Exodus*
Ralph Schindler, *Geula*
Leo Schlefstein, *Hatikvah*
Sam Schulman, *Exodus, Kibbutz Galuyot, Atzmaut*
Max Schwartz, *Haganah*
Szulim M. Schwarz, *Wedgwood*
Zeev Segal, *Exodus*
Yehuda Sela, *Haganah*
Dov Seligman, *Wedgwood*
Lou Selove, *Exodus*
David Shachori, *Geula*
Hayman Shamir
Israel Shankman, *The Jewish State*
Aaron Shapiro, *Haganah*
Abe (Avi) Sheffi, *Haganah*
Reuben Shiff, *Geula*
Doc Shmetterling, *Haim Arlosoroff*
Paul Shulman
Abe Siegel, *Exodus*
Martin Silver, *Mala*
Larry Silverstein, *Haganah*
Lennie Sklar, *Exodus*
Sholom Solowitz, *Geula*
Erling Sorensen, *Ben Hecht*
Frank Stanczak, *Exodus*
Reuben Starer, *Haim Arlosoroff*
Edward R. Styrak, *Ben Hecht*
Benjamin Sushman, *Haganah*
Ben Ami Sussman, *Geula*
Avraham Sygal, *Exodus*
Archie Taller, *Calanit*
Willie Tillow, *Haim Arlosoroff*
E. (Phil) Tsuk, *Haim Arlosoroff, Kibbutz Galuyot*
Teddy Vardi, *Exodus, Kibbutz Galuyot, Atzmaut, Mishmar HaEmek*
Irving Weingarten, *Haim Arlosoroff, Kibbutz Galuyot, Atzmaut*
Al Weingrad, *Wedgwood*
Sid Weinhaus
Harry Weinsaft, *Exodus*
Cy Weinstein, *Exodus*
Manny (Wingy) Weinstein, *Hatikvah*
Sonny Weintraub, *Hatikvah*
Charles Weiss, *Hatikvah, Atzmaut, Kibbutz Galuyot*
Marvin Weiss, *Hatikvah, The Jewish State*
Mike Weiss, *Exodus*
Samuel Wiesman, *Wedgwood*
Jack Winkler, *Ben Hecht*
Yehuda Witenoff, *Calanit*
David Wurm, *Geula*
Saul Yellin, *Hatikvah*
Sid Yellin, *Hatikvah*
Jack Yeriel (Friedland), *The Jewish State*

The shu-shu boys

(Names provided by the Clandestine Immigration and Naval Museum, Haifa)

Yosef Almog
Eliezer Armon
Yitzhak Aron (Aronowitz)
Israel Averbach
Yehoshua Baharav
Max Cohen
Bezalel Drori
Azriel Einav
Arye (Lova) Eliav
Meir Falik
Patchia Feig
Arye Friedman
Moshe Gidron
Shmuel Haram
Yossi Harel
Zvi Katzenelson
Menahem Keller
Nisan Levitan
Avraham Liconsky
Gad Lifshitz
Mordechai Limon
Dov Magen
Yehezkel Maoz
Avraham Meron
Aharon Michaeli
Nahum Mondera
Benyamin Nativ
Akiva Ofenbach
Reuven Oren
Zalman Perach
Micha Peri
Yisrael Rotem
Alexander Shur
Haim Weinshelbaum
Moshe Yerushalmi

Appendix C

Seven who lost their lives for Israel's independence

Louis Ball, of the Geula crew, was killed July 9, 1948, while taking part in a Palmach attack on Iraq Sueidan, an Egyptian stronghold controlling the north-south road to the Negev. Born Ludwig Smargad in Vienna, March 10, 1922, he came to the United States after the Germans took over Austria. He lived with relatives in New York and completed high school and college. At age 21, he became an American citizen, changed his name to Louis Ball, and joined the U.S. Army. After his discharge as a sergeant, he volunteered for Aliyah Bet. Arriving in Palestine in December 1947 from Cyprus, he lived at Kibbutz Maayan Baruch and later at Degania, where he joined the Palmach. He was reinterred in the Nahalat Yitzhak military cemetery at Tel Aviv on January 23, 1951.

William (Bill) Bernstein, chief mate of the Exodus, died July 18, 1947, after being clubbed on the head by a British marine in the boarding party that captured his vessel. Born January 27, 1923, in Passaic, New Jersey, he graduated from high school in San Francisco and attended Ohio State University. Although entitled to a deferment from military service as a pre-medical student, he volunteered for the Merchant Marine in World War II. He graduated from the Kings Point Merchant Marine Academy in 1944 as a second lieutenant. After the war, he received an appointment to the U.S. Naval Academy at Annapolis but instead volunteered for Aliyah Bet. The night before the British captured the Exodus, he expressed to his shipmates a premonition he would die in the battle that lay ahead. He was buried in Martyrs Row in the Haifa cemetery.

Arie Lashner, of the Haganah crew, was killed March 15, 1948, by a sniper firing from the eastern side of the Jordan River as he climbed an electrical pole at Kibbutz Kfar Blum. Born April 8, 1915, in New York City, he graduated from the City College of New York and became the key organizer of Habonim, the Labor Zionist youth movement. He served in the U.S. Navy from 1942 to 1945 as a radioman and returned briefly to Habonim before becoming a recruiter for Aliyah Bet. He came to Palestine on the Aliyah Bet ship

Haganah and joined Kfar Blum in August, 1946. He was buried at Kfar Blum.

Baruch Linsky, of the Haim Arlosoroff crew, was killed May 26, 1948, at Hulda. Born May 1, 1921, in Chicago, he grew up in California and graduated in psychology from the University of California at Los Angeles in 1943. He received a master's degree from the University of California at Berkeley in 1945 and moved to New York, where he volunteered for Aliyah Bet. After arriving in Palestine, he spent several months at a kibbutz in the north and then enrolled in the Hebrew University. In the spring of 1948, he volunteered for the Haganah. He was buried at Hulda and reinterred October 26, 1950, in Haifa.

Harold (Zvi) Monash, of the Haganah crew, was killed in action April 25, 1948. Born January 1, 1924, in Berlin, Germany, he emigrated to the United States in 1936 and entered the army in 1943, becoming a member of a Ranger unit. He captured three German soldiers at Anzio and was seriously wounded in the fighting for Rome. Back in the United States, he studied Hebrew in preparation for Aliyah. After his Aliyah Bet service, he studied at the Technion for a year. He joined the Palmach and was sent to the Jerusalem sector. He was buried at Kiryat Anavim.

In the book *Underground to Palestine,* the American journalist I.F. Stone wrote the following about Monash:

He was one of the few who survived Anzio Beachhead. His shipmates were proud of him, but it was hard to get him to talk about his experiences. He spoke of his many missions behind the German lines laconically: "Aw, it was just routine work. You don't want to hear about that." But his shipmates told me that he once lured 12 Germans over the American lines by pretending to be a *Wehrmacht* officer in the darkness.

The Ranger, as we called him, did tell me about one of his experiences which he didn't consider routine.

His outfit was destroyed during the Anzio landing. After his escape from Anzio a soldier walked up to him and asked what outfit he was in. He said, "I'm a Ranger."

"This other soldier took a look at me," he went on, "and asked, 'What's your religion?' I said, 'I'm a Jew.'

"He said, 'How come a Jew got into the Rangers?'

"I was so mad I pulled out my revolver and would have shot him, but my buddies interfered and held my arms, and my lieutenant walked up and knocked him out with a sock on the jaw."

Reuven (Red) Schiff, of the Geula crew, was killed in action with the Palmach. Born in 1924 in Toronto, he joined the Canadian army at 17 and served for five years. He was wounded in Germany and discharged in 1945. He was among a group of sailors from the Geula and The Jewish State who escaped November 19, 1947, from a bus convoy taking them to Athlit detention camp on their arrival from Cyprus. He went to Kibbutz Maayan Baruch and from there volunteered for the Palmach. He died

AMERICAN VETERANS OF ISRAEL FOREST

יער מתנדבי ארה"ב וקנדה למען ישראל

IN MEMORY OF THE VOLUNTEERS
FROM THE U.S.A. AND CANADA
WHO GAVE THEIR LIVES IN ISRAEL'S WAR
OF INDEPENDENCE

לזכר המתנדבים
מארצות-הברית וקנדה
שמסרו את נפשם על עצמאות ישראל
במלחמת השחרור

1948 – 1949

תש"ח - תש"ט

RALPH MUSTER	ראלף מוסטר	SAMUEL HANOVICE	שמואל הנוביק	BENNI BOGUSLAVSKY	בני בוגוסלבסקי
LEONARD PITCHET	לאונרד פיטצ'ט	RAY KUNTZ	ריי קונץ	ZEEV CANTOR	זאב קנטור
SIDNEY RUBINOV	סידני (ישעיהו) רוביגוב	SIDNEY LEIZEROWITZ	סידני לייזרוביץ	WILLIAM FISHER	ויליאם פישר
ROBERT LESTER WEECKMAN	רוברט לסטר ויקמן	SEYMOUR LERNER	סיימור לרנר	AARON HANOVICE	אהרן הנוביק

KALMAN PITTEL	קלמן פיטל	DANIEL GOODMAN	דניאל-יצחק גודמן	HANS ABRAHAM	חיים אברהם
SALLY PALKOWSKI	סלי פלקובסקי	IGO GRIFFEL	יצחק גריפל	JUSTIN ADLER	יוסף אדלר
SHMUEL POMERANZ	שמואל פומרנץ	FRED GROSS	צבי גרוס	WILLIAM ALT	ויליאם אלט
POSNER	פוזנר	ZIPORA GRUNBERG	צפורה גרינברג	STANLEY ANDREWS	סטנלי אנדרוס
CARMI RABINOWITZ	כרמי רבינוביץ	ERICH HELLINGER	אריך הלינגר	PHILIP BALKIN	פילים בולקין
HARRY ROH	שבתאי רוה	OLIVER HOLTON	אוליבר הולטון	LOUIS BALL	אריה באל
MOSHE ROSENBAUM	משה אהרן רוזנבאום	OSCAR HYMAN	אוסקר היימן	ISRAEL BERN	ישראל ברן
JACOB ROTHMAN	יעקב רוטמן	JOE KAHN	יוסף כהן	WILLIAM BERNSTEIN	ויליאם ברנשטיין
SELIG RUDOLPH	רודולף זליג	JEROME KAPLAN	יהודה קפלן	YAACOV BIELUR	יעקב ביאלור
MIRIAM SALPETER	מרים סלפטר	HERBERT KERMISH	צבי קרמיש	LESLIE BLOCH	לסלי בלוך
MOSHE SCHMUCKLER	משה שמוקלר	ERNIE KING	ארני קינג	SPENCER R. BOYD	ספנסר ר בויד
DOV SELIGMAN	דב זליגמן	JACK KLEIN	יעקב דניאל קליין	JOSHUA BROWN	יהושע בראון
IRVING SEVIN	ישראל סוין	HEINRICH KUPPERMAN	חיים צבי קופרמן	BUZZ BURLING	בז ברלינג
JACK SHULMAN	עזריאל שולמן	ARI LASHNER	אריה לשנר	JACOUB CHECK	יעקב נח שק
YOSEF STADLER	יוסף שטדלר	ALVIN LEVY	אברהם לוי	MOSHE REUBEN COHEN	משה ראובן כהן
AVRAHAM DAVID STAVSKY	אברהם דוד סטבסקי	BARUCH LINSKY	ברוך לינסקי	WILLIAM EDMONSON	ויליאם אדמונסון
SHLOMO SZIGETI	שלמה סיגטי	JOSEPH MANN	יוסף מן	BERNARD FAJERMAN	ברוך פיירמן
YECHEZKEL TESHER	יחזקאל תשר	DAVID MICKEY MARCUS	מיכאל דוד מרכוס	HENRI FERNEBOK	הנרי פרניבוק
LEONARD TROYEN	ליאונרד טרוין	MANDEL MATH	מנדל מט	ZVI FISHEL	צבי פישל
ISRAEL YAROST	ישראל ירוסט	DAVID MILLER	דוד מילר	LEN FISHER	לן פישר
REUVEN SCHIFF	ראובן שיף	HAROLD MONASH	צבי מונש	MOSHE GEBERER	משה גברר
MOSHE ZUCKER	משה צוקר	HOWARD E. MOORE Jr.	האוארד מור	WILLIAM GERSHON	ויליאם גרשון
		MOSHE PERLSTEIN	משה פרלשטיין	PHILIP GOLD	פילים גולד

JEWISH NATIONAL FUND

in the Negev, and his name appears on a memorial at Maayan Baruch.

❧

Dov Seligman, of the Wedgwood crew, was killed January 19, 1948, by a sniper while working with a tractor in the fields of Kibbutz Ein Dor. Haganah members killed the sniper the following day. Born in New York in June 1922, Seligman grew up in the Bronx. Although his parents were followers of the Bund, an anti-Zionist Jewish group, they supported his decision to join the Zionist youth movement Hashomer Hatzair. After graduating from high school, he studied agriculture at a farm school in Doylestown, Pennsylvania. Husky and athletic, he played the position of tackle on the Doylestown school's football team. During World War II, he served in the U.S. Army Air Corps, spending almost two years on the Kwajalein atoll in the Pacific. He was interred at Ein Dor, where his parents are also buried.

❧

Appendix D

Chronology

1945

Ben-Gurion holds first meeting with Sonneborn Institute founders in New York. July 1, 1945.

President Truman proposes that Britain admit 100,000 Jews to Palestine. August, 1945.

First post-war Aliyah Bet voyage; 35 immigrants reach Caesarea aboard the refugee boat Dalin. August 28, 1945.

Britain limits Jewish immigration to 1,500 per month. September 5, 1945.

1946

First capture of an Aliyah Bet ship by the British: the Enzo Sereni, with 900 aboard. January 17, 1946.

Dewey Stone is asked to transfer $125,000 to the Caribbean Atlantic Shipping Corporation. February 2, 1946.

Haganah and Wedgwood sail from New York. April 1946.

Wedgwood captured by the British and taken to Haifa. June 27, 1946.

Haganah transfers passengers at sea to the Biryah (Akbel II), June 28, 1946.

"Black Sabbath." British arrest Jewish leaders throughout Palestine. June 29, 1946.

Biryah is towed into Haifa after capture by British. July 1, 1946.

Ben-Gurion in New York asks Sonneborn Institute to become active. July 7, 1946.

Irgun blows up British headquarters at King David Hotel, Jerusalem. July 22, 1946.

Haganah leaves Yugoslavia with more than 2,700 passengers. July 24, 1946.

Haganah captured by the British and taken to Haifa. July 29, 1946.

British begin transporting captured immigrants to Cyprus. August 1946.

"A Flag is Born" opens in New York. September 5, 1946.

Weston Trading Company buys the Unalga, soon to become the Haim Arlosoroff. October 17, 1946.

U.S. Maritime Commission approves transfer to Weston Trading Company of the President Warfield, soon to become the Exodus 1947. December 3, 1946.

1947

Haim Arlosoroff leaves Trelleborg, Sweden, with 664 passengers. January 24, 1947.

Britain refers Palestine question to the United Nations. February 1947.

President Warfield almost sinks off Cape Hatteras and returns to port. February 26-27, 1947.

Haim Arlosoroff captured at Bat Galim after battle with British. February 28, 1947.

Martial law declared in Palestine after violence following Arlosoroff capture. March 1, 1947.

Ben Hecht arrives at Haifa with 600 passengers after capture by British. March 8, 1947.

Pan York and Pan Crescent purchased in New Jersey. March 17, 1947.

President Warfield sails from Philadelphia as Honduras tries to revoke registration. March 27, 1947.

Explosion aboard Pan Crescent in Venice. April 30, 1947.

Hatikvah captured by the British and taken to Haifa. May 17, 1947.

Exodus captured by British; three Jews killed in shipboard battle. July 18, 1947.

Bomb placed by Hatikvah crewmen sinks British prison ship in Haifa harbor. July 23, 1947.

Exodus passengers, deported to Port de Bouc, France, refuse to go ashore. July 28, 1947.

Exodus passengers receive British ultimatum to debark in France or be deported to Germany. August 21, 1947.

United Nations commission recommends partition of Palestine. British announce intention to withdraw. August 31, 1947.

Exodus passengers are forced to debark at Hamburg, Germany. September 8, 1947.

Geula and The Jewish State captured by British with more than 4,000 immigrants from Eastern Europe. October 2, 1947.

British try to prevent sailing of Pan York and Pan Crescent with more than 15,000 immigrants from Eastern Europe. October-December, 1947.

United Nations General Assembly votes for partition of Palestine. November 29, 1947.

Pan York and Pan Crescent sail from Bulgaria. December 25-26, 1947.

1948

Pan York and Pan Crescent arrive in Cyprus with more than 15,000 immigrants. January 1, 1948.

State of Israel proclaimed, May 14-15, 1948.

Sources of Information

Many facts in this book are from documents in the Haganah archives at Bet Golomb in Tel Aviv. Other sources of documents were the American Jewish Historical Society, the Institute of Contemporary Judaism at the Hebrew University in Jerusalem, and Tel Aviv University's project on Aliyah Bet.

A special resource was material from the files of one of the American volunteers, Yehuda Sela of Kibbutz Hatzor, whose research included interviews with many participants in Aliyah Bet. Ephraim (Phil) Tsuk of Haifa also shared his personal files.

Among those persons who supplied facts and background, in discussion, correspondence, and interviews recorded in archives, are the following:

Yosef Almog, Yitzhak (Ike) Aronowitz, Yisrael Averbach, Marvin Bacaner, Yehoshua Baharav, David Baum, Shabtai Breen, Shepherd Broad, Joe Buxenbaum, Pearl Buxenbaum, Reuven Dafni, Shaike Dan, Bezalel Drori, Heine Franz Fleigler, Arye Friedman, Morris Ginsberg, Pino Ginsburg, Sam Gordon, Mimi Grey, Murray S. Greenfield, Gottlieb Hammer, Avraham Halevi, Sam Halpern, Gad Hilb, Isaac Imber, Bea Jaffer, Harold Jaffer, David Kaplan, Eddy Kaplansky, Harold Katz, Arnold A. Kite, Joe Kramer, Benny Kulbersh, David Macarov, Dov Magen, Irving Meltzer, Kalman Michaeli, Paul Milgrom, Milton Miller, Dov Mills, Dvora Nameiry, Rudolph Patzert, Adrian Phillips, Miriam Rapaport, Stanley Ritzer, Willie Rostoker, Avraham Segal, Yehuda Sela, Shirley Lashner Shpira, Avi Sheffi, Hava Shind, Paul Shulman, Akiva Skidell, Teddy Vardi, and Jack Yeriel.

Although Danny Schind and Davidka Nameiry died long before this book was begun, both left behind first-person recollections on which we were able to draw. Schind's account of a visit to Samuel Zemurray can be found in the Haganah archives and appears in a memorial volume published in 1981 by Kibbutz Kfar Szold with the cooperation of Zim and the Jewish Agency. An English translation appears in Hadari's *Voyage to Freedom,* cited in the section headed "For Further Reading." Nameiry's recollections appear in Hebrew in *The Story of Davidka, Told by Himself and His Friends,* published in 1974 by Hakibbutz Hameuchad Publishing House Ltd.

A list of published sources follows.

For Further Reading

Readers who wish to pursue this subject can find additional information about the American volunteers and Aliyah Bet in source materials used in preparing this book. Except where noted, the references are books in the English language.

About the American vessels

Dibner, Brent, "Exodus 1947; Its History and its Voyage," article in the *Bulletin* of the American Friends of the Haifa Maritime Museum, Fall 1984.

Eliav, Arie L., *The Voyage of the Ulua,* translated by Israel J. Taslitt. New York, Pyramid Books, 1970. A memoir of the Haim Arlosoroff, the third American-manned vessel, by its Haganah commander. Briefly mentions the American crew.

Grauel, Reverend John Stanley, *Grauel, An Autobiography* as told to Eleanor Elfenbein, Freehold, N.J., Ivory House, 1983. Anecdotes and observations by a Methodist minister who sailed on the Exodus and functioned for a time as its spokesman.

Gruber, Ruth, *Destination Palestine; the Story of the Haganah Ship Exodus 1947.* New York, Current Books, 1948. A journalist's report, with stories about the American crew members.

Hadari, Ze'ev Venia, and Tsahor, Ze'ev, *Voyage to Freedom; an Episode in the Illegal Immigration.* London, Vallentine, Mitchell, 1985. (English translation). The history of the Kibbutz Galuyot and Atzmaut (Pan York and Pan Crescent) by an assistant to Aliyah Bet director Shaul Avigur. Briefly mentions the Americans.

Holly, David C., *Exodus 1947.* Boston and Toronto, Little, Brown, 1969. An American naval officer's history of the Exodus, rich in detail and background.

Stone, I.F., *Underground to Palestine.* Boni & Gaer, New York, 1946. A journalist's account covering portions of the voyages of the Wedgwood and Haganah, the first two American-manned vessels.

Isben, Sam, *Umlegalische Yidden Shpalten Yammen.* (Yiddish) The Hevrah Kadishah, Buenos Aires. Account of the Hatikvah by a Morgen-Journal correspondent who took part in the voyage.

Other background

Dinnerstein, Leonard, *America and the Survivors of the Holocaust.* New York,

Columbia University Press, 1982. Includes the text of the 1945 Harrison Report on Displaced Persons.

Grose, Peter, *Israel in the Mind of America.* New York, Knopf, 1983. Background on American attitudes toward Israel and Zionism. Mentions the Sonneborn Institute, among others.

Hammer, Gottlieb, *Good Faith and Credit.* Cranbury, N.J., Cornwall Books, 1985. Includes material on the Zionist purchasing mission in New York in 1945-48, Danny Schind, and the Sonneborn Institute.

Heckelman, A. Joseph, *American Volunteers and Israel's War of Independence.* New York, Ktav, 1974. Deals mainly with military volunteers. Contains some material on Aliyah Bet including comments from a number of volunteers.

Kimche, Jon and David, *The Secret Roads; The "Illegal" Migration of a People, 1938-1948.* New York, Farrar, Strauss and Cudahy, 1955. A survey of Aliyah Bet, with emphasis on British and Zionist policies.

Naor, Mordechai, *Ha'apalah 1934-1948.* (Hebrew) Israel Defense Ministry, 1978. A concise survey, with several references to the American role. An English translation is in preparation.

Sherman, Arnold, *The Ship.* Jerusalem, La Semana Publishing Company, 1978. A fictional voyage of an Aliyah Bet ship with characters and incidents resembling those of the American-manned Haganah.

Slater, Leonard, *The Pledge.* New York, Simon & Schuster, 1970. A detailed account of Haganah efforts to acquire arms in America in 1945-48, including the activities of the Sonneborn Institute.

United States Department of State, *Foreign Relations of the United States,* Volumes for 1945-48, Washington, U.S. Government Printing Office.

Uris, Leon, *Exodus.* New York, Doubleday, 1958. Epic novel set in 1946-49, including a fictionalized history of Aliyah Bet. The story of a fictional vessel named the General Stonewall Jackson, which resembles the actual Exodus, is told in Book I, Chapter 27.

Weisgal, Meyer W., *So Far; An Autobiography.* Weidenfeld & Nicolson, London, 1971. Briefly mentions Danny Schind and a visit to Samuel Zemurray.

Wilson, Maj. R.D., *Cordon and Search; with the 6th Airborne Division in Palestine.* Gale & Polden, Ltd., 1949. Includes section on British interceptions of Aliyah Bet vessels.

Wyman, David S., *Abandonment of the Jews.* New York, Pantheon Books, 1984. Tells of failures by American Jewish organizations and others to rescue the victims of the Holocaust.

THE PALESTINE POST

JERUSALEM SUNDAY, MAY 16, 1948

PRICE: 25 MILS VOL. XXIII. No. 6714

STATE OF ISRAEL IS BORN

The first independent Jewish State in 19 centuries was born in Tel Aviv as the British Mandate over Palestine came to an end at midnight on Friday, and it was immediately subjected to the test of fire. As "Medinat Yisrael" (State of Israel) was proclaimed, the battle for Jerusalem raged, with most of the city falling to the Jews. At the same time, President Truman announced that the United States would accord recognition to the new State. A few hours later, Palestine was invaded by Moslem armies from the south, east and north, and Tel Aviv was raided from the air. On Friday the United Nations Special Assembly adjourned after adopting a resolution to appoint a mediator but without taking any action on the Partition Resolution of November 29.

Yesterday the battle for the Jerusalem-Tel Aviv road was still under way, and two Arab villages were taken. In the north, Acre town was captured, and the Jewish Army consolidated its positions in Western Galilee.

Most Crowded Hours in Palestine's History

Between Thursday night and this morning Palestine went through what by all standards must be among the most crowded hours in its history.

For the Jewish population there was the anguish over the fate of the few hundred Haganah men and women in the Kfar Etzion bloc of settlements near Hebron. Their surrender to a fully equipped superior foreign force desperately in need of a victory was a foregone conclusion. What could not be known, with no communications since Thursday morning, was whether and to what extent the Red Cross and the Truce Consuls would secure civilized conditions for prisoners and wounded, and proper respect for the dead. Doubts on some of these anxious questions have now been resolved.

On Friday afternoon, from Tel Aviv, came the expected announcement of the Jewish State, and its official naming at birth, "Medinat Yisrael"—State of Israel, with the swearing in of the first Council of Government. The proclamation of the State was made at midnight, coinciding with the sailing from Haifa of Britain's last High Commissioner. Within the hour, President Truman announced in Washington that the Government of the United States had decided to give *de facto* recognition to the Jewish State, with all that such recognition implied. The Assembly of the United Nations, meeting since the middle of April for "further study" of the Palestine problem was thus left, by one means or another, to ratify the Two-States decision of November last year, or dissolve with nothing concrete to its credit. The Assembly adjourned with the resolution to appoint a mediator between the Jews and Arabs, to cooperate with the Security Council's Truce Commission in Jerusalem.

Russian Recognition Awaited

Russia and her allies had given early assurance of their intention to recognize the Jewish State, whoever else did or did not. As a result of Washington's action and the Eastern Bloc's stand, other countries are expected to extend their recognition to the newly born state.

Nor did the Arab Bloc remain idle. True to their promises, or threats, the members of the Arab League completed their plans for a full-scale invasion of Palestine in what has been described as a Moslem "crusade" against the Jews. Tel Aviv was bombed twice yesterday by Egyptian war planes. One of the enemy planes was shot down by a Jewish fighter plane, and the pilot taken prisoner, showing that this move against the civilian population was not a surprise, and that the Jewish preparations include anti-aircraft defences.

A black-out has been ordered for the whole of Jewish Palestine Tel Aviv itself having blacked out on Friday.

At the same time, the air was filled with reports of two Egyptian columns on the move from the south towards Gaza and Beersheba, and of intensified shelling from across the northern border of Jewish settlements in North-Eastern Galilee.

The Security Council met yesterday in a special session to consider action on the invasion of Palestine by member states of the U.N.

In the afternoon, Jerusalem was subjected to shelling from the northwest.

Haganah forces throughout the country continued mopping up, and Jewish sources claimed most of Western Galilee safe against attack. Naharayim, near Jisr el Majamie, inside Trans-Jordan, where the Jordan River works of the Palestine Electric Corporation are, is claimed by the Arab Legion. The battle for the Tel Aviv-Jerusalem Road at Bab el Wad is still on, Haganah taking two villages — Abu Shusha and Kubeib — between Ramleh and Latrun.

Converging on Old City

In Jerusalem the "cease fire" observed on both sides for six days was broken on Friday, although the more strategic buildings in Princess Mary Avenue, the Russian Compound, and Jaffa Road passed to the Jews without a shot being fired, as did the David Building commanding the road to the German Colony and Railway Station. By yesterday evening, Jewish forces were approaching some of the gates of the Old City. The Police Training School on Mt. Scopus and Sheikh Jarrah are in Jewish hands.

On Friday morning, the Truce Commission met at the French Consulate and invited Jewish and Arab representatives to confer with them. Jewish Agency delegates agreed that the "cease fire" be extended in Jerusalem for eight days. Arab representatives could not attend, they said, because of the firing in Julian's Way, and a two-hour respite was arranged from 5 to 7 in the evening. Whether they agreed or not, became academic as by that time the battle for Jerusalem had been renewed.

To Jerusalem's tension was added the aggravation of electric power failing in most parts of the city, as nearly all of the Electric Corporation's lines had been shot down. This meant, on top of the other heardships to a fuel-less city, no broadcast news yesterday, when there were no newspapers. For more than a week the city was also without piped water.

ACRE CAPTURED

Acre, the sea-coast town across the bay from Haifa, was captured by Jewish forces yesterday, the Haganah Radio reported. The surrender of the town, and subsequently two villages to the north, came after a strong Jewish attack.

Arms dumps containing enormous quantities of military equipment were captured.

The B.B.C. stated yesterday that almost all of Western Galilee was in Jewish hands, but that Naharayim, on the Jordan, had been occupied by the Legion.

Double Summer Time in Jerusalem

At midnight tonight all clocks in Jewish Jerusalem will be advanced two hours.

The Emergency Committee has instituted double summer time in order to save fuel. The measure does not apply to the rest of the country.

The Jerusalem Electric Corporation will cut off current to the Jewish Quarters from 1 to 9 p.m. as from today.

JEWS TAKE OVER SECURITY ZONES

The Battle for Jerusalem, which began when the British forces withdrew on Friday morning, continued all day Friday and yesterday. The crackle of small-arms fire and explosions of mortar shells were still being heard in the early hours of this morning as the battle entered its third day.

Repeated efforts on Friday evening and again on Saturday by the U.N. Truce Commission to bring about a "cease fire" were brought to nought when the Arab representatives failed to agree within the specified time limit.

On Friday morning, Jewish forces entered the Russian Compound and Zone C to reoccupy the buildings requisitioned from Jews last year. This operation was almost bloodless, but beyond the western edge of Zone C, Arabs engaged the Jews in Jaffa Road. The Arabs were forced back and the Barclays Bank area was taken.

In other parts of the city fighting flared up. Jews overran one after another the areas evacuated by the British. By last night, the quarters and strongpoints held by Haganah included the German Colony and part of the Baka'a Quarter in Zone A, all of Zone B except for the Red Cross area, Sheikh Jarrah (where the Jewish flag was flown from the Mufti's House), the Mea Shearim Police Station and Allenby Barracks on the Bethlehem Road. The I.Z.L. were in occupation of the Scopus Police Billet.

Yesterday afternoon eight cannon shelled Jewish Jerusalem from the Arab village of Nebi Samwil, more than 100 shells falling in the north-western quarters. Several persons were injured.

Jewish casualties in the two days of fighting were eight killed and a number of wounded. Arab casualties are not known.

EMERGENCY

A state of emergency in the Jerusalem area was declared to exist by the Haganah Area Commander as from yesterday in what is the first Order of the Day to be issued in almost 2,000 years by a Jewish Military Commander of the city.

The Order said:

With the declaration of the establishment of Medinat Israel (the State of Israel) and the setting up of its Provisional Council of Government, the Jews of Palestine have entered upon the decisive phase of the war.

In order to obviate any disturbance during the difficult time that confronts us, I hereby declare a state of emergency to exist in the Jerusalem District as from 00.01 hours on Saturday, May 15, and I hereby give the following instructions:

1. Every inhabitant must place himself at the disposal of the authorized security forces of Medinat Israel and obey their orders.
2. All property required for the needs of the Military Command may be expropriated by the security forces acting through officers carrying proper documents. Compensation for such expropriated property will be paid according to evaluation by the Jerusalem Committee and at such time as the latter shall decide.
3. The areas evacuated by the forces of the Mandatory Government and now held by the security forces are hereby declared to be Military Occupation Areas under the authority of Military Governors.
4. No person may enter any such area without permission of the Military Governor.
5. Any person found looting or committing any criminal act will be brought before a Military Court and punished with all the rigour of the law.

The Palestine Post

Despite the power failure in Jerusalem, the Electric Corporation succeeded in providing these offices with power about 10.15 last night. There was another failure about 11.15 but again the Corporation was able to restore the current.

Before the linotype machines could begin to work, however, it was 1 a.m., and in order to be able to appear this morning, The Palestine Post is published, for the third time in as many weeks, in two pages.

Egyptian Air Force Spitfires Bomb Tel Aviv; One Shot Down

Kol Israel, the Tel Aviv broadcasting station, reported at 2 o'clock yesterday afternoon that Tel Aviv had been bombed three times in the previous evening and morning, and that one plane had been shot down and its Egyptian pilot taken prisoner.

In the first raid, four planes attacked from a height of 300 feet. Two dropped bombs, while the others strafed the city. Little damage was caused. In the second attack two hours later, the airport to the north of the city was bombed, and an Air France plane parked there was damaged. The third raid was launched shortly before midday, but the planes were driven off without causing any damage.

Two settlements in the Negev had also been attacked from the air, the radio reported.

A country-wide blackout was ordered by Air Raid Precaution Headquarters in Tel Aviv.

Mr. David Ben Gurion, the Prime Minister, broadcast from Tel Aviv to the people of America yesterday morning. As he spoke, Egyptian planes were bombing the city.

In the north, the settlements of Ein Gev and Shaar Hagolan and Dan had been shelled, but no further details were available.

Kalandia airfield was taken by the Jewish army on Friday morning, shortly after the High Commissioner had left there by plane for Haifa. The field was evacuated,' together with the neighbouring settlement of Ataroth, on Friday night. The settlement itself was burnt by Arabs yesterday.

2 Columns Cross Southern Border

By WALTER COLLINS
U.P. Correspondent

CAIRO, Saturday. — A communique issued today by the Egyptian Ministry of National Defence reported that two columns of Egyptian troops, including infantry and artillery, had struck across the Palestine border, preceded by aircraft.

One column was reported to have crossed the frontier 30 miles inland and to have attacked the "Jewish village of Auja on the road to Beersheba, wiping it out because its inhabitants had refused to surrender." (Auja is a police post near the frontier, about 25 miles from the nearest Jewish settlement). The column then entrenched itself on heights east of Gaza.

Meanwhile, according to this Cairo report, another column crossed the border at midnight, travelling north along the coast road towards Gaza.

Egyptian sources later reported that their forces had reached the Negev settlements of Nirim and Kfar Darom, but could give no further details.

In Cairo, at midnight, 2,000 Egyptian Police, commanded by 370 Officers, started a round-up of suspected Zionist sympathizers and arrested 600 persons within six hours.

According to Haganah sources, Jewish soldiers beat off an Egyptian "amphibious operation," an attempt to land troops near Ashdod, 20 miles north of Gaza. The ship which attempted to make the landing was forced to turn back, these sources said.

Arab Legion Cross Border

It was reported in Jerusalem last night that troops of the Arab Legion had crossed the border into Palestine in two places, over Allenby Bridge and near the Palestine Electric power station at Naharaim.

According to Reuters, the long convoy of the first route of lorry-borne troops, artillery and armoured cars, was headed by King Abdullah, who fired a symbolic pistol shot towards Palestine and wished his troops success in their campaign.

In Cairo, a group of journalists have asked the Egyptian Premier, Nokrashi Pasha, for an interview to discuss the proposed blackout of news, the Cairo Radio has reported.

A Good Thing

CAIRO, Saturday (UP). — The Egyptian Premier, Nokrashi Pasha, told the press that advance units of the Egyptian army had entered Gaza 12 hours after crossing the frontier.

"This is a very good thing," he added.

Etzion Settlers Taken P.O.W.

Fighting in the Kfar Etzion bloc continued throughout Friday, after Kfar Etzion itself had surrendered to the Arabs on the previous day. The wounded from the settlement were evacuated to Massuot Itzhak.

The fighting was broken off on Friday on the intervention of a Red Cross representative, accompanied by a Jewish Medical Officer, who went out to the settlements and supervised the transfer of the Jews from Revadim and Ein Zurim, the wounded and women being taken to Bethlehem, and the other settlers to prison.

The settlers from Massuot Itzhak, including the wounded from the first day's fighting at Kfar Etzion, were removed yesterday.

The terms of surrender agreed on by the Jews and Arabs were:

All able-bodied soldiers to be taken as prisoners of war, and kept in "special camps," to be supervised by the International Red Cross.

Women, non-combatants and wounded to be brought to Jerusalem by the Red Cross.

War Office Says Legion Had Left

LAKE SUCCESS, Saturday. — Sir Alexander Cadogan, Britain's delegate to the U.N., read to the Security Council a telegram from the War Office today, stating that *all units of the Arab Legion had left Palestine for Trans-Jordan prior to the end of the Mandate.*

U.S. RECOGNIZES JEWISH STATE

WASHINGTON, Saturday. —Ten minutes after the termination of the British Mandate on Friday, the White House released a formal statement by President Truman that the U.S. Government intended to recognize the Provisional Jewish Government as the *de facto* authority representing the Jewish State.

The U.S. is also considering lifting the arms embargo but it is not known whether to Palestine only or the entire Middle East, and the establishment of diplomatic relations with the Jewish Provisional Government.

The White House press secretary, Mr. Charles Ross, told correspondents today that reaction so far to the recognition had been overwhelmingly favourable. He said this step had been discussed with Mr. Marshall and Mr. Lovett before action was taken, and it had their complete support.

Mr. Ross said that the President had decided several days ago to grant American recognition to the new Jewish State, but due to protocol regulations he could not announce his policy until a formal letter arrived. "We were able to move very quickly when the messenger brought the letter," he said, "because the President had already determined the course of action to be taken."

Provisional Government

A few minutes before five (midnight Palestine time), Mr. Eliyahu Epstein, of the Jewish Agency's Washington Office, handed a letter to the White House, requesting the U.S. to recognize the new Jewish State. "With the full knowledge of the deep bond of sympathy which existed and has been strengthened over the past 30 years between the U.S. Government and the Jewish people of Palestine," the letter said, "I have been authorized by the Provisional Government of the new State to tender this message and express the hope that your Government will recognize and welcome Israel into the community of nations."

In Frankfurt, General Lucius D. Clay, the U.S. Military Commander of Germany, said today that Jews in Germany and Austria would be assisted to leave for the State of Israel as soon as official word of America's recognition was to hand.

EGYPTIAN INVASION BEFORE U.N. SECURITY COUNCIL

LAKE SUCCESS, Saturday. — Israel today appealed to an emergency meeting of the Security Council to order a halt to Arab invasions into Palestine and, if necessary, to impose economic and military sanctions.

Dr. Mordechai Eliash, representing the day-old Jewish State, appealed to the Council to act fast against the invading Arab States, because "every hour counts." He stated that King Abdullah of Trans-Jordan, through the instrument of the Arab Legion, was clearly committing an act of aggression.

At the beginning of the session, Dr. Issa Nakh'eh, of the Arab Higher Committee, declared that Egyptian forces had been invited by the A.H.C. to assist in the establishment of law and order. He asked: "What right has the Jewish Agency, which represents world Jewry, to complain against this action before the Security Council?"

Mahmoud Bey Fawzi, of Egypt, declared in explanation of a cable which he had earlier read to the Council that Egyptian troops had entered Palestine by invitation and with the unequivocal consent of the Palestine people. Egyptian forces were not going to Palestine to conquer anybody, but just to restore peace.

The invasion was "not directed against the Palestine

(Continued on Page 2, Col. 7)

GROMYKO TO BE REPLACED

LAKE SUCCESS, Saturday. (UP). — M. Andrei Gromyko, the Soviet Deputy Foreign Minister and his country's representative at the U.N., will soon be replaced — probably permanently.

The 38-year-old Soviet diplomat will be replaced by M. Jacob A. Malik Deputy Foreign Minister and a major figure in the conduct of Russian Foreign policy in the Far East. M. Malik, is already en route here by plane from Berlin.

Proclamation by Head Of Government

The creation of "Medinat Yisrael", the State of Israel, was proclaimed at midnight on Friday by Mr. David Ben Gurion, until then Chairman of the Jewish Agency Executive and now head of the State's Provisional Council of Government.

David Ben Gurion, Prime Minister

The first act of the Council of Government, as announced by its head, was to abolish all legislation of the 1939 White Paper of the late Mandatory Power, particularly the Ordinances and Orders relating to immigration and land transfer.

In the declaration of independence, Mr. Ben Gurion called on the Arabs of Palestine to restore peace, assuring them full civic rights and full representation in all governmental organs of the State.

Mr. Ben Gurion prefaced the declaration with a review of the historic connection of the Jewish people with the Land of Israel and of their efforts to return, which never ceased throughout the generations of their dispersal, until the Nazi holocaust proved anew the urgency of the need for a Jewish State.

The Balfour Declaration of 1917, confirmed by the League of Nations, had given explicit international recognition to the right of the Jewish people to reconstitute its National Home in Palestine, he said.

"On November 29, 1947," continued the declaration, "the United Nations decided on the establishment of a Jewish State and an Arab State in Palestine and called upon the inhabitants of the country to take all steps necessary for the establishment of the two States.

Historic Rights

"This decision cannot now be changed. Accordingly, we, the members of the Provisio-

(Continued on Page 2, Col. 6)

Special Assembly Adjourns

FLUSHING MEADOWS, Saturday. — The Special U.N. Assembly, called four weeks ago to discuss the U.S. proposal for a temporary Trusteeship for Palestine, adjourned yesterday until its next regular meeting in September without taking any decision to alter the resolution of November 29, which called for the setting up of two states in Palestine. The Assembly adopted only one motion — to appoint a special mediator to go to Palestine and cooperate with Truce Commission.

President Truman's announcement that the U.S. was proposing to recognize the new Jewish State reached newsmen during the session before the American delegation itself knew about it.

All the afternoon, the Assembly had been tied up in knots. After much fillibustering it rejected the Franco-U.S. proposal for a special administration for Jerusalem. As the debate dragged on, correspondents sat with stopwatches to see whether a decision would be taken before the six o'clock deadline (N.Y. Summer Time) when the Mandate terminated. As zero hour was reached without a vote, they rushed to the booths, and about ten minutes later, the tickers in the local news agency offices flashed President Truman's recognition.

Gromyko and Jessup

The Assembly floor was half deserted and the American delegation had not been officially informed. The first to mention the Jewish State from the rostrum was M. Gromyko, who said he saw no need for further action on the American mediator proposal, since the Jewish State had been recognized as a reality by the U.S. He asked what was being proposed for the Arab area of Palestine which was still without a government.

Shortly afterwards, Mr. Philip Jessup, the anti-Partition fighter, mounted the rostrum and officially announced U.S. recognition of the Jewish State, insisting, however, that the passage of the American mediator proposal was more necessary now than ever.

The Assembly passed it.

Between the flash from the White House and the final vote there was an eerie atmosphere in Flushing Meadows. The lights of the television cameras played on the rostrum, lighting up one Arab speaker after another who mounted the steps and expressed in a low voice frustration and anger.

To the last minute, officials of the State Department had been lobbying right on the floor against the Jewish State, even while the President's statement was already on the wires.

The Assembly did not adopt any resolution at all which altered the U.N. decision of November 29, 1947.

2 Villages Taken In Road Battle

In the battle for the Tel Aviv-Jerusalem road, the Haganah on Friday night took Kubeib and Abu Shusha villages between Latrun and Ramle. In engagements elsewhere along the route positions near Latrun and Bab el Wad changed hands.

Jewish casualties in this area in the last two days are about 40 killed. The Iraqis suffered greater losses, but their exact number is unknown.

It was reported that Iraqi troops had entered the Trappist Monastery at Latrun, and had set up strongpoints on the grounds and the building itself.

Sir Alan Sails From Palestine

The High Commissioner's departure from Palestine on Friday went according to plan — he appeared on the steps of Government House at 8 o'clock in the morning, wearing a full General's uniform. There he reviewed a guard of honour, consisting of 50 men of the Highland Light Infantry, the last British troops to leave Jerusalem.

Sir Alan Cunningham then drove to Kalandia airfield and boarded a plane for Haifa. Spitfires and Lancasters covered his short car journey.

The last British civil servants left Jerusalem together with Sir Alan: including Sir William Fitz-Gerald, the Chief Justice, and Sir Henry Gurney, the Chief Secretary.

Sir Alan's plane was piloted to Haifa by the Air Officer Commanding in Palestine, Air Commodore Dawson.

USA

New York

Philadelphia

Baltimore

Norfolk

Cape Hatteras

Charleston

Miami

> **"...out of the 6,000,000 American Jews it
> jumped into the breach..."**
>
> *Pre*
> *at the 40th A*

(1) New York
(8) Azores
(11) Gibraltar
(23) Genoa
(24) Savona
(47) Haifa
(48) Atlit

(2) Baltimore
(8) Azores
(33) Marseilles
(37) Le Havre
(21) Copenhagen
(22) Trelleborg
(14) Algiers
(15) Philippeville
(16) Sousse
(25) Gallipoli
(26) Metaponto
(47) Haifa (Bat Galim)
(M) Cyprus

(1) New York
(35) Sete
(12) transfer point
(M) Cyprus
(18) Mylos
(19) Split
(20) Baka
(47) Haifa
(48) Atlit

(1) New York
(8) Azores
(34) Port de Bouc
(47) Haifa
(M) Cyprus

HATIKVAH

(4) Miami
(3) Charleston
(2) Baltimore
(8) Azores
(9) Lisbon
(33) Marseilles
(34) Port de Bouc
(31) Portovenere
(28) La Spezia
(29) Bogliasco
(30) Bocco del Magre
(47) Haifa
(M) Cyprus